Learning to Teach in Higher Education

This book addresses the problem of how best to evaluate and improve the standard of higher education teaching in a climate of accountability and appraisal. It links educational theory and the practical realities of teaching in an entirely new way. Designed for the use of practising lecturers, it argues that becoming a good teacher in higher education involves listening to one's students and changing one's understanding of teaching.

Paul Ramsden argues for a more professional approach to university teaching. The first part of his book provides an outline of the experience of learning and teaching from the student's point of view, out of which grows a set of principles for effective teaching in higher education. Part two shows how these ideas can enhance educational standards, looking in particular at four problems facing every teacher in higher education: organising the content of undergraduate courses, selecting teaching methods, assessing student learning, and evaluating the effectiveness of teaching. Case studies of exemplary teaching, based on the experiences of actual lecturers, are used to connect the ideas to practice and to illustrate how we can all improve our teaching – no matter how adverse the conditions in which we work. The final part of the book looks in more detail at appraisal, performance indicators of teaching, accountability and educational development and training.

Paul Ramsden is Senior Lecturer at the Centre for the Study of Higher Education at the University of Melbourne. He has taught and researched in polytechnics, universities and schools in the United Kingdom ... nally involved in acade...

Learning to Teach in Higher Education

Paul Ramsden

London and New York

To Elaine

First published 1992
by Routledge
11 New Fetter Lane, London EC4P 4EE

Simultaneously published in the USA and Canada
by Routledge
29 West 35th Street, New York, NY 10001

Reprinted 1992, 1993, 1994 (twice), 1995, 1996, 1998, 1999, 2000

Reprinted 2000, 2002 by RoutledgeFalmer

RoutledgeFalmer is an imprint of the Taylor & Francis Group

© 1992 Paul Ramsden

Typeset by GilCoM Ltd., Mitcham, Surrey
Printed and bound in Great Britain by
TJ International Ltd, Padstow, Cornwall

British Library Cataloguing in Publication Data
A catalogue record for this book is available from the British Library

Library of Congress Cataloguing in Publication Data
A catalogue record for this book is available from the Library of Congress

ISBN 0-415-06414-7 (hbk)
ISBN 0-415-06415-5 (pbk)

Contents

List of figures   vii
List of tables   viii
Preface   ix
Acknowledgements   xi

Part 1 Learning and teaching in higher education

1   Introduction   1

2   Ways of understanding teaching   12

3   What students learn   17

4   Approaches to learning   38

5   Learning from the student's perspective   62

6   The nature of good teaching in higher education   86

7   Theories of teaching in higher education   109

Part 2 Design for learning

8   The goals and structure of a course   123

9   Teaching strategies for effective learning   150

10   Assessing for understanding   181

Part 3 Evaluating and improving the quality of teaching and learning

11   Evaluating the quality of higher education   217

12   What does it take to improve teaching?   248

Appendix Course experience questionnaire   270

Notes   275
References   276
Index   286

Figures

4.1   The logical structure of approaches to learning   43
5.1   Student learning in context   83
6.1   Transparency used by Ms Ramsey   93
6.2   Differences in teaching quality by field of study   105
6.3   Scores on the 'Good Teaching' scale of the CEQ for
      thirteen Australian accountancy departments   106
7.1   A model of teaching in higher education   119
11.1 Two dimensions of evaluation in higher education   223

Tables

4.1 Different approaches to learning 46
4.2 Examples of questions in the Lancaster Approaches to Studying and the Biggs Study Process Questionnaires 52
4.3 Relationship between approach to learning and outcome of learning 54
4.4 Levels of Biggs's SOLO taxonomy 55
4.5 Approaches to learning and examination performance 57
5.1 Characteristics of the context of learning associated with deep and surface approaches 81
6.1 Categories and examples of questions in The Course Experience Questionnaire 104
8.1 Some examples of aims and objectives 134
8.2 The aims of a law course 135
10.1 A marking checklist for students' written presentations in a problem-based engineering (vibration analysis) course 202
10.2 A question designed to test understanding of some concepts in statistics 204
10.3 Example of an item used to test understanding of clinical decision analysis concepts in Balla's study 208
10.4 A test of understanding in physics, showing assessment categories derived from qualitative analysis of first year students' responses 209

Preface

The general theme of this book, illustrated in each of its chapters, is that the clear definition of problems in education is more important than the provision of solutions. Many books on teaching and learning in higher education tend to the opposite view: there is a prevailing impression that the busy lecturer or head of department has no time to acquire an understanding of the subject of education. 'Don't give me theory: just give me something that works' is a plea that there is every temptation to answer.

This plea is part of a certain way of looking at teaching, and it is approximately the reverse of the truth about how to improve it. No university chemist or historian would apply it to their own discipline. No physician or architect would apply it to their own practice. No progress in any subject, including education, can be made without the reflective application of knowledge to the right problems.

This book aims to help lecturers change their understanding of teaching. The purpose of education in teaching is the self-development of the teacher. No one but a fool or a charlatan may presume to tell lecturers the right answer to the question of how to teach students better. There are no right answers: there are only methods that may work better or worse for each individual teacher, each department, and each group of students. The idea of this book is to help readers to find their own answers through reason and judgement.

The book is addressed chiefly to practising teachers of undergraduate students in systems of higher education based on the United Kingdom model. It has been written at a period when these teachers are under pressure to demonstrate their effectiveness and efficiency. At the same time, existing methods for guaranteeing academic quality (especially highly selective admissions procedures) are becoming inappropriate as the British and Australian systems move slowly towards more open student access. The book can be read as a text on the evaluation of courses and teaching in this taxing climate of concurrent restraint and expansion. It returns again and again to issues of the quality of teaching, students' perceptions of how effective it is, and indicators of teaching performance. But it is a text written from a certain point of view. Another of its themes is that the demands of performance assessment and quality review, while they form part of the environment in which today's lecturers have to work, can never in themselves make teaching and learning better. We can only hope to improve teaching in higher education if we understand that the process and outcomes of improvement are worthwhile ends in themselves.

Paul Ramsden
Eltham, Victoria

Acknowledgements

This book is the result of my experiences with many teachers and students. I wish to express my particular gratitude to the lecturers who allowed me to talk to them about their teaching and helped me to learn from them. The names of the teachers in those case studies reported in chapters 8, 9, 10, and 11 which are based on previously unpublished material are fictitious. All these case studies represent exemplary teaching in action; but I have thought it prudent not to identify the teachers concerned, whose views, however educationally sound, may not be shared by their colleagues. The quoted material was originally transcribed from interviews, course outlines, and other curriculum material, but it has subsequently been edited in various ways. I apologise if I have accidentally misrepresented anyone's views in the process.

The majority of extracts from student interviews and students' course evaluation forms are from my own research and development work, much of it hitherto unpublished. Some of the extracts from the student interviews have appeared elsewhere, notably in *Understanding Student Learning* (by Noel Entwistle and Paul Ramsden, 1983), published by Croom Helm and now out of print.

The Course Experience Questionnaire was devised as part of a project supported by the Department of Employment, Education and Training (Australia) and directed by Professor Russell Linke. I am indebted to Dr Gerald Elsworth, Research Director of the Review of the Accounting Discipline, for access to the data on which Figure 6.3 is based. The Approaches to Studying Questionnaire mentioned in several chapters was developed at the University of Lancaster in a project directed by Noel Entwistle and Gareth Williams. Parts of chapters 11 and 12 contain material based on a keynote paper presented at the 1990 Higher Education Research and Development Society of Australasia's Annual Conference. The revisionist Confucian anecdote on page 263 is the work of Alan Chang of the Chinese University of Hong Kong.

Among the many people who have helped me in writing this book, I must mention the following particularly: John Balla, John Biggs, Pamela Eakins, Harriet Edquist, Norman Eizenberg, Noel Entwistle, Graham Gibbs, John Hyland, Richard Johnstone, Diana Laurillard, Robyn Lines, Peter McPhee, Brenda Marshall, Ference Marton, Geofferey Masters, John Milton, Michael Nott, Cliff Ogleby, Kate Patrick, Michael Prosser, Kathleen Roth, Andrew Stephanou, Keith Trigwell, Andrew Vincent, and Ken Wright. My greatest debt is to Elaine Martin. She read several drafts of the manuscript, as well as discussing my half-formed ideas, and any merit the book may possess is due to her exacting intellectual criticism and her practical wisdom as a teacher.

Part 1

Learning and teaching in higher education

Chapter 1

Introduction

You cannot be wise without some basis of knowledge; but you may easily acquire knowledge and remain bare of wisdom.

(A.N. Whitehead)

HIGHER EDUCATION TEACHING IN ITS CONTEXT

Today's lecturers work in a climate of expanding government intervention. They are told that higher education has obstinately refused to accept the need to respond to the changing economic and social conditions of the second half of the twentieth century. They are assailed with the accusation that higher education is a drain on scarce national resources; simultaneously, they are informed that it holds the key to improved economic performance. Requirements to cut public expenditure have led to less money in the system and to demands to use what there is more efficiently. Growing numbers of students and moves towards more open access have meant that the available resources have to be spread more thinly. At the same time, there has been assiduous pressure on institutions of higher education to give a formal and public account of themselves for funding purposes, and to carry out more visible types of evaluation, especially of research activity. The use of overt measures of performance, including numerical indicators of research output and the appraisal of academic staff, has become part of higher education policy.

For the most part the institutions, tied as they are to central government for much of their finance, have given in to the pressures. As a consequence, the pleasures of the academic life have dwindled for many teachers in higher education. We are likely to be preoccupied with a constant stream of demands – produce more research papers, attract more external money, conform to exacting criteria for performance appraisal, supervise more graduate students, get those students through their degrees more quickly. Special tensions arise from the requirement to do more with less. Where many polytechnic lecturers used to handle classes of 30 to 50 students, they are now faced with groups of 100 to 200. The university in which I teach currently has some first year classes of 900 students and, in some faculties, a staff to student ratio of 1:25. Today's lecturers are expected to deal with an unprecedentedly broad spectrum of student ability and background. Detailed previous knowledge, especially in mathematics and science, cannot any longer be relied on. As a result, courses and teaching methods must be amended to deal with classes that are now not only larger, but also more mixed in their attainments.

It is little exaggeration to say that these changes, taken together, mean that the average university or polytechnic teacher is now expected to be an excellent teacher: a man or woman who can expertly redesign courses and methods of teaching to suit different groups of students, deal with large mixed-ability classes, and juggle new administrative demands, while at the same time carrying a heavy research responsibility and showing accountability to a variety of masters as both a teacher and a scholar. How are we to adapt to this changed environment?

A RATIONALE FOR LEARNING TO TEACH BETTER

These pressures form an inescapable background for any discussion of better teaching in universities, colleges, and polytechnics. As you read this book, you may be wondering how to cope next week with a class that has grown to twice its former size, or how to convince your head of department that your performance is excellent in your annual appraisal. One way to address these problems would be for me to write and you to read a book about how to handle large classes, or how to present evidence in an appraisal interview. These are reasonable questions; but we should be careful not to confuse symptoms with causes. We deceive ourselves if we think that responses to new demands like these constitute our real problem, as surely as institutions and governments deceive themselves if they think that the forces of accountability will automatically improve the standard of teaching and research, and as surely as students deceive themselves if they think that passing tomorrow's examination is what learning is all about. The truth is that the stresses placed on us form an entirely inadequate basis for enhancing the quality of teaching. Something else is needed to make teaching better. If you really want to improve your own teaching, you must understand what this something is.

This book has been written because I believe that teaching is one of the most delightful and exciting of all human activities when it is done well and that it is one of the most humiliating and tedious when it is done poorly. Let us be clear about one fact: the quality of undergraduate education needs to improve, and it has needed to improve for a long time. No golden age of impeccable instruction and taken-for-granted high academic standards ever existed, except in the world of academic mythology. Appraisal or no appraisal, large classes or small, it is useless to deny that, although there is much that is and has been excellent in higher education teaching, there is a great deal that has always been frankly bad. And there is little in the world of education that is more depressing than bad university teaching. Perhaps its nadir is reached in the vision of an outstanding scholar standing before a class of brilliant, hand-picked first year students. He or she mumbles lifelessly from a set of well-worn notes while half the class snoozes and the other makes desultory jottings, or maybe – if this is an engineering or medicine lecture especially – tests new aerodynamic theories by constructing and launching paper projectiles. Everyone longs to get the hour over and get back to something serious.

The greatest fault of this sort of 'teaching' is not that it is inefficient or ineffective as a way of helping students to learn (though it is that as well) but that it is a tragic waste of knowledge, experience, youth, time, and ability. There need never be any excuse for it: every teacher can learn how to do better. Anyone who has seen really good teaching in action will not need to invoke the exigencies of performance appraisal and maintaining academic standards as reasons for improvement. I think they will begin to understand the truth of the proposition that good teaching, though never easy, always strenuous, and sometimes painful, is nevertheless its own reward.

A VIEW OF LEARNING AND TEACHING[1]

A key idea of this book is that we can improve our teaching by studying our students' learning. It will be useful to be clear from the start just what I mean by learning. One of the ideas you will meet time and time again as you read the following chapters is that learning in educational institutions should be about changing the ways in which learners understand, or experience, or conceptualise the world around them. The 'world around them' includes the concepts and methods that are characteristic of the discipline or profession that they are studying.

From this point of view, the vital competences in academic disciplines consist in *understanding*. By understanding, I mean the way in which students apprehend and discern phenomena related to the subject, rather than what they know about them or how they can manipulate them. Many students can juggle formulae and reproduce memorised textbook knowledge while not understanding their subjects in a way that is helpful for solving real problems. Merely being able to repeat quantities of information on demand is not evidence of a change in understanding – at any level of education. Learning that involves a change in understanding implies and includes a facility with a subject's techniques and an ability to remember its details. These skills become embedded in our knowledge during the slow process of changing our understanding of a topic, as anyone who will reflect on their own learning will recognise.

The idea of learning as a qualitative change in a person's view of reality is essential to an appreciation of my main argument. I shall maintain that improving teaching involves the same process that informs high quality student learning. It implies changing how *we* think about and experience teaching – it involves changes in our conceptions, in our common-sense theories of teaching as they are expressed in practice. These theories consist of sets of ideas and knowledge of their application. But they are not coherent conceptual structures inside teachers' heads; they are expressed, as far as the individual teacher is concerned, solely in their experiences of teaching. They are exemplified through individual activity in the classroom, the design and implementation of educational programmes, and even the management of teaching departments and institutions. If the way in which lecturers understand teaching determines how effectively they will teach, as I hope to show, then simple solutions that offer better teaching through such devices as training in lecturing and group work skills, or giving bonuses to good teachers, are bound to fail. In subsequent chapters I shall try to illustrate exactly what this means for improving the standard of higher education.

The aim of teaching is simple: it is to make student learning possible. Teaching always involves attempts to alter students' understanding, so that they begin to conceptualise phenomena and ideas in the way scientists, mathematicians, historians, physicians, or other subject experts conceptualise them – in the way, that is to say, that we want them to understand them. There can be no such thing as a value-free education. This book, too, embodies a central educational value. Its main object is to help improve teaching in higher education through encouraging academic staff to reason about what they do and why they do it. This argument rests on the proposition that higher education will benefit if those who teach enquire into the effects of their activities on their students' learning. This proposition, together with the idea that changes in how we think about and experience teaching are crucial to improvements in higher education, leads to this book being different from others that have been written on the subject in a number of ways.

A REFLECTIVE APPROACH TO IMPROVING TEACHING

The assumption that the primary aim of teaching is to make student learning possible leads to the contention that each and every teaching action, and every operation to evaluate or improve teaching, should be judged against the simple criterion of whether it can reasonably be expected to lead to the kind of student learning which is desired by lecturers. We shall look at what this kind of learning is in chapter 3.

This in turn leads to an argument for a reflective and enquiring approach as a necessary condition for improving teaching. Such a strategy has always been tenable good teachers down the ages have continually used what they learned from their students to improve their practice. But it is probably easier to implement it today than it was 20 years ago. During this time there have occurred some important investigations which have looked, from the students' point of view, at the processes and conditions of effective learning in higher education. These offer a valuable foundation for the development of higher-quality teaching. One result of the knowledge gained through this research is confirmation of a fact that many educators have known for years – that teaching and learning in higher education are inextricably and elaborately linked. To teach is to make an assumption about what and how the student learns; therefore, to teach well implies learning about students' learning. 'Learning and teaching are constantly interchanging activities. One learns by teaching; one cannot teach except by constantly learning' (Eble, 1988, p. 9).

A recurrent finding of this research into student learning is that we can never assume that the impact of teaching on student learning is what we expect it to be. Students' thoughts and actions are profoundly affected by the educational context or environment in which they learn. They react to the demands of teaching and assessment in ways that are difficult to predict: a lot of their 'learning' is not directly about chemistry or history or economics, but about learning how to please lecturers and gain high marks. These strategies all too often lead to them using methods of study that focus on simply recalling and reproducing information rather than the actions which will lead to changes in their understanding. An important part of good teaching is to try to understand these contextual effects and to adapt assessment and teaching strategies accordingly.

Good teaching involves striving continually to learn about students' understanding and the effects of teaching on it. Precisely because the research into student learning in higher education has studied and described the conditions which are necessary for changes in student understanding, it provides a convenient source of ideas for teaching. I shall try to show how these research insights, when harnessed together with our own experiences as teachers, can help us to decide on the best ways to organise the curriculum, evaluate teaching in order to encourage improvement, and plan satisfactory programmes for teaching lecturers to teach better.

A FOCUS ON SEVERAL DIFFERENT LEVELS OF THE SYSTEM

It is tempting to see improving the quality of teaching as requiring a single focus – on the individual lecturer. This emphasis is clear in most manuals on effective university teaching; it is common in the workshops and seminars run by the educational development units that exist in many institutions of higher education; it is seen to be very important by the institutions when they consider evaluating teaching performance and motivating staff to teach better.

I shall argue that this is too narrow a view. Improvement requires intervention at several different levels of the enterprise of higher education. The level of the individual lecturer is an important point of influence, but it is not the only one. Although university teaching is still in many cases a very private business, no lecturer works alone. Many well-intentioned changes to teaching fall foul of the apathy or jealousy of departmental colleagues. Focusing on this level alone is likely to create frustration, conflict, and ultimately regression to the status quo. To achieve change in the quality of teaching and learning, we ought rather to look carefully at the environment in which a lecturer works and the system of ideas which that environment represents. This means an emphasis on courses and departments as well as on individual academics. It is often more efficient and more practical to try and change a large course than to start by trying to change every single teacher in it. We should also look to the management of academic units: to what extent does a head of department understand and encourage effective teaching in his or her discipline? The highest point of intervention, for the purposes of this book, is the institution itself. What understanding of teaching is manifest in its public statements and its internal procedures? To what extent does a university or college vigorously promote teaching which will lead to high quality learning? If it wants teachers to change, it must direct resources towards helping them to change.

AN EMPHASIS ON HOW TO HELP STUDENTS LEARN ACADEMIC CONTENT

As I have already indicated, one approach to improving teaching in higher education involves concentrating on the various techniques of instruction – how to give a lecture, organise a laboratory class, or run a small group discussion, for example. This book takes a fresh approach to the problem. It concentrates on the best ways to teach students in relation to what we know about how they learn actual subject matter in the everyday setting of classes and assessment. Why is this such an important difference?

Much university teaching is still based on the theory that students will learn if we transmit information to them in lectures, or if we make them do things in practicals or seminars. It is therefore not surprising that improving teaching is often seen as a process of acquiring skills – how to lecture, how to run small groups, how to use computers, how to set examination papers, and so on. But effective teaching is not essentially about learning techniques like this. They are actually rather easily acquired; it is understanding how to use them that takes constant practice and reflection. And they are useful only in so far as they are directed by a clear awareness of key educational principles – in particular, the principle that the content of student learning is logically prior to the methods of teaching the content.

We shall find as we move through the book that the skills of selecting teaching methods, structuring and planning courses, assessing students, and discovering the effects of teaching on students through evaluation, may all be derived from a small number of essential teaching principles of this kind. No book can tell you how to approach a teaching problem; only you learn how to do that, for yourself. When you have learned how to approach a teaching problem, you will have learned something far more valuable than a set of rules on how to run a class of 200, or how to persuade a recalcitrant student to say something in a tutorial. You will have learned to make the technical skills of teaching part of your understanding of teaching.

MOVING TOWARDS A PROFESSIONAL APPROACH TO TEACHING IN HIGHER EDUCATION

For too long we have relied in higher education on teaching that is essentially an amateur affair. A professional approach to teaching should be seen in the same light as a professional approach to law, medicine, or engineering. From the perspective adopted in this book, it is not enough for a lecturer to be an exceptional clinician, advocate, or designer. He or she must be a distinguished teacher as well.

A distinctive characteristic of professionals is that they retain theoretical knowledge on which to base their activities. This body of knowledge is more than a series of techniques and rules. It is an ordered pattern of ideas and evidence that a professional teacher uses in order to decide on an appropriate course of action from many possible choices. The professional authority of the academic-as-scholar rests on a body of knowledge; the professional authority of the academic-as-teacher should rest on a body of didactic knowledge. This comprises knowledge of how the subject he or she professes is best learned and taught. I hope to convince you that a theoretical understanding of learning and teaching and their relationship to each other is an essential base for effective action as a university teacher. Changing students' understandings of the subject matter they learn is the answer to improving their learning: in turn, the key to improving teaching is changing the way in which the process of education is conceived by its practitioners.

'Teaching' in this book is defined in its broadest sense to include the aims of the curriculum, the methods of transmitting the knowledge those aims embody, the assessment of students, and the evaluation of the effectiveness of the instruction with which they are provided. Professional teachers in higher education display certain salient characteristics. They possess a broad range of specialist teaching skills; they never lose sight of the primacy of their goals for student learning; they listen to and learn from their students; they constantly evaluate their own performance. They understand that teaching is about making it possible for students to learn; they succeed in integrating educational wisdom and hard-headed classroom knowledge. I want to show in the following pages how every lecturer can learn to emulate the qualities of teachers like these through reflectively applying intelligence about his or her students' learning to the problems of teaching. The book will do this by linking theory and implementation at a number of different levels.

THE STRUCTURE OF THE BOOK

The following chapters invite readers to think in depth about their students' learning and their own understanding of teaching, and to undertake a journey which may lead them to change their way of understanding it. There are as many different ways to read a book as there are readers. This one tries to tell a continuous story that has a beginning, a middle, and an end – even if the end cannot be more than a glimpse into an uncertain future. It begins from the idea that there are different ways of experiencing teaching; it ends with speculations on how to make it better.

Part 1 lays the foundations. It covers some of the central ideas that have emerged from studies of students' and lecturers' experiences of learning and teaching in higher education. We shall explore how and what students learn in different academic subjects, and look at the students' views of what effective teaching consists of. This part also examines some of the different ways in which lecturers understand the process of teaching in higher education. A grasp of the main ideas about how students experience learning is indispensable for a complete understanding of the arguments about the nature and methodology of teaching that follow in the remainder of the book.

Out of these experiences of lecturers and students grows a set of principles for effective teaching in higher education. Chapters 6 and 7 isolate these principles and describe the relations between how lecturers understand teaching and the strategies they use.

Part 2 of the book shows how the ideas can be used to enhance educational quality. Its three chapters link theory and practice by covering three of the main areas, or problems, that we face in teaching: what we should teach, how we should teach it, and how we can decide what students have learned from what we have taught them. It is quite impossible to do justice to every method of teaching and assessment in higher education in one book, and these chapters do not attempt to do anything of the kind. They are highly selective (they do not consider graduate supervision and they say little about distance education, for example); and they concentrate on the application of principles in real situations rather than lists of techniques. Their aim is to stimulate thinking about methods of instruction in taught courses, first by looking critically at current methods and second by providing some case studies of good practice. These case studies of exemplary teaching, based on the experiences of actual lecturers, demonstrate that the improvement of our teaching is an entirely realistic goal.

Part 3 is also about applying theory. Here, though, the spotlight shifts to the theory's relevance to measuring performance, evaluating instruction, and educational development and training. A fairly full treatment is given of the main problems in evaluating teaching and combining self-evaluation, which is so essential for improvement, with measures of accountability. Although all evaluation, like all student assessment, has the potential to distort the curriculum, I argue that the remedy is not to turn our backs on it but to use it to our advantage to improve the quality of teaching. The concluding chapter tries to show how the arguments about improving student learning may be applied to the entire process of educational development in higher education. From the educational perspective established earlier in the book, it will become clear that much of what is now being done in the name of maintaining academic standards is based on naïve theories of learning and ignores the down-to-earth reality of good teaching. If we really want to improve the quality of higher education, the principles of effective teaching must also be applied to the task of evaluating performance, managing departments, and educating lecturers.

Chapter 2

Ways of understanding teaching

No one starts out teaching well.

(Herbert Kohl)

A good way of starting to learn more about any subject is to review what you already know about it. We quite often find that we think we know more than we actually do. We can remember an idea or a formula, but get stuck when we try to apply it to a real problem. This signals the need to go back a step and revise our earlier work.

This approach can be applied to improving teaching. Most lecturers probably think that they know more about teaching than they really do. Teaching in higher education is a very complicated and detailed subject. It takes many years of practice to learn how to do it well, and even then you will not have learned enough. Some lecturers do not know where to start improving it; at once overwhelmed by and unwilling to admit its complexity, they ask for a set of rules that will solve all their difficulties. Half the difficulty with doing it better is knowing what the real problem is, of being aware of what we do not know. In order to be clear about what we do not know, we will find it useful to ignore the details of teaching and form a picture, a simplified description, to help us to understand our problem.

In this chapter we look at a simple description of different ways of understanding teaching. Its purpose is to encourage active reflection on your own understanding of it. Later in the book, when I have described learning and teaching from several points of view, including the student's, we shall return to these ideas and consider their application to more involved problems in real life teaching.

What exactly is teaching about? What do we mean when we say we 'teach' someone something? What are the main problems we face in teaching? What methods should we use, and why? What helps our students to learn? What stops them learning? Can thinking about teaching usefully be separated from the activity of teaching itself? The case studies of teachers described below are fictionalised and each combines information from several different individuals, but all the information comes from what actual teachers have said or have been observed to do.

CASE 1

John teaches electrical engineering. He regards today's students as inferior to those of ten, or even five years ago – mainly, he says, because the schools don't prepare them as well. Asked why he thinks this can be so, when the entry standards to his department's courses are now higher, he blames falling standards in school-leaving examinations – especially maths. He also argues that today's students put less time and effort into their studies.

He has been experiencing, for the first time in his career, discipline problems in lectures:

> The students just aren't interested, aren't bothered, like they used to be. They're out to get a degree as easily as possible. They're not natural workaholics, which engineering students have got to be, because the amount of work they have to get through is reasonably strenuous. This lot think they can memorise the facts the night before the exam, spot the question types, and plug the numbers into the right formulae, and to hell with listening in lectures. They're wrong, of course, but they don't know how wrong until after the first year exams.

John wants some new techniques for delivering his content more effectively.

> Most of the things that used to work don't seem to work any more. The techniques in the book on lecturing you lent me didn't work either. They all ignored the buzz group questions and talked about Saturday's game or something. They're basically idle and won't do a thing unless it gets a mark. I tried a few labs differently, I asked them more questions and tried to explain things better, but there were problems because some

of the students reckoned I was spending too much time on explaining and not enough on getting the stuff across, covering the syllabus. Which was true of course. And now with my student appraisal coming up, I'm worried, I guess. Remembering what we tell them is the big thing for students. The amount of knowledge in this subject increases every few minutes and the syllabus is now twice as big as it was when I was a student. I'm thinking about some video presentations to get the stuff across, to transfer it more efficiently from my mind to the students' heads. If something is visual they'll remember it better. Isn't that right?

CASE 2

Andrea teaches politics. She is convinced that students learn best by doing, by being active: 'The session you ran on small group teaching was really helpful. The problem is to get them doing and talking. They come into second year expecting me to be the fount of all knowledge. They're wanting all the answers.'

She sees a main task in her teaching as being able to overcome this lack of independence by managing student learning in class.

What I'm doing now is not thinking so much about the material in the topic but about how I'm going to split this up and work out the groups. How I'm going to structure the movement from two to say, groups of six or a plenary. It's vital to get people voicing their opinions early. Once they're off, the session will be pretty much over and you're home and dry. You've treated the problem effectively.

Andrea does not talk about the subject matter, the concepts, and knowledge associated with the particular topic, in her description of her class management strategy. She assumes that if the students are talking and the class ends on a high note that they will have learned something important. The students' involvement is a measure of success, and she feels quite successful.

CASE 3

Kevin teaches physiology. He has spent the last five years restructuring the first and second year curriculum for medical students in this discipline, and has become interested in applying ideas from educational research to the practice of teaching. He has developed an ability to step back from the immediate events of the lecture room and practical class and see what is happening to the quality of students' engagement with the content. He has altered the curriculum to make it more interesting, to make its aims clearer, and to begin from students' naïve conceptions of physiological structure and systems. He has tried to change the assessment methods so that students are rewarded for (and see they are rewarded for) understanding and explanation rather than being able simply to reproduce 'correct' factual information. Student evaluations and grades have improved, and there is also some evidence of students being able to use the material more effectively when they begin the clinical component of the medical course.

He enjoys teaching but is not entirely comfortable with his course. 'I try to listen to students all the time and "read" their work as I am marking it. They are all different. It's still far from ideal. I can't get to all of them. I've come to see that teaching can never be perfect and that if you wait for the one perfect solution you delude yourself and nothing changes. In the end it's up to the teacher to keep changing. I spend a lot of time thinking "I wonder what the difference is between what I did last time and what I did this time. What caused the difference?" It's puzzling and it's enjoyable. Sometimes I realise then that what I expected students to get from the session wasn't what they actually got, so I change it next time. I try to expect the unexpected.'

WHAT JOHN, ANDREA, AND KEVIN ARE SAYING

Case 1
- Teaching is about transmitting knowledge from academic staff to students.
- Student learning is separate from teaching.
- Student learning is a process of acquiring new knowledge.
- Problems in learning are not to do with teaching.

Case 2
- Teaching is about managing student activity.
- Student learning is associated with teaching.
- Problems in learning can be fixed by adopting the right teaching strategy.

Case 3
- Teaching is about making it possible for students to learn subject content.

- Student learning is a long and uncertain process of changes in understanding.
- Teaching and student learning are parts of the same whole; understanding students' ways of thinking about the subject matter is essential to effective instruction.
- The activity of teaching and the process of reflecting on it are inextricably linked.
- Problems in learning may be addressed by changing teaching, but with no certainty of success. Constant monitoring is needed, as yesterday's solutions might not work today.

These three examples highlight important differences in the ways lecturers think about teaching and function as teachers. Success in learning how to improve your own teaching is related to the extent to which you are prepared to conceptualise your teaching as a process of helping students to change their understanding of the subject matter you teach them.

But simply thinking about teaching is not enough. Every teacher has thought about teaching: the challenging assignment is to merge thinking and doing. Constant practice informed by the study of the qualities displayed by good teachers is necessary. Everyone has progressed some way down the road represented by these three stories; theories 1 and 2 above are not so much 'wrong' as inadequate representations of the truth. They are narrow visions of teaching. Telling students about facts and ideas in science or humanities is not in itself incorrect: it is simply that it is only one part of instruction, and not by any means its most important part. Blaming students is not improper – what teacher has not done it sometimes, often with more than enough justification? But that is not the point. It is not an efficient or effective way of helping students to learn: it is not in any sense a professional approach to teaching.

Each of these ways of experiencing teaching has implications for the ways in which students will learn. In the following three chapters I shall look at these implications, from three related points of view: the different outcomes of learning, the ways in which students go about learning, and the students' perceptions of teaching.

Chapter 3

What students learn

Instead of encouraging the student to devote himself to his studies for the sake of studying, instead of encouraging in him a real love for his subject and for inquiry, he is encouraged to study for the sake of his personal career; he is led to acquire only such knowledge as is serviceable in getting him over the hurdles which he must clear for the sake of his advancement.

(Karl Popper)

QUALITATIVE DIFFERENCES IN LEARNING

We come now to examine what is known about the quality of student learning in higher education. While you are reading this chapter, it will be useful to keep in mind the different conceptions of teaching described in chapter 2 and to think about how they might be related to differences in what students learn. It may be helpful as well to think occasionally about your own teaching, and how what you do might lead to different student learning outcomes.

The central questions to be addressed here are: 'What do we want students to learn?' and 'What are the variations in the outcomes of their learning?'. An important idea is introduced: there is often an inconsistency between the outcomes of student learning as teachers and students would *ideally* like them to be and the reality of what students *actually* learn. In other words, there is a gap between what lecturers say they want from their students and what students actually accomplish. Every teacher in higher education wants students to understand important concepts and their associated facts and procedures in his or her subject, but many students are unable to accomplish these goals.

Why does this discrepancy occur? The argument developed in the next few chapters is that differences in the quality of learning are due to differences in the ways that students go about learning; and these differences can in turn be explained in terms of their experiences of teaching. We can only improve the quality of education if we study its effects on students and look at the experience through their eyes.

The issue of what students learn from higher education has been examined from many points of view – those of lecturers, educational theorists, employers, graduates, and the students themselves. A good deal of research has been carried out into what students actually remember and understand from their studies. And there is no shortage of complaint about the quality of student learning, and by implication methods of teaching. But in this area it is more than usually difficult to decide where rational enquiry ends and prejudice begins – particularly now that higher education has become more attractive to political hobby-horse riders than it used to be.

It is perhaps simplest to arrange the present selective review by looking at what students learn in terms of a series of qualitatively different levels. At the most abstract level, there are very general abilities and personal qualities – such as 'thinking critically and imaginatively' or 'being able to communicate effectively'. At the second level, there are more specific, content-related changes in understanding, linked to particular disciplines or professions – such as understanding the formal theorems of Newtonian mechanics or the inductive propositions of psychology, as well as the less easily defined ways of thinking 'like a sociologist' or 'like an electronic engineer' when faced with a typical problem in a subject. Finally, there are highly categorical proficiencies like knowledge of factual information, technical or manipulative skills, and specific problem-solving techniques. Knowledge at all these levels, and the ability to connect knowledge at each level to each of the others, is regarded as essential if a graduating student is to be considered an educated person.

GENERAL AIMS AND HIGHER LEVEL ABILITIES

The concept of excellence in higher education has remained surprisingly unchanged down the years. In 'Universities and their function', an essay first published in 1929, A.N. Whitehead described his view of the proper aims for student learning of an institution of higher education; his comments are entirely compatible with the expectations of lecturers today. Whitehead's ideas were, perhaps unexpectedly, also in harmony with the idea that higher education should be 'relevant' to the community and the economy – although there was nothing crudely utilitarian about them. His main theme was that a university education should lead students to 'the imaginative acquisition of knowledge':

> The university imparts information, but it imparts it imaginatively. . . . A university which fails in this respect has no reason for existence. This atmosphere of excitement, arising from imaginative consideration, transforms knowledge. A fact is no longer a bare fact: it is invested with all its possibilities. It is no longer a burden on the memory: it is energising as the poet of our dreams, and as the architect of our purposes.
>
> Imagination is not to be divorced from the facts: it is a way of illuminating the facts. It works by eliciting the general principles which apply to the facts, as they exist, and then by an intellectual survey of alternative possibilities which are consistent with those principles. It enables men to construct a vision of a new world, and it preserves the zest of life by the suggestion of satisfying purposes. . . .
>
> Thus the proper function of a university is the imaginative acquisition of knowledge. Apart from this importance of the imagination, there is no reason why business men, and other professional men, should not pick up their facts bit by bit as they want them for particular occasions. A university is imaginative or it is nothing – at least nothing useful.
>
> (Whitehead, 1929, pp. 139,145)

Whitehead's 'imaginative understanding' is reminiscent of the often-articulated aim that students in higher education should develop the ability to 'think critically'. The Hale Report (Hale, 1964), for example, asserted that 'an implicit aim of higher education is to encourage students to think for themselves'. Ashby (1973, pp. 147–9) described how students should develop 'from the uncritical acceptance of orthodoxy to creative dissent . . . there must be opportunities for the intellect to be stretched to its capacity, the critical faculty sharpened to the point at which it can change ideas'. More recently, an Australian Senate Report reiterated the same theme, with modern variations. Australian university graduates should possess 'a capacity to look at problems from a number of different perspectives, to analyse, to gather evidence, to synthesise, and to be flexible, creative thinkers' (Aulich, 1990, p. 3). Similarly, the CNAA has described the aims of a programme of study in higher education as:

> The development of students' intellectual and imaginative powers; their understanding and judgement; their problem-solving skills; their ability to communicate; their ability to see relationships within what they have learned and to perceive their field of study in a broader perspective. The programme must aim to stimulate an enquiring, analytical and creative approach, encouraging independent judgement and critical self-awareness.
>
> (quoted in Gibbs, 1990, p.1)

The university and polytechnic lecturers in a survey of educational objectives carried out at Lancaster University in the late 1960s (Entwistle and Percy, 1974) evidently thought along corresponding lines; in these interviews, 'there was a substantial consensus about the importance of critical thinking' (Entwistle, 1984, p. 4). Knapper (1990) summarises two studies, at Monash University in Australia and at the University of Alberta in Canada, that tell the same story about lecturers' aims for student learning. Staff were asked, among other things, to indicate their agreement or disagreement with 15 possible teaching goals. The Canadian and Australian academics were most likely to agree with the same three educational objectives:

- To teach students to analyse ideas or issues critically
- To develop students' intellectual/thinking skills
- To teach students to comprehend principles or generalisations.

Analogous statements are found in writings advocating the need for 'lifelong' or 'anticipatory' learning in higher education, particularly in professional fields. Aims such as the capacity to respond flexibly to changing circumstances, to learn throughout a career, and to integrate theory and practice by generalising from a theoretical knowledge base to deal capably with previously unmet situations, are very common (see Bligh, 1982; Knapper and Cropley, 1985; General Medical Council, 1987; Aulich, 1990; Williams, 1988). Equally ubiquitous are arguments that these goals are not being met by conventional means of instruction and course administration. Of these kinds of criticism, more in a moment.

CONTENT-RELATED EXPECTATIONS: DISCIPLINARY AND PROFESSIONAL ABILITIES

What of more specific objectives related to particular disciplines and professions? What is involved in learning a subject well? This kind of goal does, of course, overlap with the general aims described above. When lecturers are asked to describe what they expect one of their competent students to be able to do, their answers naturally vary depending on the discipline or profession being taught. However, there is also a sense in which the expectations are uniform, so that they can be related to the general aims of the kind summarised above.

Entwistle and Percy's lecturers, when speaking about their subjects more specifically, spoke of objectives involving the effective use of evidence and social awareness (history) entering into different individual and cultural conditions (English); interpreting and analysing experimental data (physics); and becoming concerned with the nature of evidence and scientific argument (psychology). Many of the lecturers interviewed were apprehensive about overemphasising factual knowledge (Entwistle, 1984, p. 3). The aims of medical and veterinary schools, and many other professional faculties, generally stress the importance of developing professional problem-solving skills and the ability to apply information to new problems, together with the development of professional values peculiar to the vocation (Heath, T., 1990).

It is clear from several studies that the ideas expressed by teachers in higher education will usually embrace knowledge of procedures and familiarity with the basic facts of the subject, but they will invariably include what the lecturers themselves describe as something more fundamental. These fundamentals can be summarised as an *understanding of key concepts*; an ability to go beyond the orthodox and the expected so that hitherto unmet problems can be tackled with spirit; a facility with typical methods of approaching a problem in the discipline; and – closely associated with previous point – an *awareness of what learning and understanding in the discipline consists of.* In other words, lecturers describe content-related versions, with a *substantive* and a *procedural* or *syntactic* element, of the general principles of 'critical thinking' and understanding. It is important to understand that the general educational goals gain their meaning through the specific subject content in which they are expressed.

What do you want *your* students to learn? In my own development work with higher education staff, I have often found it valuable to introduce ideas about teaching against a background of what lecturers themselves want their students to learn. (The importance of relating all teaching methods to particular goals for student learning is a topic which I shall be highlighting again and again.) When my colleagues and I asked a group of newly appointed lecturers in several different disciplines to describe their aims for undergraduate student learning, these were some of the things they mentioned:

- Taking an imaginative and creative approach to design problems (environmental planning)
- Understanding when a particular mathematical concept (integration) is needed for an (engineering) problem and when it is not (mechanical engineering)
- Being able to analyse different perspectives on the nature of Renaissance art (fine arts)
- Communicating professionally (listen carefully, interpret accurately, respond with concern) with a patient (medicine)
- Having an appreciation of the significance of the normal in interpreting data from a patient (medicine)
- Understanding the limitations of the concept of marginal utility in real situations (economics)
- Understanding the social, political, and economic context of legal decisions; and developing the desire to know more about them (law)
- Analysing the variety of practices and disputes that arise in the area of industrial relations (industrial relations)
- Seeing the connections between a physiological and a pharmacological way of solving a problem (pharmacology).

Content-related objectives of this type are important. They form a rather more accessible link between studies of what students have learned and the curriculum with which they are provided than the more general aims previously mentioned. It seems that high quality student learning is a concept which is well understood by teachers in higher education. The expectations all show a degree of consistency, despite their specific subject allusions. Analysing, understanding, appreciating the significance, interpreting, are recurring descriptions for explaining what students are meant to learn. It seems plain that a student who had achieved these objectives would be well on the way towards the 'imaginative understanding' of a subject as described by Whitehead. An understanding of the main issues in a subject, an appreciation of the nature of appropriate arguments in it, an awareness of what counts as relevant evidence, and the wisdom to think critically and admit one's deficiencies in knowledge – all these things are important, though they naturally vary depending on the discipline being studied.

The academic staff who expressed these objectives for their students did, with some prompting, describe acquisition of facts and techniques as well as more general skills (being able to identify and use legal rules, for example). But they were always at pains to point out that these were subordinate to and *included within* their higher level objectives. Factual knowledge had no value in itself; but the higher level objectives had no meaning unless they were taken to imply the lower level knowledge. This is also interesting, because these views are exactly compatible with the assumptions of the theory of student learning that informs this book. It seems that teachers in higher education do not ultimately judge students on the amount of knowledge in their possession, but on their self-critical awareness of what they do not know and their readiness to find out more.

In discussions with teaching staff of a more formal kind, I have found that they persist in emphasising the importance of encouraging students to undertake higher order thinking about problems in the discipline (Ramsden, Masters, and Bowden, 1988). Physics lecturers, for example, argued that first year physics learning should not simply be a matter of memorising facts and formulae and applying these to familiar types of problems. They insisted that students ought to relate experiences in the physical world to theoretical concepts: 'Students have to be able to visualise and understand the situation and say "Yes, this formula should apply to that situation"', as one lecturer put it. For these lecturers, an understanding of the role of mathematical models in physics was important; students should appreciate the importance of seeing the relationships among the equations that they encountered rather than seeing them as unrelated formulae applicable to different physical problems: 'Part of the idea that you're trying to get across is that it's profitable to start from simple situations, simple models, and see how and when things depart from this in the real world.'

Law lecturers interviewed as part of the same project described their objectives for student learning on two levels. The first included overarching substantive concepts such as the development of a sensitivity to the idea of morality in twentieth-century law, together with general procedural objectives such as learning about the dynamics of law and about methods that can be used to change its course. The second embraced more specific legal concepts (such as what 'property in trust' means to a lawyer) and related specific skills (such as arguing with legal logic). Again the emphasis was on changes in student understanding and the ability to tackle new problems with confidence.

In first year history, a fundamental goal was for students to 'think historically'. This involved a sensitivity to the ways people in other cultures understood themselves and a healthy caution about applying currently understood definitions of concepts such as 'feudalism' to the past. Developing higher order skills in analysis and historical argument was a crucial objective: a student, according to the history lecturer who was interviewed, should be able 'to pose meaningful questions about the past and answer them logically in the way a historian does, to recognise that history involves debate about how understanding is to be achieved, to eschew the idea that there is one right answer laid down by historians'.

STUDIES OF THE OUTCOMES OF LEARNING

How far do students achieve these intellectual aims, both general and specific? And to what extent is the third type of goal – mastery of particular knowledge and skills – attained? The three types overlap, of course, and so achievement in one area cannot always be precisely separated from that in another. In all cases, however, it is necessary to look at how students have experienced learning in order to judge the extent to which development takes place. There is enough evidence to suggest that there is a good deal of variation in the quality of learning. Moreover, while the general changes in ways of thinking are common enough outcomes, changes in discipline and subject-specific knowledge are often limited to basic procedural skills and the temporary mastery of factual information.

Level 1: General intellectual development

Studies of changes in thinking

William Perry's work at Harvard (Perry, 1970; 1988) clearly implies that students develop increasingly sophisticated ways of thinking as they progress through higher education. Initially, many students appear to conceptualise knowledge as a set of conveniently packaged and static facts and techniques. Learning these packages implies gaining authoritative information about them; the 'right' answers exist, are held by teachers and text-books, and the student's first task is to discern these answers. It is then necessary to remember the information and accurately reproduce it.

Although this conception of knowledge and learning may have served intelligent students well in their time at school, it is, as Säljö (1984) observes, not an invention of the school system, but a part of common-sense thinking. Perry describes a gradual change in students' conceptions, away from the absolutistic view of knowledge and learning towards a relativistic conception. Knowledge is then seen to be uncertain; the truth always remains provisional. Altogether, Perry identified nine 'positions' along a spectrum of ethical and intellectual development in college students. After having passed from the stage of basic duality through a stage of confusion about the nature of knowledge and belief, at the highest level, students will have learned to commit themselves to personal values and particular interpretations of evidence, while at the same time acknowledging the existence of alternative interpretations of 'reality' and being capable of continuing to learn.

A similar pattern of intellectual change emerged in Heath's interviews of students at Princeton (Heath, R., 1964). His ideal type of student (the 'reasonable adventurer'), which other students gradually came to resemble, alternated between curiosity and critical thinking. This conception is comparable to Whitehead's description of the imaginative consideration of knowledge. We may assume that at least part of this development is due to the experience of higher education.

Remaining at this macro level of analysis, we find other studies that show the existence of demonstrable effects on intellectual development. Hasselgren (quoted in Dahlgren, 1984) studied student teachers' abilities to interpret videotape sequences of children at play. Four categories were identified, ranging from partial, impressionistic accounts that mentioned only what was immediately observable, to accounts that considered the events observed as concrete instances of abstract educational ideas. The majority of students showed evidence of development from the lower to the higher categories during their course.

Säljö (1979) carried out an interview study which led to his describing five different understandings of what learning consists of among adults (see also Van Rossum and Schenk, 1984). When students were asked to say what they understood by learning, their replies could be classified into different categories:

1 Learning as a quantitative increase in knowledge. Learning is acquiring information or 'knowing a lot'.
2 Learning as memorising. Learning is storing information that can be reproduced.
3 Learning as acquiring facts, skills, and methods that can be retained and used as necessary.
4 Learning as making sense or abstracting meaning. Learning involves relating parts of the subject matter to each other and to the real world.
5 Learning as interpreting and understanding reality in a different way. Learning involves comprehending the world by reinterpreting knowledge.

You will probably be able to see immediately that conceptions 4 and 5 in Säljö's system are qualitatively different from the first three. The first three conceptions imply a less complex view of what learning consists of. They resemble the early stages of Perry's and Hasselgren's schemes; learning in these conceptions is something *external* to the learner, and at its most extreme (conception 1) is understood to be something that just happens or is done to you by teachers. Conceptions 4 and 5 emphasise the *internal*, or personal aspect of learning: learning is seen as something that you do in order to understand the real world. These conceptions imply a more relativistic, complex, and systematic view of knowledge and how it is achieved and used. And indeed, as we would expect from Perry's work, Säljö found that the adult students who had experienced higher education were more likely to express conceptions 4 and 5. Säljö points out that an important aspect of his system is that it is hierarchical: in other words, students who conceive of learning as understanding reality are also able to see it as increasing their knowledge. Each higher conception implies all the rest beneath it.

Students' and employers' views

Complementary studies of the influence of higher education have been carried out by asking students to describe their attitudes and the significant changes they have experienced as a result of their studies, and by collecting employers' descriptions of the value of graduates. The findings tend to point in the same general direction. West *et al.* (1986), for example, reported the results of an enquiry into mature students' attitudes. Using data from the same students at the beginning and at the end of their courses, they found that the experience of higher education was associated with perceptions of an increase in academic interests, self-esteem, liberal attitudes, and general life satisfaction – and a decrease in dogmatism.

Powell (1985) examined autobiographical accounts written by graduates, and reached the conclusion that students attached most importance to the acquisition of general intellectual skills, attitudes, and values. Specific propositional knowledge was rarely mentioned and was presumably taken for granted; descriptions of the development of problem-solving, logical thinking, and information-gathering skills, together with a growth in self-confidence and independence, dominated the accounts. For example:

I think I learnt to organise my work and myself, to think theoretically and evaluate concepts, to look things up before I made statements, and that first draft work should be left in a drawer for a week before being re-read and totally re-written several times more.

I have realised since finishing at university that I didn't gain so much a body of knowledge as an approach. I became a problem-solver.

What I believe I learnt was a capacity to apply logical principles.

. . . self-directed research, flexibility of approach and resourcefulness and tenacity in grappling with the varying demands of university and family life.

(Powell, 1985, pp. 133–5)

The picture was by no means uniformly satisfactory, however. Negative effects attributed to excessive competition and inappropriate assessment were described. They give a foretaste of the kind of student comments on the quality of university teaching that we meet in subsequent chapters. For example:

I latched on to the idea that to pass you got a clear view of what you were expected to know, and learnt it, word for word. Not much thinking. Just learn the sacred texts. I had no more trouble passing university examinations. Unfortunately, the apparent success of this mind-stunting technique impressed me and retarded my mind's development for years to come.

(Powell, 1985, p. 133)

It is popularly supposed that employers are highly critical of their graduate recruits and the 'irrelevance' of higher education to the world of work, but research into their actual views does not support quite such simple conclusions. In fact, there seem to be many variations in employers' views of the quality of graduates. In Kogan's major study of expectations of higher education in England and Wales (Kogan, 1985) there were certainly some minority views among employers that non-graduates were better employees than graduates, and that university students did not grasp the importance of the market and its forces. On the other hand, the majority of employers seemed to think that higher education did improve their employees' general skills. They believed that it enhanced academic ability and personal qualities, especially flexibility and motivation; they supported educational experiences that increased general understanding:

Few had doubts about the value added by higher education . . . . There were explicit comments approving the opportunity that higher education gave to students: in one accountant's terms, the opportunity 'to study a subject because they love it'. When asked about the advice they would give students about their choices of subject, some employers felt that students would be best studying something they were interested in or good at.

(Kogan, 1985, p. 103)

Many of these employers' views resemble those expressed by the more satisfied students in Powell's study. However, other studies of graduates' skills at work have been less positive: Brennan and McGeevor (1988), for example, found that graduates themselves were critical of experiences of higher education which had emphasised individual work at the expense of collaborative skills in teams (see also Williams, 1988). A recent HMI report on teaching in English polytechnics (DES, 1989) was similarly critical of the over-dependence of students on teachers as sources of knowledge and the effects of this lack of independence on the quality of graduates.

Lecturers' views

Rather surprisingly, though, it is the lecturers themselves who are the least enthusiastic of all about the qualities that their students develop. Both Entwistle and Percy (1974) and Hounsell and Ramsden (1978) report numerous comments criticising students for their lack of intellectual development and their inadequate motivation even at the end of their degree courses. Many students, Entwistle and Percy's lecturers believed, showed a disappointingly low level of understanding after three years of university study. The lecturers in both studies were quick to attribute poor progress to weaknesses in students' natural abilities or personalities.

On balance, it seems that many students' understanding of what learning consists of does change during the course of their studies, and that the changes are in a direction that lecturers and others, including many employers of graduates, find desirable. There is also some evidence of movement towards general intellectual competence and a more open-minded attitude to knowledge and a tolerance of differing values; and there is a degree of satisfaction with these aspects of the outcomes of higher education. But the evidence indicates considerable variation in quality. The effects of higher education are not uniformly positive or strong; some employers, students, and (especially) teachers are dissatisfied with the results of the experience of higher education. Weak development of skills in working cooperatively and independently appears to be one important concern. There is also another problem in taking an optimistic view of the effects of higher education on students from these studies. A nagging anxiety recurs: how well will students have understood and remembered the knowledge and professional skills they supposedly acquired in the early years of their university studies, when their views of learning were so undeveloped? Yet such basic knowledge may be critical to expert judgement. It would seem clear that one of the outcomes of effective teaching will be that it encourages rapid development of more sophisticated conceptions of learning, but there is no evidence that such changes occur until late in most students' experiences of higher education. The third difficulty concerns the level of analysis. The strength of these structural analyses is that they are highly general and not tied to any particular subject content. This is also a weakness, however: differences in intellectual development that are tied to specific subject matter are invisible.

Levels 2 and 3: Content-related outcomes

A depressing picture emerges from studies of the quality of students' understanding in academic disciplines and professional subjects. It seems that many students often do not change their understanding in the way their lecturers would wish.

Set against the epistemological and educational position that was taken in chapter 1 of this book – that learning is fundamentally about changes in understanding of reality, and that teaching should be directed towards helping students to understand phenomena in the way subject experts do – these findings represent a serious indictment of the effectiveness of higher education. It seems that it has not been as successful as it could have been in helping students to change their understanding of, for example, the nature of the physical world, or to grasp the nature of the scientific process. In recent years, it has become clear from numerous investigations that:

- Many students are accomplished at complex routine skills in science, mathematics, and humanities, including problem-solving algorithms.
- Many have appropriated enormous amounts of detailed knowledge, including knowledge of subject-specific terminology.
- Many are able to reproduce large quantities of factual information on demand.
- Many are able to pass examinations.

- But many are *unable* to show that they understand what they have learned, when asked simple yet searching questions that test their grasp of the content. They continue to profess misconceptions of important concepts; their ideas of how experts in their subjects proceed and report their work are often confused; their application of their knowledge to new problems is often weak; their skills in working jointly to solve problems are frequently inadequate. Conceptual changes are 'relatively rare, fragile and context-dependent occurrences'

(Dahlgren, 1984, p. 33).

In summary, the research indicates that, at least for a short period, students retain vast quantities of information. On the other hand, many of them soon seem to forget much of it (see, for example, Saunders, 1980), and they appear not to make good use of what they do remember. They experience many superficial changes – acquiring the jargon of disciplines, for example – but they still tend to operate with naïve and erroneous conceptions. Moreover, many students are unaware of what they do not know: they have not developed self-critical awareness in their subjects.

These lacunae are not confined to higher education students – but that is small consolation. A complete description of the findings would occupy the remaining pages of this book. Among the studies that lead to these conclusions are those of the Gothenburg group of researchers on text-related analysis of the content of learning (see Marton and Säljö, 1984; Dahlgren, 1984; Säljö, 1984); numerous investigations of science and mathematics students' learning; research into medical students' clinical skills and the outcomes of other professional education courses; and studies of humanities and social science students' misconceptions. These studies show that there exist genuine qualitative differences in student learning outcomes.

It may be best to begin this brief summary by recalling the statements made by the physics teachers earlier in this chapter. Remember how they highlighted the importance of students relating physical and mathematical models to each other and to the real world, rather than simply slotting memorised equations into typical problem types. But their views of what their students actually did were in stark contrast to these ideals. Their students, rather like those described in Entwistle and Percy's study, were described as generally incapable or uninterested in higher order thinking or relating ideas to reality. They were perceived to spend their time searching for recognisable problems to which they could apply the 'right' formulae:

> A lot of them seemed to get swamped with formulas. They tried to learn every formula, get every formula in the world – but they didn't know where to go from there.

> If you just have to plug in formulas, you never learn how to analyse and interpret . . . A lot of them didn't understand. They just tried formula shoving.

> They knew every formula, but didn't know the situation to which it applied. Sometimes they recognised it from the symbols, which didn't always work, because symbols change in different situations. They got confused there. They'd try to shove in Density instead of Distance!

The students in this study did not disagree that they adopted this way of learning:

> You learn the formulas, as many as you can. You could say that's the whole exam. You have to understand the question and put in the right formula. So that's all I have to know – the formulas.
>
> (Ramsden *et al.*, 1988)

Teachers in an Australian accountancy course with which I was involved were also critical of their students' understanding, their ways of learning, and their general attitude to studying:

> In the final exam, students are weak on conceptual points, such as the matching principle. It is possible to pass without being competent in handling Debit and Credit, or accruals. Students can't write; this may be because they don't understand the concepts. So they concentrate on number-crunching in order to pass.

> Many students go from week to week, from topic to topic, without being able to see how anything fits together. Therefore they find the subject difficult, and this reduces their motivation to work at it.

> Tutorials are largely wasted. Many students don't prepare for them, but just come to copy the answers from the board. This would apply to one third of the best groups, two-thirds of the worst ones.

They believe they already know accounting, when all they have learned is rules and techniques dogmatically.

In a previous investigation of lecturers' perceptions in the United Kingdom, I found that staff were easily able to distinguish the learning outcomes of their weaker students (the majority) from those of their stronger ones (a small minority) using similar terms. Engineering lecturers, for example, spoke of students' inability to relate technical knowledge to realistic applications and their tendency to handle every new problem as a special case. A psychology teacher observed a comparable phenomenon:

> The general impression I get is that they don't seem to see how things hang together. They seem to treat the articles they read as if they were all disparate and not related to the same topics – there's no coherence in it, they don't see a pattern. They don't see why somebody's done something in relation to somebody else's experiment, or they don't see any kind of systematic approach to the kind of reading they're doing, or the kind of material they're being offered. They aren't able to tie it together into a package.
>
> (Hounsell and Ramsden, 1978, p. 138)

The studies summarised above focus chiefly on the methodological aspects of students' learning – their inability to use the explanatory frameworks of their disciplines to achieve understanding. West (1988) described several examinations of the outcomes of university science education and reached analogous conclusions about the quality of students' understanding of specific concepts. Gunstone and White (1981) interviewed science graduates about simple physics concepts related to gravity, and identified several outright misconceptions. West, Fensham, and Garrard (1985) reported serious gaps in the learning of apparently excellent first year chemistry students when asked to apply their new knowledge of phase changes to simple real-world situations (such as the effect of different pressures on the boiling point of water when cooking vegetables).

In other investigations, the belief that 'motion implies a force' (contrary to Newton's conception of force as expressed in his first law) among American, British, Swedish, and Australian college students has been widely reported (see, for example, di Sessa, 1982). In one of these experiments, Johansson *et al.* (1985) asked mechanical engineering students to answer the following question:

A car is driven along a motorway in a straight line at a high constant speed. What forces act on the car?

Two main categories of conceptions of a body moving at a constant velocity were identified. The first was that all the forces counterbalanced each other (the car is in equilibrium because it is moving at constant speed; therefore no net force exists). The second was that the car required a net pushing force to keep going (the forces directed forwards have to be greater than those in the opposite direction). The second conception is non-Newtonian and would get no marks from a physics teacher. Of the seven students in this study who expressed this belief at the beginning of a course in mechanics, six still held it at the end.

McDermott (1984) found that students who did well in course examinations were often incapable of demonstrating a qualitative understanding of acceleration as the ratio $\Delta v/\Delta t$ when they were asked to apply this concept to an example of actual motion. The fact that some higher education and senior secondary students may have quite severe difficulties in understanding frames of reference and relative velocities also has been demonstrated in studies at Melbourne (see Ramsden *et al.*, 1991).

Even simple algebraic thinking seems to prove problematic for many higher education students. As soon as they are set free from the straightforward manipulation of symbols, and are forced to consider the meaning underlying them as well, many appear to flounder. The classic example is Lochhead's. He reports that 80–90 per cent of US college students do not really understand ninth-grade algebra, although they can meet standard behavioural objectives in the subject. If they are asked to express the equation $A = 7S$ in an English sentence, nearly three-quarters will interpret it incorrectly (i.e. backwards) (Lochhead, 1985).

The biological sciences appear to fare no better than the physical ones. Barnett and his colleagues (Barnett, Brown, and Caton, 1983) asked zoology students, from third year to graduate level, to answer questions on biological theory and the philosophy of science. Students were invited, for example, first to state whether they agreed that 'All biological phenomena are in the long run explicable in terms of the physical sciences' (and to comment on the statement); second, to discuss the concept of

natural selection; and lastly, to comment on the proposition that
'A theory is scientific only if it can, in principle, be refuted.'

The results were surprising, to say the least. None of the
students had failed conventional assessments, yet few proved to
have a satisfactory grasp of central biological concepts or the
fundamentals of scientific process. More than half of them
accepted the extreme reductionist position that all biological
phenomena could eventually be reduced to physical science. If
this were true, there would be no organisms remaining to be
explained. Confusion about evolution was evident: two-thirds of
students accepted natural selection uncritically, as an axiom or
dogma. More than 80 per cent were baffled by the question on
scientific theory, being unable to distinguish different categories
of propositions (Popper, 1972) and consider the different ways
theories are actually used. These students seemed to have a
narrow and absolutistic conception of science. The findings are
similar to those of other studies (such as Brumby, 1982) and
probably have general application.

Professional courses are not exempt from criticism either. In
medicine, for example, Balla (Balla 1990a; 1990b) explains how
the available evidence shows that learning in traditional curricula
is often unsatisfactory. In most medical schools the biomedical
sciences are introduced before clinical experiences; it is assumed
that students will apply the theory to practice. In fact, students
often use basic science knowledge incorrectly or not at all in
formulating and revising diagnoses; when they become practising
clinicians, they continue to use their theoretical knowledge only
rarely and with difficulty. Numerous investigations show that both
students and clinicians make errors and possess systematic biases,
ignoring probabilities and basic science in favour of other sources
of information.

Heath (1990) describes another problematic area of student
learning, this time in the context of veterinary science – the
development of professional values and understanding of clients'
and colleagues' needs. Both teachers and students regard these
aspects of professional competence highly, but students and
novice veterinarians complain that they feel inadequate in their
dealings with clients and superiors. A major review of
engineering education (Williams, 1988) came up with similar
findings. The review found that both graduates and students felt
that they had not developed enough self-awareness, self-

confidence and understanding of other people and their motives, nor gained sufficient skills in management, team work, and industrial relations, as a result of their courses.

Social science and humanities subjects have been less closely researched, but numerous cases of misconceptions and misunderstandings of the syntax of disciplines that survive years of instruction have been reported. It would be tiresome, though, to give more and more details of the many other studies of this kind here. Suffice it to say that we are talking about the fundamentals of learning, and the portrait that the research paints of what many students know about these fundamentals is bleak. When a physics student discerns the relation between, say, a mathematical model and a physical reality, and sees the causal principles behind a formula (such as $\sum F = ma$) she has been taught – whereas previously she saw the formula as simply a handy tool to solve problems set by the lecturer – then it seems to make sense to say that she has learned something. Similarly, when a student begins a course in economics by thinking that price is determined by the value of an object, and ends it by having a conception of price as system-dependent, then learning has occurred. There has been a movement from one way of conceptualising a phenomenon to another, qualitatively distinct one. The student looks at the phenomenon, at some aspect of the world, quite differently. The same thing could be said to occur when a medical student develops a capacity to use biomedical science knowledge, together with knowledge of prior probabilities, to revise an early diagnostic formulation and solve a diagnostic problem imaginatively. From seeing diagnosis as matching a pattern, he comes to understand it as a much more complicated process of relating many parts to form a whole; a qualitatively different conception of reality has become established. The development of professional skills associated with ethics and human relationships (including strategies for collaborating with colleagues) may also be seen as a shift from a narrowly technical view of the professional role to a broader, more liberal and qualitatively different one.

It seems evident that, from a perspective on learning as changes in understanding, many students in higher education are not learning as effectively as they should be. There is clear variation in quality, and the developments of the last decade and a half in describing qualitative differences enable us to be much clearer about what this variation is like. It is true that some students understand better than others, and it seems certain that some courses are more successful in promoting changes in conceptions of subject matter than others. Nevertheless, very large numbers of students appear to be learning an *imitation* of at least some of the disciplines they are studying, a counterfeit amalgam of terminology, algorithms, unrelated facts, 'right answers', and manipulative skills that enables them to survive the process of assessment. Evidence of inadequate skills in working cooperatively to solve problems, over-dependence on teachers as sources of information, and a lack of that self-critical awareness of one's own ignorance in a subject area that is the only true precursor of further enquiry – together these indicate that the standards achieved by our graduates in relation to the resources invested in educating them are often less than satisfactory.

Why do students just come to classes to copy from the board? Why do they think they understand accounting or history when all they know is a set of narrow rules or one accepted explanation? Why do they use the wrong formulae in physics? Why are they poor at working on real problems? Why can't they see the wider picture? One way of trying to understand these defects is to ask the students to tell us about their learning and how it is affected by our teaching. The connection between how students experience our teaching and how they learn will accordingly be the subject of the next two chapters.

Chapter 4

Approaches to learning

Nearly every subject has a shadow, or imitation. It would, I suppose, be quite possible to teach a deaf and dumb child to play the piano. When it played a wrong note, it would see the frown of its teacher, and try again. But it would obviously have no idea of what it was doing, or why anyone should devote hours to such an extraordinary exercise. It would have learnt an imitation of music. And it would have learnt to fear the piano exactly as most students fear what is supposed to be mathematics.

What is true of music is also true of other subjects. One can learn imitation history – kings and dates, but not the slightest idea of the motives behind it all; imitation literature – stacks of notes of Shakespeare's phrases, and a complete destruction of the power to enjoy Shakespeare . . .

(W.W. Sawyer)

REAL AND IMITATION SUBJECTS

In the preceding chapter we saw how teachers in higher education expect their students to develop intellectual abilities that go beyond the possession of technical skills and subject knowledge. In all subject areas, these abilities involve combining and relating ideas so that the knowledge can be used effectively. Lecturers want their students to learn how to analyse what is unfamiliar to them, to assess proposed solutions to problems critically, to recognise the style and persuasiveness of concepts that describe the physical or social world, and to be able to apply ideas learned in formal classes to the world outside the classroom. They expect students to change their interpretations of the world in which they live through developing their understanding of the subjects they have studied.

Why do these changes not always happen? Why do students so often obtain quantities of knowledge, yet fail to change their understanding of what it means? How can it be that they can keep their academic knowledge separate from their experience? Why is the quality of undergraduate education deficient in these respects? Sawyer's little book, first published in 1943, holds the essence of the answer. Anyone serious about improving their teaching should think about the implications of the idea of an 'imitation subject' carefully. Students who have learned imitation subjects have been involved in a certain process that has enabled them to acquire factual knowledge which is useful in a very limited range of situations. Much of what they have learned has no personal relevance to them (except as a form of gaining qualifications) or any connection with the real world it is supposed to explain.

In this chapter and the next one, I try to show how we can use the idea of different approaches to learning to explain the perplexing phenomenon of students' misunderstandings, and to learn how to tackle its causes. We must do this by examining in detail the students' own experiences of learning and teaching – by looking, in other words, at learning from the student's perspective. It will become clear that the quality of our students' understanding is intimately related to the quality of their engagement with learning tasks.

HOW STUDENTS LEARN: THE CONCEPT OF APPROACH TO LEARNING

We now meet one of the most influential concepts to have emerged from research into teaching and learning in higher education during the last 15 years. You must fix clearly in your mind the concept of *approach to learning* in order to understand and get full value from the recommendations for better teaching in this book. It is unquestionably a key concept in teaching and learning. The main idea is not at all recondite, but it is somewhat abstract. The explanation of it is inevitably a little technical, but of much interest.

In previous chapters I introduced the idea that learning might be thought about as a change in the way we conceptualise the world around us. According to this way of looking at learning, a conception of an aspect of subject matter can be thought of as a sort of *relation* between a person and a phenomenon. In the academic world, a conception describes how an individual makes sense of something such as classical conditioning, irregular German verbs, integral calculus, or the anatomy of the upper arm. A conception is not a stable entity within a person's mind; it is a way that the person relates to the world outside the person. The 'world outside' includes the subject matter of academic disciplines: the principles and concepts the discipline uses to explain phenomena and ideas, and its characteristic ways of discovering and explaining. When we talk about a student understanding something, what we are really saying is that he or she is capable of relating to a concept or topic in the way that an expert in that subject does.

We can think about approaches to learning in exactly the same fashion. The way in which anyone goes about learning is a relation between the person and the material being learned. I am not talking about psychological differences between people, but about how someone makes sense of a particular learning assignment. Learning, from this perspective, is always the learning of *something*. There is no such thing as 'learning' in itself. The assignment in question might be almost anything in the world of academic learning – finding out about relativity, writing an essay about Chaucer, solving an economics problem, doing a project on pressurised water reactors, reading this book. The concept of approach describes a qualitative aspect of learning. It is about how people experience and organise the subject matter of a learning task; it is about 'what' and 'how' they learn, rather than 'how much' they remember. When a student learns, he or she relates to different tasks in different ways.

Review your own experiences of learning. There will have been times in all our experiences of formal schooling when, for example, we have seen the task before us as temporarily memorising facts or formulae for an examination; and others, when we took delight in mastering an idea, representing an interesting concept in our own words, painstakingly practising until we got a proof or an essay just right. Most lecturers in higher education will have become teachers because of the pleasure they experience in doing the second type of learning within their specialist subjects. That sort of relationship with what is to be learned is hard work; it is no harder nor easier a relationship than learning in the dull way. But because it leads to a command of the genuine subject, not its imitation, it is profitable hard work.

APPROACHES TO READING ACADEMIC TEXTS

In the last chapter I mentioned some different outcomes of learning in experiments at Gothenburg University where students were asked to read academic texts. One of these experiments involved reading an article about pass rates and educational reforms. Students' answers could be classified into four categories representing a hierarchy of understanding. The first two of these showed that students had grasped the meaning the author intended to convey; they both involved a focus on the *conclusions* that the author drew from the evidence he presented. The second two categories focused on *describing* parts of the text alone. These students did not understand the point of the article; they merely remembered some vestiges of it.

Why did these differences occur? Because of the nature of the relation between the student and the task of reading this particular article. The students in the second group were not looking for the meaning of the text which embodied the intention of its author. *They could not understand the article because they did not intend to understand it. They concentrated on its constituent parts rather than the whole in relation to the parts.* They defined their job as if they were empty vessels into which the words on the page would be poured. They focused on the separate words and sentences of the text, rather than on the meaning those words and sentences were intended to convey; they 'skated along the surface of the text', as Marton and Säljö express it. They were not personally involved in the task. They saw it as an external imposition – a job to be completed for some purpose outside themselves. They anxiously tried to memorise what was in the article, because they knew they would be asked questions on it later and felt that they would need to recall all its details. One said: 'You get distracted. You think "I've got to remember this now". And then you think so hard about having to remember it – that's why you don't remember it.' As a consequence of using this approach, these students found it hard to distinguish between principles and examples, between evidence and conclusions, between main points and secondary details. They were also less likely than the others to remember the ideas and facts.

The other group engaged with the task in an entirely different way. They experienced the learning situation as one that required them to extract personal meaning from the article. They were not dominated by a requirement to answer questions later. They tried to understand the author's message by searching for connections within the text, looking for an underlying structure, or by relating the text to something in the real world or in their previous reading. They defined their job as actively making sense. *They stood more chance of understanding because they intended to understand and organised the information they read to that end.* They were not trying to memorise the points made by the author, yet they remembered the ideas and the evidence used to support the ideas very well when they were asked to recall them. From their perspective, the text was not an end in itself, but a means to understanding the author's message: 'The whole aim of the article was what I was thinking of.'

This original concept of approach to learning was narrowly focused on the task of reading a text. It has since been broadened to include all the different sorts of learning tasks that students carry out, as we shall see below. The two contrasting ways of relating to a learning assignment described above have become known as surface and deep approaches to learning respectively. Strictly speaking, there are two different aspects of an approach to learning. One is concerned with whether the student is searching for meaning or not when engaging with a learning task; the second is concerned with the way in which the student organises the task. The first aspect is what the original researchers meant by deep and surface approaches (which they at first called 'deep-level and surface-level processing'). The second aspect, which derived from the work of Lennart Svensson, is about differences in how students organise the information, and particularly about whether they distort and segment the framework of the task. They may confuse, for example, the author's argument with the evidence he or she uses to support it, and perhaps see each separate component as a single sequence of 'facts'. This approach is called an *atomistic* one. The alternative is to maintain the structure through integrating the whole and the parts: this is known as a *holistic* approach.

We therefore have two related aspects of an approach to

Figure 4.1 The logical structure of approaches to learning

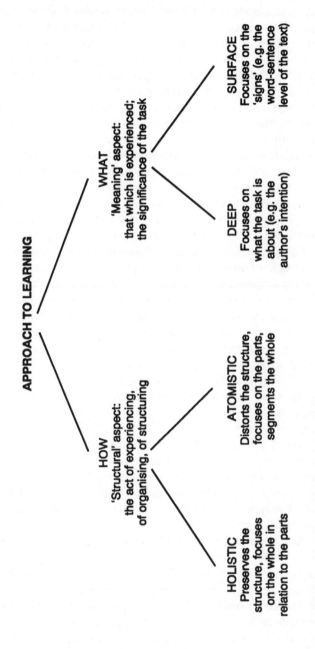

APPROACH TO LEARNING

HOW
'Structural' aspect:
the act of experiencing,
of organising, of structuring

WHAT
'Meaning' aspect:
that which is experienced;
the significance of the task

HOLISTIC
Preserves the
structure, focuses
on the whole in
relation to the parts

ATOMISTIC
Distorts the structure,
focuses on the parts,
segments the whole

DEEP
Focuses on
what the task is
about (e.g. the
author's intention)

SURFACE
Focuses on the
'signs' (e.g. the
word-sentence
level of the text)

Source: Based on Figure 1 in Marton (1988), p. 66

learning, one concerned with *what* the student refers to (actively trying to understand or passively trying to reproduce – a focus on the signs or words of the text versus what is signified by it) and the other with *how* the student structures the task (relating its components in a connected structure or keeping them isolated). In practice, these two aspects of approaches are fused together. In order to understand, a student must integrate and organise and see the text or other learning task as a whole. It makes no sense to talk about the meaning attributed to something unless one also talks about how the meaning is constituted. On the other hand, how a student structures a task cannot be considered in isolation from what he or she is intending to structure. In the literature on student learning, we sometimes meet the terms 'deep-holistic' and 'surface-atomistic' to describe the combination of the two aspects, although deep and surface alone are often used to describe the same mixture. The logical structure of the categories used to describe approaches to learning is summarised in Figure 4.1.

The fate of many seminal ideas in education has been to acquire a common-sense significance remote from their original meaning. The idea of an approach to learning is very frequently misunderstood. The most common mistakes are to believe that an approach is a characteristic of an individual person, like the colour of a student's hair; to believe that the approach can be inferred from a student's observable behaviour; to concatenate 'low ability' and surface approaches; or to think that surface and deep approaches to learning are in some way complementary or sequential.

The only way to overcome these misconceptions is to understand the concept for yourself. Approaches to learning are not something a student *has:* they represent what a learning task or set of tasks *is* for the learner (see Marton, 1988, p. 75). This may sound like playing with philosophical definitions, but it is a very practical difference. Everyone is capable of both deep and surface approaches, from early childhood onwards. An approach describes a relation between the student and the learning he or she is doing. It has elements of the situation as perceived by the student and elements of the student in it (how else can a situation be perceived?), but you cannot reduce it to the sum of these two sets of elements. It would be just as impossible to do this as it would be to reduce the baking of a cake to the heat in the oven and the raw ingredients. There is no escaping the fact that a baked cake is something qualitatively different from each of these elements, while at the same time it cannot exist without both of them.

The distinction between characteristics of students and the nature of different approaches to learning is an absolutely critical one for teachers to understand. Its implications run right through how we should teach. In trying to change approaches, we are not trying to change students, but to change the students' experiences, perceptions, or conceptions of something.

Take care also with the differences between knowing facts or understanding concepts and the different approaches. An approach is not about learning facts versus learning concepts: it is about learning *just* the unrelated facts (or procedures) versus learning the facts *in relation to* the concepts. Surface is, at best, about quantity without quality; deep is about quality and quantity. As John Biggs has put this:

> Knowing facts and how to carry out operations may well be part of the means for understanding and interpreting the world, but the quantitative conception stops at the facts and skills. A quantitative change in knowledge does not in itself change understanding. Rote learning scientific formulae may be one of the things scientists do, but it is not the way scientists think.
>
> (Biggs, 1989, p. 10)

It may be helpful in trying to understand these distinctions to return to the idea of an imitation subject, and to remember that imitation subjects, like surface approaches, cannot occur in an ideal educational environment. They cannot ever be acceptable as long as the educational value position represented in this book, and made tangible in the statements of higher education lecturers about their goals, is maintained. Surface approaches are uniformly disastrous for learning, as we shall observe below; yet they may permit students to imitate authentic learning and to bamboozle their teachers into thinking that they have learned. So, depending on one's point of view, a surface approach might be the best bet sometimes (the night before an exam in a subject you missed all the lectures for, maybe). The snag is that you may survive the exam but you will almost certainly forget everything you memorised for it after a few days. As Marton and Säljö say: 'We are not arguing that the deep/holistic approach is always "best": only that it is the best, indeed the only, way to *understand* learning materials' (1984, p. 46).

Table 4.1 Different approaches to learning

Deep approach

Intention to understand. Student maintains structure of task.

Focus on 'what is signified' (e.g. the author's argument,
    or the concepts applicable to solving the problem).
Relate previous knowledge to new knowledge.
Relate knowledge from different courses.
Relate theoretical ideas to everyday experience.
Relate and distinguish evidence and argument.
Organise and structure content into a coherent whole.
Internal emphasis: 'A window through which aspects of reality
    become visible, and more intelligible' (Entwistle and Marton, 1984).

Surface approach

Intention only to complete task requirements.
Student distorts structure of task.

Focus on 'the signs' (e.g. the words and sentences of the text, or
    unthinkingly on the formula needed to solve the problem).
Focus on unrelated parts of the task.
Memorise information for assessments.
Associate facts and concepts unreflectively.
Fail to distinguish principles from examples.
Treat the task as an external imposition.
External emphasis: demands of assessments, knowledge cut off from
    everyday reality.

STUDENTS' EXPERIENCES OF SURFACE AND DEEP APPROACHES IN HIGHER EDUCATION

The variations in approaches to learning that were noted in the original experiments can be observed in many educational contexts. The last 15 years have seen the important concept of approach to learning extended and applied to all kinds of learning tasks in higher education, from writing essays in history to problem-solving in science. It has also been generalised to describe the ways students engage with clusters of learning tasks and complete courses of study. 'Text' takes on a metaphorical sense when approaches to learning in everyday studies are considered (see Marton and Säljö, 1984, p. 45). A student may focus on passing a course or completing a particular learning assignment, such as a laboratory report or examination, as an end in itself, or alternatively on the meaning the course or assignment has in relation to the subject matter and the world that the subject matter tries to explain.

The defining features of the different approaches in the context of everyday academic studying are summarised in Table 4.1.

In order to illustrate the nature of these differences, some university and polytechnic students' descriptions of their approaches to normal learning tasks are given below. Think about what the student in each of these extracts is trying to do. What meaning is he or she imposing on the task? How is the content being organised? What messages about learning do these students seem to be getting from the tasks they have been set to do?

Subject matter: geography, essay preparation
Well, I read it, I read it very slowly, trying to concentrate on what it means, what the actual passage means. Obviously I've read the quotations a few times and I've got it in my mind what they mean. There's a lot of meaning behind it. You have to really get into it and take every passage, every sentence, and try to really think, 'Well, what does this mean?' You mustn't regurgitate what David is saying, because that's not the idea of the exercise. I suppose it's really original ideas in this one, getting it all together.

Physics, practical work
I suppose I'm trying to imagine what the experiment is talking about, in a physical sense, sort of get a picture of what it's about. This one says an ultra-violet lamp emits one watt of power; it says calculate the energy falling on a square centimetre per second. I'm just thinking of the light and the way it spreads out, so therefore I know it's the inverse square law .

Engineering, problem solving
It's an operation research exercise, a programme to find a minimum point on a curve. First I had to decide on the criteria of how to approach it, then drew a flow diagram, and checked through each stage. You have to think about it and understand it first. I used my knowledge of O.R. design of starting with one point, testing it and judging the next move. I try to work through logically . . . I chose this problem because it was more applied, more realistic. You can learn how to go about O.R. You get an idea of the different types of problem that exist from reading.

(Laurillard, 1984, pp. 134–5)

Computer Studies, lecture notes/revision
[Learning in this course is] getting enough facts so that you can write something relevant in the exam. You've got enough information so you can write an essay on it. What I normally do is learn certain headings. In an exam I can go: 'Introduction' and I'll 'look' at the next heading, and I know what I've got to write about, without really thinking about it really. I know the facts about it. I go to the next heading and regurgitate.

Physics, exam revision
Formulae. You just have to go into the exam with as many formulae as possible. So you learn those parrot-fashion. And approaches to the way you work out problems, techniques involved in maths. I seem to remember these just sort of one day or two.

Engineering, problem solving
This problem is not to be handed in . . . I knew how I'd do it from looking at it; it practically tells you what equation to use. You just have to bash the numbers out. I knew how to do it before I started so I didn't get anything out of it. There's not really any thinking. You just need to know what you need to solve the problem. I read through the relevant notes, but not much because you don't need to look at the system.

(Laurillard, 1984, pp. 134–5)

Can you categorise these extracts into the different approaches previously described? The first three show typical characteristics of deep approaches. The students are focusing on the content of the task and how it relates to other parts of the course or previous knowledge; they are trying to understand the task and relate its component parts to the whole. The process is internal: the students are concerned with integrating the new material with their personal experiences, knowledge, and interests. The remaining three quotations are classic surface: the assignment is a chore, the focus is on reproducing bits and pieces of memorised or textbook knowledge. The process of learning is external to the student: it is one in which alien material is impressed on the memory or manipulated unthinkingly with the intention of satisfying assessment demands.

How many students are talking here? Is this is a distinction between bright and weak students? In fact, there are three students represented in these extracts, and each one of them is describing first a deep approach and then a surface approach. His or her relation to the task differs from one situation to another. Each student is using deep and surface approaches in response to different circumstances. We can see that one cannot be a deep or surface learner; one can only learn the content in a deep or surface way.

APPROACHES IN DIFFERENT SUBJECT AREAS AND IN RELATION TO DIFFERENT ACADEMIC TASKS

The same student learns differently in different situations; but there is a further complication. What constitutes an approach to learning, surface or deep, varies according to the academic task. This is also implied by the relational character of the concept. The content of the subject being learned is inextricably linked to the approach: learning, as I have emphasised, is always the learning of some particular content. Since typical tasks vary between different disciplines, we find that the way in which approaches manifest themselves also varies. The extent to which these differences are in some way a function of the essential nature of the discipline or have a socio-cultural origin is not important – for our purposes. The fact that the differences exist *is* important, however.

It may be instructive to work out some of the characteristic ways in which different approaches reveal themselves in tasks associated with your own discipline. You would be likely to find, if you compared the defining features of approaches in science and humanities areas, that they reflected some of the typical differences in the ways of thinking that characterise practitioners of these different specialisms. The conclusion reached by the research into student learning is that while the general difference between deep and surface approaches is as applicable to English and politics as it is to chemistry and engineering, the meaning of the distinction has to be reinterpreted in relation to different subject areas.

For example, an initially narrow concentration on detail and logical connections as part of a deep approach is common in subjects typified as cumulative, paradigmatic, replicable, and capable of being summarised in terms of general laws (such as physics); while in subjects usually described as being particularistic, idiographic, and reinterpretive (such as history) a deep approach is more likely to involve the student in stressing, right from the start, an intention to elucidate material in a personal way. In describing surface approaches, students of science are more likely to speak of a narrow focus on techniques, procedures, and formulae, while humanities and social scientists tend to report a more generalised and vague approach, which frequently includes an oversimplification of main ideas in reading and essay writing, or memorising unrelated generalities in preparation for examinations. I listed many specific examples of these sorts of differences, extracted from my student interviews at Lancaster, in a previous book (Entwistle and Ramsden, 1983). It was also clear from these interviews that students have implicit theories about the disparate demands of different disciplines which map neatly on to what is known about differences in teaching and assessment practices in different subject areas (see Ramsden, 1988a).

Recent studies show that in professional subjects, which usually involve a large amount of problem-solving activity, in an important sense the approaches used are also the outcomes of learning: in other words, students are learning a process which will be an essential part of their work as professionals. For example, they are learning how to gather clinical information, relate it to theoretical knowledge (such as disease prevalence rates), and form a diagnosis. Analogues could be identified in architecture, law, engineering, accounting, and other professional subjects – including teaching. It is clear that the dichotomy typically appears in the context of clinical education tasks, for example, in relation to the integration or separation of theoretical and practical knowledge. In clinical medicine, and specifically diagnostic problem-solving, a deep approach typically appears as the establishment of a complex chain of associations which links symptoms to theoretical knowledge, while a surface approach implies a focus on specific isolated symptoms, linking and sequencing these parts in order to arrive at a conclusion. In using a surface approach, a student may address the task of clinical information-gathering by listening for a cue from the patient, and then using a routine, predetermined list or 'case-matching' strategy (Whelan, 1988).

ORIENTATIONS TO STUDYING

Deep and surface approaches in the original sense in which Marton and Säljö used them are about a student's immediate engagement with a particular learning task, such as reading a social science text or solving a mathematical problem. However, as we have already seen, the fact that the concept of approach has at its heart the idea of learning as an experience of *something* does not prevent us from looking at approaches in a more general fashion, as propensities to address a range of different learning tasks – say all the tasks making up a course of study – in a certain way. Although it is abundantly clear that the same student uses different approaches on different occasions, it is also true that general tendencies to adopt particular approaches, related to the different demands of courses and previous educational experiences, do exist. Variability in approaches thus coexists with consistency. This should not really be too surprising a paradox to live with; it is no different from saying that you generally support the Conservative party but that you decided to vote for the Labour candidate in a local election because she happened to have a special interest in a community issue that concerned you. We shall see later how the existence of these general approaches, or orientations to studying, has important consequences for the effects of changes to teaching on the quality of student learning.

Students' approaches to courses of study have been investigated using both interviews and questionnaires. Svensson (1977), Prosser and Millar (1989), and Ramsden (1981), for example, asked students questions in interviews such as 'How did you read the books set for the course?', 'What sorts of things do you usually do when studying for [this course] and why?', and 'What kinds of things do you do in tutorials and seminars?' Clear differences between students emerged; while some of them stressed memorising and arranging disconnected pieces of course content in order to increase their amount of knowledge, others stressed the process of linking together and abstracting personal meaning from the same material. Several researchers have used questionnaires to examine these different orientations to studying. The two best known of these questionnaires were designed by Biggs (at Newcastle in Australia) and Entwistle and his colleagues (at Lancaster in the United Kingdom). In these similar instruments, students are asked to agree or disagree with questions about their typical approaches to studying. Many of the questions were derived from what students have said in interviews about how they study.

Examples of the questions in the Entwistle and Biggs questionnaires appear in Table 4.2. (Both the Biggs and the Entwistle

Table 4.2 Examples of questions in the Lancaster Approaches to
Studying and the Biggs Study Process Questionnaires

Orientation to studying *(General approach to learning)*	*Indicative items*
Meaning orientation (Deep approach)	• I try to relate ideas in one subject to those in others, whenever possible. • I usually set out to understand thoroughly the meaning of what I am asked to read. • In trying to understand new ideas, I often try to relate them to real-life situations to which they might apply. • When I'm tackling a new topic, I often ask myself questions about it which the new information should answer. • In reading new material I often find that I'm continually reminded of material I already know and see the latter in a new light. • I spend a lot of my free time finding out more about interesting topics which have been discussed in classes.
Reproducing orientation (Surface approach)	• I find I have to concentrate on memorising a good deal of what we have to learn. • I usually don't have time to think about the implications of what I have read. • Although I generally remember facts and details, I find it difficult to fit them together into an overall picture. • I find I tend to remember things best if I concentrate on the order in which the lecturer presented them. • I tend to choose subjects with a lot of factual content rather than theoretical kinds of subjects. • I find it best to accept the statements and ideas of my lecturers and question them only under special circumstances.

questionnaires each include items concerning a third aspect of student learning, known as the 'strategic orientation' or 'achieving approach', but these need not concern us here.) Questionnaires of this type can be used as a form of course evaluation, because they provide direct information about students' responses to particular curricula and the way they are taught and assessed.

The two main orientations have been identified in a whole series of studies, too numerous to describe here, in the USA, Australia, the UK, New Zealand, Hungary, Venezuela, and Hong Kong, not only in higher education but in secondary schools as well. The deep (meaning) and surface (reproducing) components show impressive stability across age groups and national boundaries. There is little room for doubt that they describe a primary difference in how our students learn.

RELATIONS BETWEEN APPROACHES AND OUTCOMES

What is the effect of different approaches to learning on the quality of student learning? There is no uncertainty about the answer. Many research studies have shown that the outcomes of students' learning are associated with the approaches they use. *What* students learn is indeed closely associated with *how* they go about learning it. It does not seem to matter whether the approaches are measured by means of questionnaires or interviews, whether the subject area is engineering or history or medicine, or whether the outcomes are defined in terms of grades or in terms of some qualitative measure of learning (as in the first Gothenburg study). It is also evident that approaches are related to how much satisfaction students experience in their learning. Deep approaches are related to higher quality outcomes and better grades. They are also more enjoyable. Surface approaches are dissatisfying; and they are associated with poorer outcomes.

Qualitative measures of understanding

In the original Gothenburg studies, deep and surface approaches to learning were functionally related to the outcomes of learning. There was a logical inevitability about the association in Marton's original experiment – the students who 'did not get the point' of the text were not looking for it. They focused on the text itself, rather than the main points and the relations between the details and conclusion. They could not achieve understanding because they defined their task in a way that excluded the possibility of understanding. It was overwhelmingly clear as well, however, that outcome and process were empirically linked. Although there were cases where students' approaches could not be classified, the links between the four main types of outcome and the approach used were clear. Table 4.3 summarises these relations. The main dividing line between outcomes is between B and C: the fact– conclusion structure of the article is understood in types A and B, but not in types B and C (see Marton and Säljö, 1984, p. 42).

Comparable results, using students' written responses rather than interviews, were reported by Entwistle and Ramsden (1983). Watkins (1983) also described positive relations between approaches and outcomes. It has also been found that students who use deep approaches retain more of the factual material presented in the text when tested on their knowledge of it several weeks later.

Table 4.3   Relationship between approach to learning and outcome of learning

Level	Approach to Learning			
of outcome	Surface	Not clear	Deep	Sub-totals
A (conclusion-orientated, detailed)			5	5
B (conclusion-orientated, mentioning)	1	6	4	11
C (description, detailed)	8			8
D (description, mentioning)	5	1		6
Sub-totals	14	7	9	30

Source: Based on Marton and Säljö (1976; 1984)

Van Rossum and Schenk (1984) analysed learning outcomes of reading text in a rather different way, using a taxonomy developed by Biggs and Collis (1982) to classify students' answers.

This SOLO taxonomy (SOLO is an acronym for 'Structure of the Observed Learning Outcome') is a hierarchy that contains five levels of outcome which are used to classify the structural complexity of students' responses. Unlike the outcome measures used by the Gothenburg group, the categories are not content-specific, but are assumed to apply to any kind of subject matter. The system is summarised in Table 4.4. The main dividing line is between levels 3 and 4: at level 4 and above, the responses involve evidence of understanding in the sense of integrating and structuring parts of the material to be learned. Biggs has shown how this system can be applied to learning outcomes, curriculum design and assessment in many different subject areas. We shall meet it again below and in subsequent chapters.

Table 4.4 Levels of Biggs's SOLO taxonomy

1	Prestructural	Use of irrelevant information, or no meaningful response.
2	Unistructural	Answer focuses on one relevant aspect only.
3	Multistructural	Answer focuses on several relevant features, but they are not coordinated together.
4	Relational	The several parts are integrated into a coherent whole: details are linked to conclusions; meaning is understood.
5	Extended abstract	Answer generalises the structure beyond the information given: higher order principles are used to bring in a new and broader set of issues.

Van Rossum and Schenk (1984) showed that approaches to learning were strongly associated with SOLO outcomes. In their experiment, 27 of the 34 students who used a deep approach achieved a relational or extended abstract outcome, while none of the 35 students using a surface approach gave a response higher than multistructural. Van Rossum and Schenk also classified students' conceptions of learning (see above, p. 54), and found that most of the students who used surface approaches saw learning as a process of increasing knowledge or memorisation, while deep approaches were associated with views of learning as understanding reality and abstracting meaning.

Biggs's work on students' essay-writing (Biggs, 1988) extends studies of the relationship between approach and outcome to the task of essay writing. The analogy with reading text is very close.

When students feel dominated by external assessment demands and define their task as listing points or reproducing information, then planning, composing, and reviewing are not complex; but when they see writing the essay as a learning experience in its own right, careful attention is given to the audience, style, and discourse structure. Biggs shows how surface approaches to essay-writing in history restrict the quality of outcome to a low level, while deep approaches provide the writer with the opportunity to obtain high quality outcomes. Very similar results have been reported by Hounsell (1984; 1985).

Whelan (1988) and Balla *et al* (1990) have described comparable associations in their studies of medical students' problem-solving. Whelan identified two main levels of outcome in an interview study of students' diagnostic procedures: *description*, which was characterised by short associative links between symptoms and diagnosis, purely descriptive answers, or failure to make a diagnosis; and *understanding*, which involved complex causal chains of reasoning using pathophysiological links. Students were more likely to demonstrate understanding if they used a deep-holistic or 'structuring' approach (including relating previous knowledge to the problem and maintaining the problem's structure) than if they used a surface-atomistic or 'ordering' approach to the two cases presented.

A recent study by Prosser and Millar (1989) examined approach-outcome associations in first year physics students. This study is of particular interest as it looked at *changes* in students' conceptions of phenomena concerning Newtonian mechanics (such as identifying forces in cases of reducing and constant velocity). Tests of understanding were carried out before and after the course. Prosser and Millar show that students who adopt surface approaches to the course of study are less likely to show high level conceptions of the particular concepts involved. They also provide strong evidence of a causal connection between the approach used and the level of understanding reached. They found that *development* in conceptions as the course proceeded was related to the approach used. Students who used deep approaches were more likely to change their understanding in the direction that lecturers desired – away, for example, from Aristotelian views of force and motion towards Newtonian ones. Twenty-one of the 23 students classified as using surface approaches showed no development, while eight of the nine students using deep ones did.

Grades and degree results

There is equally convincing evidence that students who use deep approaches get better marks. Svensson (1977) identified deep and surface approaches in the context of both reading experiments and normal studies, and found that there were close relationships between approaches and outcomes in both contexts (see Table 4.5). Ninety per cent of students classified as using deep approaches in both the experiment and in normal studies passed all their examinations.

Table 4.5 Approaches to learning and examination performance

| Approach | | Examination Performance | | Total |
Experiment	Normal studies	Passed all	Some failure	
Surface	Surface	3	10	13
Deep	Deep	9	1	10
Deep	Surface	4	2	6
Surface	Deep	1	0	1

Source: Based on Svensson (1977)

It is impossible to discuss all the studies of associations between approaches and academic performance here, but some examples of the range of investigations will give a flavour of the findings. Entwistle and Ramsden (1983) found that British university students classified in interviews as using 'consistent deep' approaches were more likely to obtain first or upper second class honours degrees. Comparable findings, for British, Australian, and American students, have been reported by Watkins and Hattie (1981); Hounsell (1984; 1985); Schmeck (1983); Biggs (1987); and Ramsden, Beswick, and Bowden (1986). Ramsden and Entwistle (1981) at Lancaster, and Biggs (1987) in Australia also described links between students' self-ratings of their own academic progress, compared with their peers, and their approaches. The Lancaster investigation suggested that meaning orientation was more effective, and reproducing orientation more heavily penalised, in arts than in science. A recent study of adaptation to higher education in Melbourne (Ramsden, 1991a) found that a group of students who described themselves as high on deep approaches and low on surface ones, both at school and at university, also reported conscientious and well-organised study habits (compare Svensson's finding below, p. 58); obtained better school-leaving examination results; and, in the first year of higher education, gained better average grades.

None of the relationships between results and approaches reported in the literature is as strong as the associations established using measures of the quality of learning, for reasons which are discussed below. Their consistency is nevertheless remarkable.

Attitudes to studying

No one reading the interview material reported in books such as *The Experience of Learning* (Marton, Hounsell, and Entwistle, 1984) could fail to be struck by the regularity with which students obliged to use a surface approach to a task, or to an entire course, describe their feelings of resentment, depression, and anxiety. In contrast, deep approaches are almost universally associated with a sense of involvement, challenge, and achievement, together with feelings of personal fulfilment and pleasure. Svensson (1977) showed that this relationship helps to explain the connection between examination performance and approach. Students who are taking a deep approach find the material more interesting and easier to understand, and are therefore more likely to spend 'time on task'. But studying using a surface approach is a tedious and unrewarding activity: persisting with this approach leads to procrastination and delay. Surface approaches thus mean that students spend less and less time in private study, and consequently are more likely to fail their exams. When students appear to be 'unable to study' we should examine their approaches to learning before blaming them for being idle and unmotivated, particularly in view of the effect of our teaching on their approaches – as we shall see in the next chapter.

The Lancaster study established that surface approaches were linked to negative attitudes to studying: students adopting a reproducing orientation were more likely to agree with questionnaire statements such as 'Often I find myself wondering whether the work I am doing here is really worthwhile' and 'When I look back, I sometimes wonder why I ever decided to come here'. My work with students in Melbourne has shown identical associations. Students who describe the use of surface approaches, both in the sixth form and in higher education, are less satisfied with university study. Students who use deep approaches are best adapted to the demands of higher education, and most committed to studying. Similarly, Biggs (1987) reported that surface approaches were related to a high degree of dissatisfaction, and deep approaches to satisfaction with performance.

The interview evidence from several studies makes it clear that the approach–satisfaction connection is reciprocal. While the approach used determines the level of enjoyment and commitment, interest in the task for its own sake encourages a student to use a deep approach. These connections between approach and attitude were also captured in a few concise sentences by William Sawyer:

> Real education makes howlers impossible, but this is the least of its advantages. Much more important is the saving of unnecessary strain, the achievement of security and confidence in mind. It is far easier to learn the real subject properly, than to learn the imitation badly. And the real subject is interesting. So long as a subject seems dull, you can be sure you are approaching it from the wrong angle. All discoveries, all great achievements, have been made by men who delighted in their work.

> (Sawyer, 1943, p. 9)

Taken as a whole, the relationships discovered in these various studies of the connection between approaches to learning and the outcomes of learning are extremely robust, with two qualifications: surface approaches are usually more strongly linked to poor learning than deep ones are to effective learning; and the connections between grades and approaches are less marked than those between measures of learning quality and approaches. The reasons for both qualifications are plain. In the first place, although using a surface approach logically prevents the student from achieving understanding, using a deep approach does not guarantee it. Other things, such as a well-structured knowledge base in the area being studied, are necessary. In other words, *surface approaches can never lead to understanding*: they are both a necessary and a sufficient condition for poor quality learning. Deep approaches are a necessary, but not a sufficient condition, for high quality outcomes.

The explanation for the second qualification is that grades or degree results are a much less reliable and valid measure of outcome than a test of understanding based on the same study material that was used to classify the students' approaches. Many assessment methods do not test understanding, even though we may believe that they do. Students may succeed in an examination or a degree course *despite* using a surface approach; alternatively, they may not be given the opportunity to display the full range of their understanding because of the assessment methods used – two facts that are worth reflecting upon in themselves. Several investigations of approaches and outcomes show that surface approaches are often effective for recollecting unrelated facts and details over a short period. This, of course, explains the popularity of surface approaches as a form of revision for unseen examinations and as a way of coping with excessive amounts of curriculum material. It also sheds light on the genesis of the examination howler.

CONCLUSIONS

The ubiquity of surface approaches in higher education is a very disturbing phenomenon indeed. 'In my own work at universities,' said Whitehead, 'I have been much struck by the paralysis of thought induced in pupils by the aimless accumulation of precise knowledge, inert and unutilised . . . . The details of knowledge which are important will be picked up *ad hoc* in each avocation of life, but the habit of the active utilisation of well-understood principles is the final possession of wisdom' (Whitehead, 1929).

Surface approaches have nothing to do with wisdom and everything to do with aimless accumulation. They belong to an artificial world of learning, where faithfully reproducing fragments of torpid knowledge to please teachers and pass examinations has replaced understanding. 'Paralysis of thought' leads inevitably to the misunderstandings of important principles, weak long-term recall of detail, and inability to apply academic knowledge to the real world. A surface approach shows itself in different ways in different subject areas, but it leads down the same desolate road in every field, from mathematics to fine arts. Once the material learned in this way is reproduced as required, it is soon forgotten, and it never becomes part of the student's way of interpreting the universe. Through this concept of approach to learning, we can begin to unlock the puzzle of poor quality learning described in the previous chapter. The outcome of a surface approach is essentially quantitative – a list or unstructured grouping of pieces of disparate knowledge. Such outcomes tend to be associated in markers' minds with errors in calculation, the use of incorrect procedures, recapitulation (sometimes inaccurate) of material presented in lectures, linear narration techniques in essay writing, misapplied concepts, and so on. These are the sort of results of which university and college teachers spoke so deprecatingly when they identified their 'weaker students' (the majority) (Entwistle and Percy, 1974); their views were echoed by the physics and accountancy lecturers also quoted in an earlier chapter.

It is clear that, in contrast, deep approaches embody the type of learning that lecturers expect students to practise. It seems certain that the imaginative, flexible, and adaptive skills which higher education is supposed to develop in students can only be properly established in this way. It is also apparent from what we have heard from students that a deep approach is a very much more satisfying way to study. It allows students to use academic knowledge to control and clarify the world outside academic knowledge. Deep approaches are connected with the qualitatively superior outcomes which we associate with understanding a subject: the making of an argument, the novel application of a concept, an elegant solution to a design problem, an interplay between basic science knowledge and professional application, mastery of relevant detail, relating evidence correctly to conclusions. These outcomes share certain general characteristics, among which are high structure, a strong knowledge base, ability to apply one's own and other people's ideas to new situations, integration of knowledge. These common elements are almost identical to the subject-related aims of teachers in higher education described in chapter 3.

Our knowledge of the nature of approaches to learning thus enlightens our search for means to improve the quality of higher education. Good teaching implies engaging students in ways that are appropriate to the deployment of deep approaches. Later in the book we shall see how improving teaching implies engaging lecturers in ways that are appropriate to the development of their understanding of teaching. We must start, however, by examining in some detail the students' own experiences of teaching and how these influence their approaches to learning.

Chapter 5

Learning from the student's perspective

Schools teach you to imitate. If you don't imitate what the teacher wants you get a bad grade. Here, in college, it was more sophisticated, of course; you were supposed to imitate the teacher in such a way as to convince the teacher you were not imitating.

(Robert Pirsig)

THE CONTEXT OF LEARNING

If the quality of student learning is crucially dependent on the approach taken, how can we encourage students to use deep approaches? Deep and surface approaches are responses to the educational environments in which students learn. This is implied by the relational nature of the idea of an approach to learning. In phenomenological jargon, an approach is an 'intentional' phenomenon, in that it is directed outside the individual to the world outside, while simultaneously being defined by that world. It is not something inside a student's head; it is how a student *experiences* education. The most important thing to keep in mind is that students adapt to the requirements they perceive teachers expect of them. They usually try to please their lecturers. They do what they think will bring rewards in the systems they work in. All learners, in all educational systems and at all levels, tend to act in the same way.

The educational environment or context of learning is created through our students' experience of our curricula, teaching methods, and assessment procedures. Remember that we are dealing here with the students' own *perceptions* of assessment, teaching, and courses, and not with 'objective' characteristics such as the division of teaching methods into tutorials, practicals, and lectures, or assessment methods into examinations and assignments. There happen to be good reasons for believing that some teaching and assessment methods really are better than others. But it is more important at this juncture to understand that the effects of different teaching methods on students are – from their teachers' point of view – often unpredictable. Students respond to the situation *they* perceive, and it is not necessarily the same situation that we have defined. It is imperative to be aware of this routine divergence between intention and actuality in higher education teaching. In fact, as we shall see, becoming aware of it is part of what it means to teach well.

UNINTENDED CONSEQUENCES OF INTERVENTIONS

Can we instruct students in the use of deep approaches? Because of the inevitable gap between our intentions and students' perceptions of the context of learning, the answer is probably no. This fundamental point is illustrated in one of the experiments carried out by Marton's research team (summarised in Marton and Säljö, 1984, p. 47). When the Gothenburg researchers tried to give students hints about how to take a deep approach to reading a text – by inserting questions that encouraged students to relate the various parts – a curious thing happened. The students in question actually adopted a rather extreme form of surface learning. They 'invented' a way of answering the inserted questions without engaging with the text. The research team's questions, which were intended to be a means of helping students to understand what they were reading, were perceived by the students as ends in themselves. And in order to answer them expeditiously, the students adopted a superficial approach to reading, focused on being able to mention the parts of the text.

One of the studies at Melbourne produced somewhat similar results (see Ramsden, Beswick, and Bowden, 1986). Attempting to train first year students to adopt more effective learning strategies had the practical effect of increasing their tendencies to use surface approaches. Our interviews of students showed that they perceived first year courses to require the accurate retention of large amounts of content. They took from the learning skills programmes what they believed would help them to pass these courses. What they thought would be useful was the inverse of what the programmes were trying to teach.

In each of these interventions, the effects on student learning were the opposite of those that were intended by the designers, precisely because the students saw things differently. It would be fruitless to blame the students for perceiving the situation in a way we did not predict; they acted with perfect rationality. These results do not necessarily mean that all attempts to help students develop better learning skills are a waste of time. What they do imply is that we cannot train students to use deep approaches when the educational environment is giving them the message that surface ones are rewarded. We deceive ourselves if we think we can tell students not to imitate when they look around them and see that imitation, suitably disguised, appears to them to be what teachers want.

Neither, it would seem, can we train students to use particular approaches in all contexts. Approaches to learning are not skills that students possess or do not possess regardless of the subject matter they are learning. They are more domestic phenomena than that. They are inseparable from both the content and the context of student learning, both as previously experienced and as currently experienced.

DIFFERENT KINDS OF CONTEXTUAL EFFECTS

There is a long tradition behind the idea that teaching and assessment has a weakening influence on the quality of student learning. Much anecdotal and research evidence points towards the mostly negative effect of the academic environment on students. Whitehead, for example, pointed to the 'evil path' in education of easy texts and unimaginative teaching which leads to rote-learning of ill-understood information for examination purposes. Experiences of bad teaching and bad assessment practices dominate many of the stories. Tales of the unintended, and negative, consequences of teaching and assessment in higher education appear with alarming regularity.

In everyday studying, the context of learning is an ever-present influence on students' activities. Students do not simply read a textbook or write a practical report, for instance. They read or write for a particular audience and they do these things in response to the implicit or explicit requirements of their teachers. They are enrolled for courses of study and degree programmes. They have had previous experiences of the subject matter and tasks associated with it, as well as previous experiences of other educational institutions. It may be helpful to think about the relation between students' perceptions and their approaches at several interconnected levels. These are the learning task itself (including students' previous experiences of dealing with similar tasks), the quality of interaction with lecturers, the curriculum and assessment, and, at the most general level, the atmosphere or 'ethos' of the course, programme of study, or institution. Each of these levels suggests a point at which interventions can occur to change students' approaches. In chapter 12, I shall show how similar ideas might be applied to improving the quality of teaching.

Student interest, knowledge base, and previous experience

Students' approaches depend partly on their previous experiences and the nature of their interest in the task in hand. It is often hard to separate the context of learning and previous experiences in describing learning in its everyday setting. Deep approaches are closely related to a student's interest in the task for its own sake. Intrinsic interest and a sense of ownership of the subject matter provides fertile ground for attempts to impose meaning and structure. Deep approaches are in addition associated with a well-developed base of knowledge in the field of study. If there are gaps in your understanding of basic concepts, then it is obviously much more likely that your attempts to understand new material that assumes knowledge of those concepts will be frustrated. A learner may then resort to strategies requiring the minimum of interaction with the task, as this Lancaster student makes clear in his description of how he tackled two different parts of the same problem:

> It was like one of the questions from a previous course, which I could relate. It was a Shrödinger equation for a particle in a box, which we'd solved generally before in chemistry, so I could see a picture of what I wanted. I knew basically what sort of answer I should get, and from that I could work my way through it . . . . The other bit was different; I couldn't do it. Basically I gave up with it, because it was a function, which I've never really understood. I looked at it and I thought, 'That looks complicated'. It was very short. It looked like it would need a lot of rearranging.

Another Lancaster student, after describing a deep approach to writing essays in one course in whose subject matter she felt personally involved, spoke of a quite different way of tackling an apparently similar assignment in another course:

> This subject's a bit confusing. When it comes to writing essays, because I'm not very interested in it, I tend to rush through the books I'm reading, so I don't really understand it when I've finished reading. And because there's so much information I think you can either tend to oversimplify or get into too much detail.

Fransson (1977) also showed (this time in an experimental setting) that intrinsic motivation and absence of anxiety – as perceived by the student, although not always as intended by the experimenter – were related to the use of a deep approach. Failure to perceive relevance, however, was associated with surface approaches.

Background knowledge and interest in the subject matter are, of course, related to each other. Both are also affected by the student's previous educational experiences. Occasionally it is argued that because students sometimes use either deep or surface approaches consistently across different tasks, then the statement that approaches to learning are adaptive responses, rather than student characteristics, is wrong. This is a misunderstanding. The way in which a student perceives a learning task, or a whole course of study, is partly determined by his or her previous experiences. This is important for teaching, not so much because we can repair a student's past experiences but because we can influence his or her future approaches. Intrinsic interest in a learning assignment seems to lead to a deep approach; a concern with external demands to a surface one. But interest or extrinsic motivation are themselves related to previous experiences of learning.

Marton and Säljö tried to manipulate students' approaches to reading by asking one group of them a series of questions that were highly factual and specific, and the other group questions that focused on relations between conclusions and evidence. But not all the second group used deep approaches; it would seem that they interpreted what was demanded of them in different ways. This was presumably because, in spite of the attempted manipulation, they perceived the task differently. These students must have brought with them a predisposition to use a surface approach which they had previously developed in response to similar situations. Like all of us, they carried their history of learning along with them.

The approaches to studying that students deploy in higher education are certainly influenced by their experiences of learning in secondary school. One study in Melbourne found that experiences of school environments which encouraged deep approaches led to the persistence of these approaches in the first and subsequent years of university study, although they were also associated with perceptions of the quality of teaching in higher education. The same was true for surface approaches (see Ramsden, 1991a). The fact that some students begin higher education with habitual tendencies to use surface approaches has implications for how effectively they will be able to engage with the learning tasks they are set. This in turn implies that we must make special efforts to design learning contexts for first year students that rapidly develop more sophisticated approaches to academic learning.

The effects of assessment

'If we wish to discover the truth about an educational system, we must look into its assessment procedures,' said Derek Rowntree (Rowntree, 1977, p. 1). This statement could with advantage be written in large letters over every lecturer's desk. The methods we use to assess students are one of the most critical of all influences on their learning. There are two related aspects to consider: the amount of assessed work and the quality of the tasks.

As I have already suggested, it seems that a good deal of student 'learning' is not in fact about understanding biology or political science or engineering, but about adapting to the requirements of teachers. It is as if two different worlds existed – a manifest one, defined by the staff and the written curriculum, and a latent one, defined by the students' perceptions. This contrast between intent and actuality was represented by Benson Snyder (1971) as the formal versus the 'hidden' curriculum. The formal curriculum at the Massachusetts Institute of Technology in the 1950s, according to Snyder, emphasised excellent educational goals of the kind that were mentioned in chapter 3 – goals such as independent thinking, analysis, problem-solving ability, and originality. Students received a different message. The hidden curriculum, manifested in their perceptions of assessment and teaching procedures, involved memorising facts and theories to appease teachers and achieve success in examinations.

Howard Becker and his colleagues described a similar situation. In the students' 'definition of the situation', the grading system was all-powerful. Students learned strategies which enabled them to earn high grades – at the cost of understanding the material. They were pushed away from the kind of learning they would have liked to undertake towards surface approaches. As one said:

> There's an awful lot of work being done up here for the wrong reasons. I don't exactly know how to put it, but people are going through here and not learning anything at all . . . . There are a lot of courses where you can learn what's necessary to get the grade and when you come out of the class you don't know anything at all. You haven't learned a damn thing really. In fact, if you try to really learn something, it would handicap you as far as getting a grade goes.
>
> (Becker, Geer, and Hughes, 1968, p. 59)

Parallels between these findings and the conclusions of Fransson, and Marton and Säljö, will be evident. Unsuitable assessment methods impose irresistible pressures on a student to take the wrong approaches to learning tasks. It is our assessment, not the student, that is the cause of the problem.

Many contemporary studies of how students learn have registered this tendency of assessment methods and excessive amounts of assessed course material to have a harmful effect on students' attitudes to studying and approaches to learning. Laurillard (1984) describes how approaches to problem solving in science are related to students' perceptions of marking criteria. Some of the problem-solving tasks in her study at a British university were seen by students to require only the barest of interaction with the content if satisfactory marks were to be obtained. Students tackled what Laurillard calls the 'problem-in-context', not necessarily the problem set. The problem-in-context consisted of much more than the microelectronics content intended by the lecturer: it also included the students' interpretations of the lecturer's behaviour and second guessing of what the lecturer would like:

I thought of a diagram drawn in a lecture and immediately referred back to it. Then I decided which components were wanted and which were not and started to draw it out, more or less copying without really thinking.

I decided since X was setting the question, block diagrams were needed.

(Laurillard, 1984, p. 131)

While some problem-solving tasks are perceived to require preserving the structure of the problem, others can unfortunately be answered in a way that distorts the structure, and essentially involves manipulating isolated elements. It is not apparent that this helps students to learn anything useful about the subject. As one of the students interviewed at Lancaster said, on reading down a list of physics problems handed out the previous week:

The first one – well, I know that formula off from last year. It's just a simple formula. You shove in a number and it comes out straight away.

In problem-solving tasks, the structural aspect of the dichotomy between different approaches to learning (see p. 43) is crucial to an awareness of the unintended negative effect of the context on students' understanding. A learning task must employ a student constructively. 'Shoving in a number', while it may have some advantages right at the start of learning a new topic in removing a sense of fear, more often implies poor quality engagement with the material. It teaches you little you don't already know about the behaviour of elementary particles or electronic systems. If the student responds to the problem-in-context *rather than* the content of the problem, a qualitatively inferior outcome learning is inevitable. The task is at best inefficient, in that it takes up time the student could be using more productively, and at worst positively harmful in that it reinforces undesirable attitudes to the subject. As Laurillard puts it: 'The whole point of problem solving as a learning task is that it should engage the students actively in thinking about the subject matter, and in operating on the relations within it, so that personal meaning can be created' (Laurillard, 1984, p. 136).

In a series of investigations carried out in Lancaster in the late 1970s, I interviewed many students about the ways in which assessment influenced their approaches to learning. Several of the published extracts from these interviews have been widely quoted in the literature, and I apologise to any readers who may be familiar with them already for repeating some of them here. One of the most memorable interviews for me was with a brilliant second year psychology student who passed with first class honours. He described his approaches to essays and unseen tests in very different ways:

> I think I tend to relate quite a lot of the reading (for the essay) to my own experiences; I try and think of instances where these experiments would be proved right. So it takes a bit of time reading. I think if they're talking about things like field independence I try to think about whether people I know are field dependent or independent. . . . As I was writing I was thinking about how the final product was going to come about, and that sort of directed my reading, in fact.
>
> In the class test, if you can give a bit of factual information, so-and-so did that, and concluded that, for two sides of writing, then you'll get a good mark. I hate to say it, but what you've got to do is have a list of the 'facts'. You write down ten important points and memorise those – then you'll do all right in the class test.

The point of this story is not that examinations are bad and essays good, but that inappropriate assessment methods may push students towards learning in ineffective and dispiriting ways. Students will study what they think will be assessed; but no student enjoys learning counterfeit subjects. Additional comments from Australian and British students make the negative effects of our assessment methods very apparent:

> I look at the topic and think to myself, 'Well, I can do that if I can be bothered to hunt through hundreds of textbooks and do the work' – and you sort of relate that to the value of the work in the course, which is virtually zero because it's so much exam assessment . . . . My revision is basically for the exams, purely and simply aimed at passing the exams without bothering too much about studying the subject.
>
> (A physics student)

> When I revise, I just write my notes till I've got about four copies and then try old questions and write essay plans for every conceivable question, and learn those. And when I write the exam, I can often picture the pages of my notes. I know I've written about a subject and it's on a particular page and I can

'see' it and recall it. That sort of learning I don't like having to do, because it's very false, and I forget it very quickly. But you have to learn like that to pass the exams on this course.

(A student on a vocational course at an English polytechnic)

I'd say the thing that would get you through [this subject] is not what you know but how good you are at learning. Techniques involved in learning how to cut down on the understanding and just aim at the marks. How quickly you adapt to the techniques involved in passing exams, in getting assignments in with good marks.

(Humanities student)

I don't think you have to understand, you just have to be able to recite, which is unfortunate. You can spend all your time memorising things and then you'll go really well, but you might not know much about it.

(Medical student)

I just memorise a few facts to get through the courses I need to pass . . . for some coursework you can get it straight out of the textbook and you give them a result, just copying down something if you're lucky – which lots of people do.

(Geology student)

Closely related to the quality of assessment tasks is the amount of curriculum material that is taught and assessed – the workload and pace of a course. Overloading syllabuses with content leads to poor learning (the following extracts include written comments from students on course evaluation forms):

In very few of the lectures was I picking up the principles as we did them. It took me all my time to get the notes down. The pace is so fast that you get the notes down and that's it. You don't really follow what's going on. You can't do two things at once. You can't sit back and listen to what's being said. I put this down to the very keen desire to cover that much work.

(Engineering student)

There is far too much content especially for those who have not studied this subject since year 10. The course should cover less but explain the part that is covered so we understand it better, and can remember and thus use it better.

(Physics student)

I think the course could be improved by reducing the content quite substantially. After all it is the quality of what one learns not the quantity. I have bits and pieces of memorised knowledge but no real understanding of the concepts. From past experience I will soon forget the things I have 'learned' like this. I found that there was quite a heavy reliance on teaching students in one semester the amount it would personally take me a year to fully comprehend.

(Economics student)

I'd really much prefer to be able to study by thoroughly understanding the work. It becomes so much more interesting and worthwhile if there is some meaning behind it. Unfortunately, the large amount of knowledge that we are expected to have leads me to simply memorise facts for the exams.

(Medical student)

The dominant effect of students' perceptions of assessment requirements is graphically illustrated in the above examples. Notice especially how the students themselves are often painfully aware of the fact that the approaches to learning they are using will lead to inferior outcomes. Whatever we may say about our ambitions to develop understanding and critical thinking in our disciplines, it is in our assessment practices and the amount of content we cover that we demonstrate to undergraduate students what competence in a subject really means. There, starkly displayed for students to see, are the values academic staff attach to different forms of knowledge and ways of thinking. Assessment methods that are perceived to test the ability to reproduce accurately large quantities of information presented in class, or to manipulate procedures unthinkingly, tell students that our fine aims for conceptual understanding are but a veneer on the solid material of recalling facts.

The process of assessment influences the quality of student learning in two crucial ways: it affects their approaches and, if it fails to test understanding, it simultaneously permits them to pass courses while retaining the conceptions of subject matter that teachers wished to change. Should the assessment of students' learning go no further than testing what can be unreflectively retained in their memories, misunderstandings will never be revealed. These two aspects interact to support a stable system: the undetected misunderstandings are a result of superficial engagement with the subject matter and they in turn set the scene for the future use of surface approaches.

Dahlgren's explanation of the inadequate understanding of concepts displayed by economics students (see also chapter 3, p. 30–1) brings together these aspects. Students who had passed end-of-year examinations could not answer questions that tested their understanding:

> If a more thorough understanding is required in order to answer a question [about phenomena such as price determination and equilibrium], the number of acceptable answers is very low . . . . In many cases, it appeared that only a minority of students had apprehended basic concepts in the way intended by teachers and textbook authors. Complex procedures seem to be solved by the application of memorized algorithmic procedures . . . . In order to cope with overwhelming curricula, the students probably have to abandon their ambitions to understand what they read about and instead direct efforts towards passing examinations. . . which reflect the view that knowledge is a quantity.
>
> (Dahlgren, 1978)

Nevertheless, as we shall see in chapter 10 and elsewhere, assessment need not be cast as arch-villain in the saga of higher education; it can also be used as a positive force for improvement, both of teaching and of learning. It is a potent agent for enhancing or injuring the quality of higher education; it is an agent that must be handled with infinite care.

Students' experiences of teaching and teachers

The next level at which we can conveniently examine the effects of the learning context on approaches and attitudes to studying is that of the individual lecturer or tutor. There is a ubiquitous belief that a student's sense of interest and involvement with a topic will be increased if the lecturer is stimulating and communicates a sense of his or her own interest. There are numerous accounts in the literature of higher education of the way in which enthusiastic teaching may lead to greater student involvement and commitment to the subject, while its lacklustre and rambling counterpart results in negative attitudes and a sense of futility.

Here is a typical example of these stories, from a student's experience at University College, Liverpool (later to become the University of Liverpool) in the late nineteenth century. The lecturer is John Macdonald Mackay, professor of history, 'an impressive and formidable figure . . . a great man, the most dominating personality I had ever met':

> As a lecturer Mackay was not good. He could not survey a wide field: in the course of a year we never got further than Henry III. He could not make the past come alive. He could not give his students any idea of the way in which the facts set forth in the text-book were obtained. Although it would have seemed to me, at that time, positive blasphemy to admit all this, I found his lectures incoherent and boring . . . I attended many of Mackay's lectures during the three years when I was living on the chopped straw of a pass degree course, and, without losing my respect for his greatness, I gradually realised that his lectures were a futile waste of time. His sole object seemed to be to get rid of the prescribed hour when he had to be in the classroom, without the trouble of preparing for it . . . .
>
> Mackay had caused me to waste three years on a pass degree, which gave me no real intellectual discipline, and taught me habits of laziness.
>
> (Muir, 1943)

Will teaching that engages students lead to interest, commitment, and deep approaches to the subject matter? The research findings of studies of learning from the student's perspective tend to confirm pictures of the kind provided above, but they show that the real situation is rather more complicated. While sterile and lifeless teaching is hardly conducive to the development of understanding, colourful presentation is by no means sufficient for effective student learning. A good performance is not necessarily good teaching. In fact, an entertaining lecturer may leave students with a sense of having been entertained, but with little advancement of their learning. (Students are, however, quite competent to distinguish effective teaching from diverting exhibition: I return to this issue in the next chapter.)

It is worthwhile thinking at this point about the effects of the different kinds of teaching described in chapter 2 on students' approaches to learning. Which is more likely to lead to changes in students' understanding?

The research suggests that deep approaches are associated with quite specific characteristics of the experience of being taught. Teaching which is perceived to combine certain human qualities with explanatory skills is the most likely to encourage deep approaches. The emotional aspect of the teacher–student relationship is much more important than the traditional advice on methods and techniques of lecturing would suggest. For example, the science students in Bliss and Ogborn's study (Bliss and Ogborn, 1977) reported that they were more likely to understand the content of lectures if the lecturer interacted with them in a way that encouraged involvement, commitment, and interest. Various studies of student ratings of teachers in higher education also identify a recurring factor variously labelled 'student-centredness', 'respect for students' and 'individual guidance', and 'lecturer–student rapport' among other aspects of teaching such as the ability to explain things clearly, explain requirements fully, provide a reasonable workload, and encourage student independence (see Ramsden, 1988a).

Marris (1964, quoted in Hodgson, 1984) concluded that the effective lecturer helped students to make sense of their subject matter through enabling them to see its relevance:

He [sic] can provide a more personal context, showing why the subject interests and excites him, how he has used it in his own experience, how it relates to problems whose importance his audience already understands. From this, the student can more easily imagine how he himself could use it: he develops his own context of motives for mastering a problem.

(Marris, 1964, p. 53)

Hodgson (1984) developed this idea of the quality of the relationship between student and teacher, identifying two categories of student engagement with lectures analogous to deep and surface approaches: an intrinsic and an extrinsic experience of relevance. She argued that teaching which focuses on the use of vivid illustrations and demonstrates personal commitment may encourage students to see the content as having meaning in the real world. Thus it seems that lecturers can help their students to use deep approaches through enabling them to experience the meaning of the subject matter vicariously.

My research at Lancaster and subsequent development work in both the UK and Australia has shown similar connections between students' perceptions of teaching quality and approaches to learning. Interest in undergraduate students, help with difficulties in understanding, using teaching devices that encourage students to make sense of the content, creating a climate of trust, a proper balance between structure and freedom, and conscientious, frequent and extensive evaluative comments on assignments and other learning tasks – all these aspects of teaching are related, in students' experiences, to the use of deep approaches and the development of interest and commitment to the subject matter. The opposite is just as surely true for poor quality teaching. The students' comments, both written and oral, speak for themselves; there is much to learn from them:

> We looked at Renaissance art in terms of universal concepts that are important and relevant to people now. Doing this made it accessible, helped me to get into it and feel for it, rather than just looking at it from outside. I think this organising of the topics was very important in developing our understanding . . . . The staff weren't concerned to push a particular view; they were just very concerned to help you come to a personal understanding, to get to know your own viewpoints through art. I thought their background knowledge was very good, but it was their concern for us as students that I was most impressed by.
>
> (Art history student)

> The method of feedback on assignments was unacceptable. No comments were put on the assignments, leaving students wondering what was wrong – in particular, what areas their assignment fell down in. Although a circular was handed out re assignments, this is no substitute for comments. Each assignment's faults are peculiar to itself. If the university is to remain an education centre and not become just a degree machine assessing the 'pass-fail' of students, the usefulness of feedback cannot be ignored.
>
> (Economics student)

> All too often the lecture or series of lectures would present a string of unrelated points with no structure. These lectures were full of details which were both boring and soon forgotten and they did not make clear what the major points were that we had to understand. To make things worse, many of the

lectures seemed to be made deliberately uninteresting, as if the lecturers did not care about whether we understood or not, or as if they wanted to show how ignorant and stupid students were . . . . I guess they proved their point with many of them. The —— course was just the opposite – the lecturer bothered about whether we learned, and was around to help, and commented on ideas, and I worked a lot harder at this subject. And I definitely will be able to use what I learned as it still stands out so clearly.

(Medical student)

Luckily I'm doing some courses with good tutors on them. They can make the books come alive because they can talk about them and they can direct you to a chapter or a passage, and that's important. If you get a guideline from the tutor, then it's a godsend.

(History student)

When we asked questions, if the tutor regarded them as being too basic, we were told off. But tutorials are to learn, not to be told off when you are wrong! A student should be encouraged, not discouraged. The tutor had a strong influence on my lack of interest.

(Industrial relations student)

We had a problem sheet to hand in for yesterday which was really hard, because the guy that's lecturing is really terrible. He's given equations and in the lecture notes there's nothing about them, because he just goes on and on and mumbles to himself. Then you're asked questions on it, and you don't know where to start.

(Science student)

I gave in two essays at the beginning of the second term and I didn't get those back till this term. It's a bit difficult when you're writing the next essay, because you want to know where you've gone wrong and the points that have been all right. By the time you've got it back after waiting a whole term you've forgotten what it's all about, and it doesn't really mean much then.

(Humanities student)

If tutors have enthusiasm, then they really fire their own students with the subject, and the students really pick it up.

I'm really good at, and enjoy ——, but that's only because a particular tutor I've had has been so enthusiastic that's he's given me an enthusiasm for it. And now I really love the subject.

(English literature student)

I think a lot of the lecturers are just not particularly interested in you. Some tutors don't really bother whether you learn or not. They just prefer to sit there and wait for you to think of what you don't know. I mean, if you knew what you didn't know you'd probably learn it anyway. I've got a tutor like that at the moment – it's no good at all.

(Physics student)

The positive approach of the teaching staff and their own commitment to teaching always made me feel supported and this made me take more risks than I otherwise would have done during discussions. No one dominated at any time and we could learn from one another. So I learnt more and understood more and can already use what I learnt in my own classes, and it *works!* The theory was difficult but after a while I started to see how it was immediately vocationally relevant. I can appreciate for about the first time the applicability of educational research to my work. The excellent organisation led to me reading much more widely and deeply. I have changed the way I teach my students.

(Education student)

The effects of courses, departments, and institutions on students' approaches

While each individual lecturer's teaching and assessment methods will influence the quality of his or her students' learning, it is also possible to consider the effects of the context of learning at a more general level. Students' approaches to learning are also determined by the teaching policies and practices of academic departments, courses, and institutions – as, in fact, several of the quotations from students given above suggest. The existence of these relations has important implications for how we improve the quality of undergraduate education.

In chapter 4, I described the use of questionnaires to look at students' general approaches to learning or *orientations to studying* in a school, course, or academic programme. The Approaches to Studying Questionnaire described in the previous chapter was completed by a national sample of over 2,000 undergraduates following programmes of study in academic departments in UK higher education institutions during 1980. These students also replied to a questionnaire on course perceptions which contained categories, derived from a programme of interviews, concerning the context of learning in the departments. This questionnaire included items asking students to describe their perceptions of the quality of teaching (how helpful students felt the staff were in dealing with academic problems, for example), of the degree to which they felt they were encouraged to exercise responsibility and independence in learning, and of the amount of assessed work and curricular material they were required to address. The two questionnaires were completed by students in 66 departments, the disciplines represented being engineering, English, physics, economics, psychology, and history.

What happened when the departments were compared with each other? The answer can be predicted from what you have already learned from this chapter. The departments differed from each other in terms of the perceived quality of teaching and in terms of the preferred approach to learning. I looked at whether the departments whose students had high average scores on the meaning orientation were also thought to have effective teaching, and whether the departments with high reproducing scores were thought to be places where students were placed under too much pressure. It turned out that the prediction was generally correct. Even within the different subject areas, the context of learning did seem to affect students' orientations in the expected way. Reproducing orientations were more common in units perceived to combine a heavy workload with a lack of responsible choice over learning. Meaning orientations were more common in units perceived to combine high quality teaching with opportunities to study independently.

These relationships are remarkably similar to the ones identified among students in the Lancaster interview study. But the level of analysis has now changed: we are now dealing with aggregates of students and teachers rather than individuals. It is evidently possible for students to describe the effects of teaching both at the level of the individual lecturer and at the level of the course, and, moreover, it is possible to measure the average quality of teaching and learning using a course or department as the unit of analysis. Further evidence to confirm this conclusion will be presented in chapter 6, and its implications will be considered in Part 3.

The Lancaster questionnaire investigation also showed that students in the less highly rated departments (where surface approaches were more common) were more likely to express negative attitudes to their studies. This, of course, is just what we would expect from what we have learned about the relationships between the approaches to learning and satisfaction with studying. Surface approaches are dull and boring; deep ones are a pleasure.

Marton and Säljö (1976) found in their experimental studies that it was rather easy to push students into using surface approaches by altering the context of learning, but that changes in the questions asked did not necessarily lead to students using deep approaches. Exactly as we might expect from these findings, the connection between the high workload, low independence departments, and the reproducing orientation was much stronger than the connection between the good teaching, high independence departments, and meaning orientation. In other words, some types of teaching and assessment definitely induce narrow, minimalist approaches to studying. But deep approaches are fragile things; while we can create favourable conditions for them, students' previous experiences and other unmeasured factors may mean that they remain unexercised. This is a warning worth heeding, both in evaluating our own teaching and when it comes to measuring the effectiveness of other people's. No one can ever be certain that teaching will cause students to learn. In the last analysis, excellence in teaching cannot guarantee that students will understand.

Several subsequent studies of different institutions and departments have revealed differences in students' orientations and attitudes to studying which are only explicable in terms of the powerful effects of contexts of learning. As yet unreported research on Australian students shows exactly the same associations between approaches and the perceived quality of teaching in first and second year university level study (Ramsden, in preparation). Relations between graduates' and students' satisfaction with courses and perceptions of good teaching were confirmed by the results of the teaching performance indicator study (which will be described in chapter 6). A particularly significant investigation of the effects of different medical school environments (Newble and Clarke, 1985) established that a problem-based curriculum – one where the focus of student learning is on problems of the type met in professional life, rather than on academic disciplines taught separately from professional practice – was more likely to encourage students to employ deep approaches than a conventional curriculum. Cross-sectoral differences in approaches to learning, apparently due to differences in teaching quality, have also been observed in undergraduate students in English universities and polytechnics (Ramsden, 1983).

Results of this kind have substantial implications for our choice of teaching methods, as will be seen in chapters 6 and 9. In the meantime, it will be useful to summarise the main influences on deep and surface approaches that have been established by these various researches into how students learn (see Table 5.1).

Table 5.1   Characteristics of the context of learning associated with deep and surface approaches

---

Surface approaches are encouraged by:

- Assessment methods emphasising recall or the application of trivial procedural knowledge
- Assessment methods that create anxiety
- Cynical or conflicting messages about rewards
- An excessive amount of material in the curriculum
- Poor or absent feedback on progress
- Lack of independence in studying
- Lack of interest in and background knowledge of the subject matter
- Previous experiences of educational settings that encourage these approaches

Deep approaches are encouraged by

- Teaching and assessment methods that foster active and long-term engagement with learning tasks
- Stimulating and considerate teaching, especially teaching which demonstrates the lecturer's personal commitment to the subject matter and stresses its meaning and relevance to students
- Clearly stated academic expectations
- Opportunities to exercise responsible choice in the method and content of study
- Interest in and background knowledge of the subject matter
- Previous experiences of educational settings that encourage these approaches

---

SUMMARY: A MODEL OF LEARNING IN CONTEXT

Much research evidence has been presented in the last three chapters. It is now advantageous to consolidate some main themes concerning associations between students' learning outcomes, their approaches to learning, and the context of institutional learning in higher education. This summary is preparatory to the analysis of the characteristics of good teaching that follows in the next chapter.

Very early in the book it was argued that learning is best conceptualised as a change in the way in which people understand the world around them, rather than as a quantitative accretion of facts and procedures. This view harmonises with many statements about the mission of higher education and with lecturers' own aims for student learning. We have seen, however, that there is a large body of evidence indicating that some central goals of higher education – students' understanding of key concepts and ways of thinking in a discipline, and the development of abilities to integrate theoretical and practical knowledge in professional subjects – are by no means always achieved.

The source of this problem was traced to the quality of students' engagement with learning tasks. The fundamental concept of approach to learning was used to demonstrate how the student's intention (to understand or to reproduce) interacted with the process of studying (to maintain the structure of the subject matter of the learning task, or to distort it), and how in turn these processes and intentions were reflected in the quality of understanding reached. Deep approaches generate high quality, well-structured, complex outcomes; they produce a sense of enjoyment in learning and commitment to the subject. Surface approaches lead at best to the ability to retain unrelated details, often for a short period. As they are artificial, so are their outcomes ephemeral. The precise descriptions of surface and deep approaches differ from task to task, and so from subject area to subject area, just as learning outcomes in different subjects obviously vary. But the approaches have enough in common across different tasks to allow us to speak confidently about the universal relevance of the dichotomy they delineate. An understanding of the meaning and application of the distinction is indispensable to teachers in higher education.

In the present chapter we saw how approaches are intimately

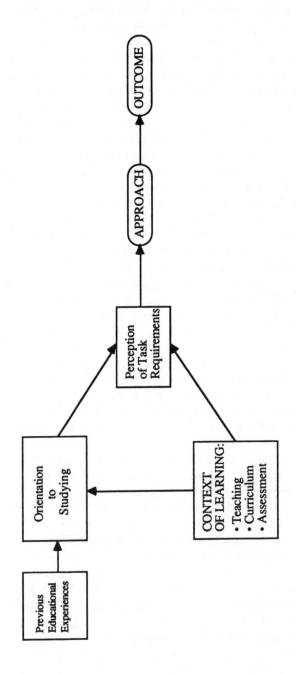

Figure 5.1 Student learning in context

connected to students' perceptions of the context of learning. Perceptions of assessment requirements, of workload, of the effectiveness of teaching and the commitment of teachers, and of the amount of control students might exert over their own learning, influence the deployment of different approaches, which are very clearly adaptive responses to the educational environments defined by teachers and courses. Students' perceptions are the product of an interaction between these environments and their previous experiences, including their usual ways of thinking about academic learning. Adaptation may lead to a student understanding the topic or subject, or to learning merely a counterfeit version of it.

Figure 5.1 outlines a model of learning in context that brings together many of these ideas. Reading from the left we begin from the students' previous experiences and trace the source of the outcomes of their learning through their general approach or study orientation and their perception of the demands of specific tasks. The diagram is heuristic, not deterministic: it is supposed to help us to reason about possible relations between different aspects of learning and teaching. It does not imply an inevitable or single causal sequence of events, but rather a chain of interactions at different levels of generality. It could be useful at this point for you to think of some specific examples of students' perceptions, approaches, and outcomes in relation to teaching and assessment in your own subject area.

These connections establish points of intervention to enhance the quality of student learning by changing the curricula we construct, the teaching methods we use, and the ways in which we assess our students. In so far as contextual variables are in the control of academic staff, it should be possible to structure the environment rationally so that students' adaptive responses are congruent with our aims. Although it is easy to encourage surface approaches, and harder to help students towards deep ones, in practice it will be most efficient if our efforts are directed simultaneously towards removing incentives for reproductive approaches and towards providing inducements for meaningful learning. Several teaching strategies can be used in order to help students to change their understanding; most of them revolve around the careful diagnosis of misunderstandings and a focus on a small number of key concepts. Yet none of them will work unless attention is paid to setting the right conditions for the development of deep approaches.

In subsequent chapters we shall see how almost exactly the same arguments can be applied to evaluating and improving teaching. I have used Sawyer's idea of an imitation subject to point up the contrast between deep and surface ways of learning academic subject matter; but evaluation and the improvement of teaching each has its imitation and its genuine version as well. In all three cases, an understanding of what is involved in coordinating theoretical and practical knowledge is required in order to encourage authentic learning.

Chapter 6

The nature of good teaching in higher education

> Bad teaching is teaching which presents an endless procession of meaningless signs, words and rules, and fails to arouse the imagination.
>
> (W.W. Sawyer)

THE IDEA OF GOOD TEACHING

The dominant theme of my argument so far has been that the quality of student learning in higher education should be improved and can be improved. How can it best be improved? It is unnecessary, and it may be misleading, to appeal to expensive instructional technologies and sophisticated 'learning skills'. The answer is nearer to home: it lies in the connection between students' learning of particular content and the quality of our teaching of that content. Through listening to what students have said about their learning, we have observed how real this connection is. Good teaching and good learning are linked through the students' experiences of what we do. It follows that we cannot teach better unless we are able to see what we are doing from their point of view.

Good teaching encourages high quality student learning. It discourages the superficial approaches to learning represented by 'imitation subjects' and energetically encourages active engagement with subject content. This kind of teaching does not allow students to evade understanding, but neither does it bludgeon them into memorising; it helps them respectfully towards seeing the world in a different way. Later in the book I shall try to show how these basic ideas can be applied to the design of curricula, teaching methods, and assessment.

First, though, we must be quite clear about *how* teaching might encourage deep approaches, interest in the subject matter, and changes in student understanding. Thus, we start this chapter with a survey of what is known about the characteristics of effective teaching in higher education. How does this knowledge relate to what students say about their learning? What does good teaching mean in practice? What actually happens to students when different teachers approach teaching from contrasting perspectives, such as those described in chapter 2? This review and these case studies lead us to six key principles of effective higher education teaching. Finally, I want to look at the idea of good teaching at the level of an academic department or programme of study, and describe some recent work on variations in teaching performance in different courses and departments.

In the next chapter we shall see how the essence of good teaching and that of its less effective counterparts as described here can be understood in terms of different theories of teaching. One reminder about terminology: as in the rest of the book, 'teaching' or 'instruction' is defined in a broad way. It includes the design of curricula, choice of content and methods, various forms of teacher–student interaction, and the assessment of students.

SOME MYTHS ABOUT TEACHING IN HIGHER EDUCATION

It suits many lecturers to believe that because learning is ultimately the student's responsibility, effective teaching is an indeterminate phenomenon. There is a cherished academic illusion, supported by abundant folk tales, that good teaching in higher education is an elusive, many-sided, idiosyncratic and ultimately indefinable quality. Now I take it for granted throughout this book that there cannot be one 'best' way of teaching. Like studying, it is too complicated and personal a business for a single strategy to be right for everybody and every discipline. So far so good. It is folly, however, to carry this truism beyond its proper territory and to suggest that there are no better or worse ways of teaching, no general attributes that distinguish good teaching from bad. The fallacy of this belief will become apparent below.

A related myth in the culture of university teaching is that because the greater part of learning in higher education takes place apart from lectures and other formal classes, then teaching is not very important after all. Learning is what students do; its relation to teaching is unproblematic. This convenient illusion draws on two very prevalent misconceptions about teaching at this level: that it consists in presenting or transmitting information from teacher to student, or demonstrating the application of a skill in practice; and that students in higher education must not be too closely supervised, lest the bad habits of dependent learning they are supposed to have acquired at school are reinforced. The myth argues that learning is something separate from teaching – learning is the student's job, and teaching the teacher's, and they should stay in different boxes. It is said in support of this myth that able students understand and apply the skills and information they have been exposed to. If the rest don't learn, they have a difficulty that the teaching cannot be blamed for; after all, they are in higher education now. This belief is associated with the view that unpopular, even dreadful, teachers in higher education are *actually* better than popular and helpful ones (because the latter force students to be 'independent', while the former 'spoonfeed').

Other fallacies about higher education teaching include the one that teaching undergraduates (especially first year ones) is easier than teaching postgraduates; that knowledge of the subject matter is sufficient as well as necessary for proficient teaching; and that the quality of teaching cannot be evaluated. There are good reasons why these myths persist: they serve specific interests, such as administrative convenience and the dominant cultures of academic departments; and they provide excellent excuses for not doing anything much to make teaching better. Not doing things about improving teaching, making things administratively easy, and educational values often conflict with one another. The prime examples are in the area of the evaluation of student and staff performance, as we shall find in chapters 10 and 11.

OUR KNOWLEDGE OF GOOD TEACHING

The reality, as opposed to the mythology, is that a great deal is known about the characteristics of effective university teaching. It is undoubtedly a complicated matter; there is no indication of one 'best way'; but our understanding of its essential nature is

both broad and deep. Research from several different stand-
points, including studies of school teaching, has led to similar
conclusions. The research supports what good teachers have
been saying and doing since time immemorial. Among the
important properties of good teaching, seen from the individual
lecturer's point of view, are:

- A desire to share your love of the subject with students
- An ability to make the material being taught stimulating and
  interesting
- A facility for engaging with students at their level of under-
  standing
- A capacity to explain the material plainly
- A commitment to making it absolutely clear what has to be
  understood, at what level, and why
- Showing concern and respect for students
- A commitment to encouraging student independence
- An ability to improvise and adapt to new demands
- Using teaching methods and academic tasks that require
  students to learn actively, responsibly, and cooperatively
- Using valid assessment methods
- A focus on key concepts, and students' misunderstandings of
  them, rather than on covering the ground
- Giving the highest quality feedback on student work
- A desire to learn from students and other sources about the
  effects of teaching and how it can be improved.

Before looking at how these discrete attitudes and behaviours are
interrelated, we might ask how they mesh with students'
experiences and with the more persistent academic myths.

As a matter of fact, the research findings on good teaching
mirror with singular accuracy what your students will say if they
are asked to describe what a good teacher does. College and
university students are extremely astute commentators on
teaching. They have seen a great deal of it by the time they enter
higher education. And, as non-experts in the subject they are
being taught, they are uniquely qualified to judge whether the
instruction they are receiving is useful for learning it. Moreover,
they understand and can articulate clearly what is and what is not
useful for helping them to learn. The evidence from students
provided in chapter 5 is perfectly convincing on this point.

There is also evidence of the authenticity of students' views from studies of evaluations of teaching, particularly in that they are known to be sensitive to variations in teaching processes (Dunkin, 1986) and that they are associated with student achievement (Marsh, 1987). Moreover, when students are asked to identify the important characteristics of a good lecturer, they identify the same ones that lecturers themselves do: organisation, stimulation of interest, understandable explanations, empathy with students' needs, feedback on work, clear goals, encouraging independent thought. Down at the bottom of the list are the lecturer's personality and sense of humour. Taken together, these findings tend to undermine the widespread views that students confuse popular lecturers with good lecturers and don't appreciate the hard work that goes on behind the scenes. Of course, students do not see every aspect of teaching, such as effort put into curriculum design, directly; nor are they necessarily able to comment validly on matters such as the relevance and up-to-dateness of the content. But those aspects they do see comprise a very important part of the whole.

Why is the academic myth about students confusing 'good performance' with effective teaching so persistent? Maybe because it feeds on a belief somewhere deep down in certain lecturers (perhaps a little of it is in us all) that learning at undergraduate level has got to be a hard and unhappy business. Some lecturers do seem to suppose, for whatever reason, that learning English or chemistry mustn't be made too attractive. Pleasure in learning, they appear to think, is something that comes later, when undergraduate tedium is well behind you. This belief may draw in its turn on the view that students will only come to see the true value of the teaching they received at university in subsequent years.

I assert that these beliefs are entirely wrong. If we cannot help students to enjoy learning their subjects, however hard they may be, we have not understood anything about teaching at all. It is abundantly clear from comparative studies of graduates' and students' reactions to courses (see, for a recent example, Mathews *et al.*, 1990) that anecdotes to the effect that bad teaching is 'really' good teaching (when students reflect on it a year or so later) have no foundation in fact. Graduates rate the same courses similarly to current students. And, in spite of a whole series of attempts to popularise the view that students can be fooled into giving those lecturers who are superficially

attractive presenters of wrong content high ratings as teachers –
the existence and prominence of these studies is an intriguing
phenomenon itself – it is evident from the correctly controlled
enquiries that students rarely fall into the trap. They can easily
differentiate the empty performer from the good teacher (Marsh,
1987, provides a ruthless critique of the studies that say they
can't). These conclusions are important for choosing methods of
evaluating teaching, as well as for understanding its nature.

DIFFERENT TEACHING STRATEGIES: TWO CASE STUDIES

Later in this chapter we shall examine the properties of effective
teaching in more detail. It might be helpful first to make some of
the assertions about good teaching more tangible by looking at
two cases of actual teaching. In particular, we need to consider
what it means to say that a teacher's application of knowledge
about students' understanding, and his or her ability to focus on
key concepts, is a vitally important part of high quality instruction. The examples are not from higher education; in fact they
are from American middle schools. However, I think that you will
immediately understand their significance, particularly to tutorial
and seminar teaching.

Neither of the teachers involved shows a lack of concern for
her students, but there are important differences in their
effectiveness. The two teachers in question were trying to help
their pupils understand scientific explanations of light and seeing
(Roth and Anderson, 1988). The extract from Ms Lane's teaching
is a good example of what occurs if a teacher does not consider
what students might misunderstand about what she is trying to
teach them. Ms Lane's classes were carefully planned around
what 'had to be covered' in the text that accompanied the course.
Her lesson plans presented one idea after another, in rapid
succession, without challenging pupils' common misunderstandings of science concepts. The breadth of coverage placed a
heavy load on both teacher and pupils, especially as Ms Lane also
used many experiments and demonstrations to supplement her
teaching. She did not attempt to integrate these hands-on
activities with the concepts she presented, however. This lack of
integration, combined with the mountain of information and the
constant pressure to get through it, conveyed a clear message to

pupils. This was that science was about memorising facts and ideas introduced in the classroom and the textbook, and that it had little to do with the real world outside.

In the extract shown below, the teacher's initial question asking for an explanation is changed into a series of factual questions. The teacher misses the opportunity to discover pupils' misunderstandings and structure the discussion around them, because she does not *listen* to what the pupils have to say. She hints at the right answers when they do not come up with them, and once the pupils have given her what she wants – even when the wording of her question has already given the answer away, and even when, as in Bob's case, the pupil is referring to the wrong thing (the colour of the iris of the eye, not the pigment-containing cells in the retina) – she goes on to the next topic, as if the answer signified understanding.

Ms Lane's teaching

Ms Lane:	What is the function of the optic nerve? [Waits; no response] What is it that a nerve does? What do they do?
Heidi:	Tells whether it is hot or cold.
Ms Lane:	Uh . . . OK, they send what?
Pupils:	[calling out] Messages.
Ms Lane:	Where do they send them?
Pupils:	[calling out] To the brain.
Ms Lane:	Without the optic nerve, could you see?
Pupils:	[unison] No.
Ms Lane:	Because it sends messages of the image to the brain. [She writes on the board: Optic nerve leads from the back of the eye to the brain.]
Ms Lane:	Then there are cells that contain pigments (in the retina). What do you think they do?
Jim:	They store.
Ms Lane:	What might they do? What does pigment have to do with?
Bob:	The colour of the eye.
Ms Lane:	So you think they might help us see colour?
Pupils:	Yeah.

(Ms Lane goes on to the next type of cells, light-sensitive cells)

(Roth and Anderson, 1988, pp. 121–2)

These pupils soon learned to respond to this learning context. They learned that there was no real problem with how they understood; they came to believe that they were just adding more details to what they already knew. They learned that using isolated words and phrases from their textbook would lead to more satisfactory answers than trying to make sense of the ideas. They engaged with the task of learning about light and seeing, in other words, in a way that ensured they could not change their understanding. They performed poorly on tests of their understanding of the application of their knowledge to everyday phenomena (Roth and Anderson, 1988, p. 132).

Now consider Ms Ramsey's classroom. Ms Ramsey also used the science textbook chapter about light and seeing, but she used it differently. She made use of a set of overhead transparencies developed by a researcher who was trying to help teachers improve their teaching of these topics. These were specially designed to focus instruction on a few key concepts that were known to be problematic for pupils at this level (fifth grade, the equivalent of the top end of the primary school). Figure 6.1 illustrates one of the transparencies, which each included an overlay showing the scientific explanation of the problem so that pupils could immediately contrast their own conception with the scientific one.

Figure 6.1 Transparency used by Ms Ramsey

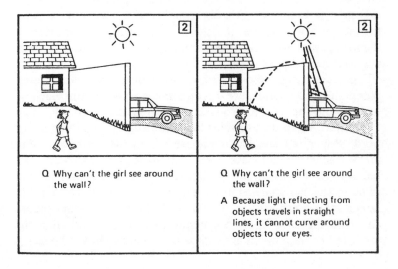

Q Why can't the girl see around the wall?

Q Why can't the girl see around the wall?

A Because light reflecting from objects travels in straight lines, it cannot curve around objects to our eyes.

Ms Ramsey's teaching emphasised entirely different things from Ms Lane's. As Roth and Anderson put it:

> Ms Ramsey's teaching focused on getting key concepts across rather than on covering all the pages in the text. Unlike Ms Lane, Ms Ramsey focused on the key issues that seemed to represent critical barriers to student learning. Her content coverage could be described as narrow and deep compared to Ms Lane's. This focus conveyed to students that science was about understanding and making sense of a few ideas, rather than a process of collecting and memorizing facts and words.
>
> (Roth and Anderson, 1988, pp. 127–8)

This teacher's way of questioning and responding to her pupils was also quite different. Like Ms Lane, Ms Ramsey asked many questions, but her questions encouraged pupils to use scientific concepts to explain real-world phenomena; they required understanding if they were to be answered correctly ('Using what you know about light, why do you think your thumb looks bigger under the magnifying glass?', for example). Like Ms Lane, she got pupils to talk about their everyday experiences, but she always prompted them to relate their stories to the relevant scientific concepts. This encouraged pupils to try to impose meaning on academic ideas and to see their relevance to the world: it gave the message time and time again that deep approaches were simultaneously more fun and what she would reward. Ms Ramsey listened carefully to her pupils' responses; this enabled her to detect the use of surface approaches and the existence of misconceptions. She could then challenge pupils who tried to get by with answers that merely involved reproducing facts or vague explanations, while hiding misunderstandings, and urge them to give more complete responses.

The interchange shown below, based on the overhead transparency illustrated in Figure 6.1, epitomises aspects of this teaching strategy and the different context of learning it created. Although 11-year-old Annie tries to show her knowledge off by using a 'big word' ('opaque') she has memorised from the textbook – and many teachers might have been content with that answer – Ms Ramsey is not satisfied. She probes Annie's understanding, testing whether she has attached any meaning to the word. The teacher listens to the explanation, correctly diagnoses a misconception, and uses the class firmly but gently to help her underline the preferred conception ('I like that answer better. Why is it better?').

Notice that, even though this is an example of highly teacher-centred instruction, there is a real dialogue between teacher and pupils, rather than a set of questions and answers, as in Ms Lane's class. Do you see any implications for your own tutorial, seminar, or practical teaching here?

Ms Ramsey's teaching

Ms Ramsey:	[puts up transparency] Why can't the girl see around the wall?
Annie:	The girl can't see around the wall because the wall is opaque.
Ms Ramsey:	What do you mean when you say the wall is opaque?
Annie:	You can't see through it. It is solid.
Brian:	[calling out] The rays are what can't go through the wall.
Ms Ramsey:	I like that answer better. Why is it better?
Brian:	The rays of light bounce off the car and go to the wall. They can't go through the wall.
Ms Ramsey:	Where are the light rays coming from originally?
Pupils:	The sun.
Ms Ramsey:	So you think her position is what is keeping her from seeing it. [She flips down the overlay with the answer]. Who was better?
Pupils:	Brian.
Ms Ramsey:	[to Annie] Would she be able to see it if she moved out beyond the wall?
Annie:	Yes.
Ms Ramsey:	Why?
Annie:	The wall is blocking her view.
Ms Ramsey:	Is it blocking her view? What is it blocking?
Student:	Light rays.
Ms Ramsey:	Light rays that are doing what?
Annie:	If the girl moves out beyond the wall, then the light rays that bounce off the car are not being blocked.

(Roth and Anderson, 1988, pp. 129–30)

Ms Ramsey also responded to pupils with careful, precise feedback; she gave them repeated opportunities to work with a single concept in many applications; and, although she taught the same number of classes as Ms Lane, she used experiments and demonstrations much less frequently. But when she did use them, she used them for a precise purpose: observation and activity was only one step in 'doing' experiments in Ms Ramsey's class. They were structured so that they helped pupils to think about, test out, and discuss with each other the relationships between concepts and everyday events.

Ms Ramsey's knowledge about her students enabled her to be a more effective teacher. She did not give them more ideas and facts to memorise; instead, she tried to diagnose their misunderstandings and use what she found out to help them change their conceptions. Her different teaching strategies led to better student learning outcomes. Her pupils easily outperformed Ms Lane's on tests of their understanding of scientific concepts.

SIX KEY PRINCIPLES OF EFFECTIVE TEACHING IN HIGHER EDUCATION

The list of properties provided on p. 89 can now be usefully condensed into six principles related to students' experiences.

Principle 1: Interest and explanation

The first group of characteristics contains elements described in studies of student evaluations as quality of explanation and stimulation of student interest. Few people will disagree that a facility for giving clear explanations of complex subject matter is a mandatory part of a lecturer's repertoire. It is evident that this facility can be learned (see Brown, 1978). Even more important, however, would appear to be the related ability to make the material of a subject genuinely interesting, so that students find it a pleasure to learn it. When our interest is aroused in something, whether it is an academic subject or a hobby, we enjoy working hard at it. We come to feel that we can in some way own it and use it to make sense of the world around us. We are more likely to focus on the subject matter itself rather than the institutional context surrounding it. And this is even more likely if an explanation is added as to why the particular method or fact that has to be learned will be useful in the future. These attitudes and behaviours are, of course, part-and-parcel of deep-holistic approaches to learning. We can all be helped to find meaning if our teachers show us how it can be done, and how exciting it is to do it.

Our old friend Sawyer ensnares this aspect of good teaching, and its converse, and presents them with exactly the stimulating qualities they imply:

> To master anything – from football to relativity – requires effort. But it does not require *unpleasant* effort, drudgery. The main task of any teacher is to make a subject interesting. If a child left school at ten, knowing nothing of detailed information, but knowing the pleasure that comes from agreeable music, from reading, from making things, from finding things out, it would be better off than a man who left university at twenty-two, full of facts but without any desire to inquire further into such dry domains. Right at the beginning of any course there should be painted a vivid picture of the benefits that can be expected from mastering the subject, and at every step there should be some appeal to curiosity or to interest which will make that step worthwhile.
>
> (Sawyer, 1943, p. 9)

Principle 2: Concern and respect for students and student learning

The second set of qualities is mainly about our consciousness of students and our consideration for them. These personal qualities are mandatory for every good teacher; it is sad that they are often scarce commodities in higher education. The archetypal arrogant professor, secure in the omnipotent possession of boundless knowledge, represents a tradition that dies hard. Certain lecturers, especially new ones, seem to take a delight in trying to imitate him; I sometimes meet his image in classes designed to prepare new academic staff for teaching. They are under pressure to show toughness, stringency and inflexibility in the face of student mystification; they are full of the haughtiness that their effortless mastery of their subjects permits; and it presumably gives them a feeling of superiority to adopt a condescending posture like John Macdonald Mackay (see chapter 5, p. 74). The educational culture of some disciplines, notably engineering and medicine, and to a lesser extent the physical and some social sciences, adds further external pressure to behave in this way.

Exactly the contrary attitude and behaviour is desirable, no matter what the discipline. Eble calls it 'generosity':

> Aristotle made much of what is commonly translated as *magnanimity*, the sufficiency of person or possessions that makes generosity possible . . . . The right attitude toward knowledge is surely a generous one, an attitude powerfully urged from the fact that knowledge, while permitting feelings of acquisition and ownership, suffers no loss when it is shared with and given to someone else. Teaching, by this basic attitude, is always a giving out, always a chance for benefaction. And as to generosity to students, few people are ever hurt by being regarded too generously. The shaky confidence about what one can learn, about how much one knows compared with someone else, needs constant shoring up.
>
> (Eble, 1988, p. 207)

Research on higher education unquestionably upholds these views. Among many other studies, Feldman's meta-analysis of student ratings (Feldman, 1976), the Lancaster investigation, and Entwistle and Tait's research on Scottish students (Entwistle and Tait, 1990) all underline the vital importance of respect and consideration for students in effective university teaching.

In fact, truly awful teaching in higher education is most often revealed by a sheer lack of interest in and compassion for students and student learning. It repeatedly displays the classic symptom of making a subject seem more demanding than it actually is. Some people may get pleasure from this kind of masquerade. They are teaching very badly indeed if they do. Good teaching is nothing to do with making things hard. It is nothing to do with frightening students. It is everything to do with benevolence and humility; it always tries to help students feel that a subject can be mastered; it encourages them to try things out for themselves and succeed at something quickly. The humility that every university teacher has felt in the presence of his or her subject, the honest awareness of what one does not know, is exactly the quality we need to display in our teaching. There is again nothing new in this statement; it embodies what good teachers have been doing, and say they have been trying to do, for thousands of years.

Related to generosity are honesty and interest in teaching, versatility in teaching skills, and availability to students. Of critical importance to students and student learning, as we have already seen, is the accessibility of staff for consultation about academic work. And if a teacher is to be generous and available, a sense of enjoyment in teaching one's subject and the adventures that teaching it presents are indispensable. Teaching like this therefore requires developing a keen interest in what it takes to help other people learn; it implies pleasure in teaching and associating with students, and delight in improvising. Teaching is nothing if it is not enjoying the unpredictable. It is futile to plead that these things are impossible to achieve in a climate of ever-reducing resources. If we want high quality teaching and learning, we cannot do without them.

Principle 3: Appropriate assessment and feedback

Giving really helpful feedback on students' work is an equally essential commitment. It is plainly related to our accessibility to students. Of all the facets of good teaching that are important to them, feedback on assessed work is perhaps the most commonly mentioned. 'Quality of assessment procedures' was one of the key features of good teaching as perceived by students noted in Marsh's authoritative review of the student evaluation literature (Marsh, 1987); similar factors also appeared in the Lancaster interviews. It is significant that the most salient question – the one that differentiated most effectively between the best and worst courses – in the Australian teaching performance indicator study (described below) was concerned with the quality of feedback on students' progress.

Setting appropriate assessment tasks, as we have seen from students' experiences, is evidently a difficult but crucial skill. It implies questioning in a way that demands evidence of understanding, the use of a variety of techniques for discovering what students have learned, and an avoidance of any assessments that require students to rote-learn or merely to reproduce detail. We shall be looking in detail at how to assess students, applying these standards, in chapter 10.

Principle 4: Clear goals and intellectual challenge

Principles 4 and 5 form a pair analogous to the 'rhythmic claims of freedom and discipline' in education that Whitehead identified.

All education may be seen to proceed in a triple cycle of growth, from a stage of absorbing, discursive, romantic discovery, through a stage of precision (which, according to Whitehead, is the sole stage in the traditional scheme of university education) to a stage of generalisation and application, where again initiative and enquiry dominate. The teacher's task is to recognise these equal claims of freedom and discipline, and their cyclical ordering, without overemphasising one or the other; to create a system in dynamic equilibrium. 'The real point', says Whitehead, 'is to discover in practice that exact balance between freedom and discipline which will give the greatest rate of progress over the things to be known'. The implication is that control over learning should reside both with the teacher and with the student.

Research into effective schooling overwhelmingly shows that consistently high academic expectations are associated with high levels of pupil performance. Lecturers in higher education should find this aspect of effective teaching relatively straightforward, so long as they remember to make the challenge interesting rather than dull. Romance must never be presumed dead, even when there are definite truths to be learned. What they are likely to have more difficulty with is explaining to students what must be learned in order to achieve understanding and what can be left out for the time being. All too often students begin a higher education course with only the vaguest notion of what key concepts they must master. Breakneck attempts to 'cover the ground' in the absence of a clear structure focused on key concepts intensify their confusion and deaden their excitement.

Principle 5: Independence, control, and active engagement

High quality teaching implies a recognition that students must be engaged with the content of learning tasks in a way that is likely to enable them to reach understanding. Perceptions of choice over how to learn the subject matter, and of control over which aspects may be focused on, are related to high quality learning.

Good teaching fosters this sense of student control over learning and interest in the subject matter. It understands the truth of Bruner's statement that 'Instruction is a provisional state that has as its object to make the learner or problem solver self-sufficient' (Bruner, 1966, p. 53). It provides relevant learning tasks at the right level for students' current understanding; it recognises that each student will learn best in his or her own way; it avoids creating over-dependence. It helps students to understand the essence of scholarship and investigation in their subjects by providing an opportunity for them to practise the art of enquiry. Trying to practise enquiry is the only way to learn how to enquire. It is also a way of arousing the imaginative spirit, differently constituted within each individual intellect, without which deep approaches to learning are impossible. It is impossible to quantify how many students have been discouraged from pursuing the learning of their chosen subjects by denying access to the art and enjoyment of enquiry.

Once again, the significance of independence and choice emerges repeatedly in research on student ratings and perceptions of favourable academic environments, at higher and upper secondary education levels. Yet most prevailing systems of learning in higher education adopt mass production standards; they handle each individual student in the same way, even though we know for certain that they operate in different ways. Active engagement, imaginative enquiry, and the finding of a suitable level and style are all much more likely to occur if teaching methods that necessitate student activity, problem solving, and cooperative learning are employed. These kinds of method permit a degree of student control over learning and can thus accommodate individual differences in preferred ways of reaching understanding, as well as having within them the potential to free students from over-dependence on teachers. They are also likely to result in students becoming engaged with what they are learning at a high cognitive level.

The positive effects on achievement of cooperative learning as compared to competitive and individualistic learning are very well established in the educational literature (see Johnson *et al*, 1981). Recently, Tang (1990) has reported similar effects for higher education students who cooperated in group discussions in preparing for assignments. They perceived their activity to be useful for understanding the content to be learned and used deep approaches to learning it. These were in turn related to higher quality learning outcomes.

All this is rather bad news for the traditional lecture, practical class, and tutorial, as well as for orthodox approaches to the professional curriculum, as will be seen in chapters 8 and 9. It seems that we often encourage poor learning in higher education through overstressing individual competition while at the same time using teaching methods that both foster passivity and ignore the individual differences between students.

It is worth stressing that we know that students who experience teaching of the kind that permits control by the learner not only learn better, but that they enjoy learning more. That is surely how it should be in higher education, as in any education; if we love our subjects, we must want other people to find them enjoyable rather than dull. Learning should be pleasurable. There is no rule against hard work being fun.

Principle 6: Learning from students

None of the foregoing principles is sufficient for good teaching. Effective teaching refuses to take its effect on students for granted. It sees the relation between teaching and learning as problematic, uncertain, and relative. Good teaching is open to change: it involves constantly trying to find out what the effects of instruction are on learning, and modifying that instruction in the light of the evidence collected.

That is the single most important message, the one you should remember if you forget everything else, of the case studies of the two science teachers summarised above. Like Ms Ramsey, a competent teacher should try to diagnose students' misunderstandings, in class and from the work they hand in, and then set about trying to change them through structuring the curriculum and assessment correctly. Knowledge about students should be actively used to select and deploy teaching strategies.

This is what 'evaluation' in relation to teaching is about, though the term has gradually become debased so that it applies to the task of collecting data rather than collecting, interpreting, and using it – both immediately, in the classroom, and in a more considered way when planning a curriculum. Evaluation of teaching in its true sense is no more or less than an integral part of the task of teaching, a continuous process of learning from one's students, of improvement and adaptation. Were we to lose all our knowledge about the nature of good teaching, it would be possible to reconstruct every other principle from a complete understanding of this one.

It is not likely that lecturers will find out much from students unless they arrange opportunities for finding out, such as talking to students and studying the products of their learning. We cannot change our understanding of anything, including our students' learning, unless we spend time and effort learning about it and going over it in several different ways.

GOOD TEACHING IN DIFFERENT DISCIPLINES AND IN DIFFERENT DEPARTMENTS: DIFFERENCES IN STUDENTS' PERCEPTIONS OF ACADEMIC COURSES

Most of the discussion so far in the present chapter has implicitly focused on one level – the level of the individual lecturer and his or her teaching skills and beliefs. I have said nothing either about how good teaching might vary in different subject areas. But we are dealing throughout with matters that can be conceptualised at more than one level, and which must be seen in relation to the cultures of different disciplines. It is timely to conclude with some evidence that sheds light on these issues, especially as this evidence brings us firmly back into the area of accountability and the evaluation of teaching quality. The principles outlined above are just as applicable to academic departments as to individual lecturers.

In chapter 5 we saw how the Lancaster investigation into British students' perceptions of teaching showed that study orientations, or general approaches to studying, were associated with the quality of teaching in different academic departments. The interview results, some extracts from which were also given, confirmed that these relations were functional – students learned better in departments that had better teaching because of the effectiveness of the teaching. But how different *are* different courses? What is the range of quality, and how is it related to subject areas? What are the characteristics of a good course, as seen by students?

A recent investigation of Australian students' evaluations of their courses provides some of the answers. During 1989, a Course Experience Questionnaire (CEQ) was tested in 50 institutions, the total sample comprising nearly 4,500 students in a range of subject areas (including humanities, natural sciences, social sciences, and professional programmes such as medicine, engineering, and accountancy) as part of a trial of performance indicators and a national review of the accounting discipline (Linke, 1991; Mathews *et al*, 1990; Ramsden, 1991b).

One version of the questionnaire appears in Appendix 1. The questions fall into five groups: Good Teaching, Clear Goals, Appropriate Workload, Appropriate Assessment, and Emphasis on Independence. These roughly correspond to the important aspects of teaching in higher education identified in previous work, such as the Lancaster study, and, of course, they represent many of the principles of good teaching outlined above. The meaning of each of the groups of questions is shown in Table 6.1.

Table 6.1 Categories and examples of questions in The Course Experience Questionnaire

Category	Example of question
Good teaching	Teaching staff here normally give helpful feedback on how you are going.
Clear goals	You usually have a clear idea of where you're going and what's expected of you in this course.
Appropriate workload	The sheer volume of work to be got through in this course means you can't comprehend it all thoroughly (negatively scored).
Appropriate assessment	Staff here seem more interested in testing what we have memorised than what we have understood (negatively scored).
Emphasis on independence	Students here are given a lot of choice in the work they have to do.

Source: Ramsden (1991b)

Three important outcomes from this study are relevant to our concerns here. The first is that students' perceptions of the relative quality of teaching vary by field of study. The differences are illustrated in Figure 6.2. The scale scores are 'standardised'; the average for the whole sample has been made equal to zero and is marked by the central horizontal line. Thus, we can see that fields of study such as medicine and engineering are rated below average, natural sciences are about average, while humanities and visual arts are rated above average. These are quite large differences in perceived teaching quality and they are congruent with the findings of other investigations. There were also differences observed *within* the fields of study. Electrical engineering was typically rated lower than other branches of

Figure 6.2 Differences in teaching quality by field of study

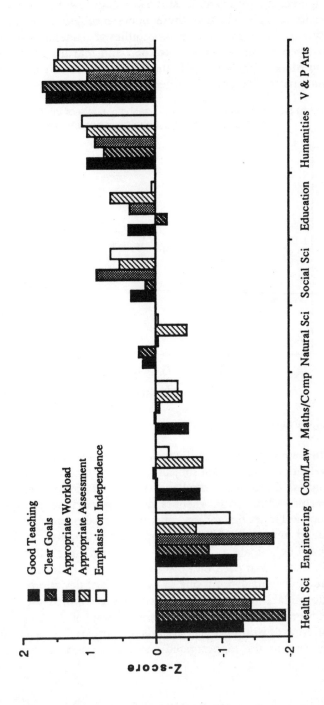

Good Teaching
Clear Goals
Appropriate Workload
Appropriate Assessment
Emphasis on Independence

Z-score

Health Sci   Engineering   Com/Law   Maths/Comp   Natural Sci   Social Sci   Education   Humanities   V & P Arts

Source: Ramsden (1991b)

engineering, for example, and psychology lower than other social sciences. The fact that these between-subject area differences have also been found in related studies of academic staff attitudes to teaching and research (Bowden and Martin, 1990; Ramsden and Moses, 1991) suggests that there are indeed differences in the quality of teaching in different academic cultures.

Figure 6.3 Scores on the 'Good Teaching' scale of the CEQ for thirteen Australian accountancy departments

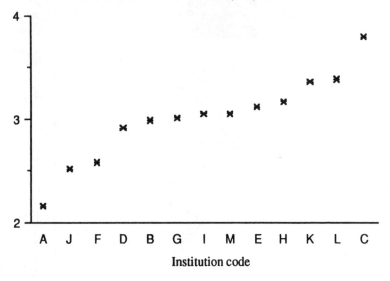

Source: Ramsden (1991b)

The second main finding is that differences in students' evaluations exist *within* subject areas and disciplines. In the CEQ studies, there were excellent, average, and poor examples of teaching within social sciences, medicine, engineering, and so on. Look at Figure 6.3, for example. It depicts the enormous range of quality among the 13 departments of accountancy on the 'Good Teaching' scale. Statistically speaking, the few extreme departments at each end of the distribution differ from those at the other end by from one to two standard deviations – certainly a formidable variation, whose validity was confirmed by interview and graduate survey data. Another way of looking at these differences within subject areas is to compare the proportions of students in the highest-rated and lowest-rated courses agreeing with the questions appearing in Table 6.1. Then we find, for example, that 70 per cent of commerce students at institution L agreed with the defining item of the 'Good Teaching' scale ('Teaching staff here normally give helpful feedback on how you are going'); at institution A, only 8 per cent agreed. Sixty-four per cent of education students at institution D agreed that 'The sheer volume of work to be got through in this course means you can't comprehend it all thoroughly' compared with only 31 per cent at institution L. Differences of this size are not only most unlikely to have occurred by chance; they are unquestionably of substantive importance. These departments really do have, in their students' perceptions, entirely different standards of teaching.

Thirdly, since there are differences within subject areas as well as across them, it makes sense to look at what constitutes more and less effective instruction at departmental or course level by looking at students' answers to each group of questions, and comparing the highly-rated courses with the lowly rated ones. The answers to the 'Good Teaching' group of items, for example, show that the courses differ in the following ways:

- Teaching staff here normally give helpful feedback on how you are going. (In the 'good' courses, students agree with this statement. In the 'bad' courses, students disagree with it. This item most clearly differentiated the best and worst courses.)
- The staff make a real effort to understand the difficulties students may be having with their work. (Good courses: students agree.)
- Our lecturers are extremely good at explaining things to us. (Good courses: students agree.)
- Teaching staff here work hard to make their subjects interesting to students. (Good courses: students agree.)
- This course really tries to get the best out of all its students. (Good courses: students agree.)
- Staff here put a lot of time into commenting on students' work. (Good courses: students agree.)
- The teaching staff of this course motivate students to do their best work. (Good courses: students agree.)
- Staff here show no real interest in what students have to say. (Good courses: students *disagree.*)

The general conclusions to be drawn from this particular study are that:

1 There are real variations in teaching quality in different courses and subjects. It is meaningless to talk about teaching quality being uniformly bad or good in higher education institutions.

2 It makes sense to talk about the relative effectiveness of teaching at the level of courses and combinations of courses *as well as* at the level of the individual teacher: the differences at aggregate (department) level mirror those at individual (lecturer) level.

3 There are differences in teaching quality between different subject areas.

4 There are also differences within subject areas. As in the study of students' approaches to learning and perceptions of courses described in the previous chapter, there are better and worse departments in science, social science, and humanities subjects.

These conclusions suggest two others – that comparisons of the effectiveness of teaching in academic departments and courses of study can legitimately be made, but should preferably be within subject areas, rather than across them; and that the less effective units can probably learn from the example of the more effective ones. Some general implications of these results for the measurement of performance and the improvement of quality will be discussed in chapters 11 and 12.

Chapter 7

Theories of teaching in higher education

I merely utter the warning that education is a difficult problem, to be solved by no one simple formula.

(A.N. Whitehead)

We are now ready to develop the preliminary representation of different theories of teaching provided in chapter 2 into a more coherent model of instruction in higher education that consolidates the principles of effective teaching outlined in chapter 6. Its propositions, each based on our knowledge of how students learn, will guide the recommendations made in Parts 2 and 3 of the book.

This model is a simple one: it is a sort of ordered common sense. It is based on the idea that there are different theories of teaching represented in lecturers' attitudes to teaching and their instructional strategies. It is a prescriptive and normative model, as any representation of instruction must be (Bruner, 1966). It describes the most effective ways of teaching in higher education and implicitly criticises less effective ways. It makes general statements about the conditions for efficient and effective learning and teaching. These statements are compatible with the descriptions of how students learn that we have examined, but they go beyond them. The foundations of good teaching outlined in this model can be applied to evaluating teaching performance, to developing the skills of lecturers, and to managing departments for high quality education. Attempts to do these things while ignoring the fundamental properties of effective instruction are likely to have unfortunate consequences.

LEARNING TO TEACH

A chain of connections has been established between learning and teaching in higher education. It should now be possible for you to see how each component of good teaching helps to bring about the kind of learning that leads to changes in understanding – and hence to the outcomes that lecturers and students value. Chapters 3 to 5 provided the basis for understanding these relationships. We saw how student learning was often of a mediocre quality, in terms of outcomes, approaches, and student satisfaction. The conclusion was that its quality was a function of the context of learning – otherwise known as students' perceptions of what we do in teaching.

In chapter 1 we met the idea of a 'conception of reality' – the way in which a student interprets a phenomenon, or structures and understands some aspect of the world around her. Learning is a change in one's conceptions – a change in one's understanding of something. Teachers cannot in the normal sense of the word tell students what a right and a wrong understanding is; the students have to make sense of it for themselves. The same reasoning applies to teaching. I can tell you what good teaching is: but only you can come to realise what it means. Thinking about teaching in the way described in the previous paragraph will imply for many lecturers a change in their conceptions – a change in their understanding of what teaching means. The case studies of the two middle-school science teachers in the Roth study summarised in the previous chapter strongly suggest that the interaction between teachers and pupils described there is directed by this latent factor of the teacher's theory of instruction. Readers will no doubt agree that the instructional strategies used by Ms Ramsey, taught as a set of stand-alone skills to teachers like Ms Lane, would have small chance of success. The skills are important, but like a car without a steering wheel, they require something else; they only have effect when they are managed by a sophisticated theory of teaching.

Thinking about teaching as a process of changing students' understanding in a general way is insufficient to ensure that good teaching actually happens. Teaching always takes place within particular contexts (such as in the physics classroom, or in writing comments on your student's political science essay, or in discussing a new form of assessment with other members of your engineering department). And, of course, it always involves a particular subject matter. Becoming skilled at teaching requires developing the ability to deploy a complex theory of teaching in the different contexts relevant to the teaching and learning of that subject matter. A lecturer who is able to do this may be said to have changed his or her understanding of teaching.

HIGHER EDUCATION TEACHERS' THEORIES OF TEACHING

Chapter 2 introduced the idea of different ways of experiencing and understanding teaching, presenting three vignettes based on what lecturers have said about the problems and possibilities of improving learning and teaching. The vignettes were derived from the structure of lecturers' theories of teaching suggested in recent research and writing on the subject, notably the work of Margaret Balla, Gloria Dall'Alba, and Elaine Martin in Melbourne (all of whom have undertaken interviews asking lecturers to describe teaching and learning in their disciplines), and John Biggs in Hong Kong. Bringing together these studies with the work in the area of students' approaches to learning, we can describe three generic ways of understanding the role of the teacher in higher education, each of which has corresponding implications for how students are expected to learn.

Theory 1: Teaching as telling or transmission

Many teachers in higher education implicitly or explicitly define the task of teaching undergraduates as the transmission of authoritative content or the demonstration of procedures. The knowledge to be handed on to students at this level (in contrast to the knowledge constituted in research and scholarship at higher levels) is seen as unproblematic. Subject content exists *sui generis*. It must be instilled in students. Much of the folklore of university teaching follows a similar line; even the Robbins Report, subsequently endorsed by the 1987 White Paper, defined key functions of higher education in terms of transmission of culture and instruction in skills. The traditional didactic lecture, of course, is a supreme representation of a perspective on teaching taken from the point of view of the teacher as the source of undistorted information. The mass of students are passive recipients of the wisdom of a single speaker. There are some more modern versions of this theory too: the belief that the fundamental problems of university instruction inhere in the amount of information to be transmitted, and that these problems can be solved by technical fixes designed to transmit more of it faster (typically nowadays some form of computer-assisted learning or sophisticated video presentation is one of them).

This way of looking at teaching has been identified in several studies of school teachers in training (see, for example, Russell and Johnson, 1988). It focuses on *what the teacher does to students*. The lecturer's role is seen as communicating knowledge smoothly; it is both necessary and sufficient that he or she should be an expert in the subject matter. Knowledge about subject content and knowledge of the techniques for teaching it are kept in separate compartments. The theory shows some affinities with the superficial engagement with content that typifies a surface approach. Learning, it seems to be saying, will occur as long as a quantity of information gets across to students.

Consistent with this view of how learning occurs, lecturers who use this theory of teaching will typically attribute any failure to learn to faults in the student. These lecturers conceptualise the relationship between what the teacher does and what the student learns as an intrinsically unproblematic one, a sort of input–output model with the works hidden away. If no student learning after exposure to teaching takes place, their theory cannot really explain why it does not. Occasionally I hear of lecturers, on being presented with evidence of student ignorance on a topic that has been the subject of a previous series of lectures, saying to the students (with astonishment) 'But you did *go* to the lectures last term, didn't you?'

We are also reminded of the lecturers in chapter 3 who appeared to believe in the existence of 'good learners' and 'poor learners' – who thought that the quality of student learning was determined by ability and personality, and could not be changed by teaching (see Bloom, 1976, for convincing arguments against this belief). Laziness, unwillingness to work at a particular topic, inability to absorb new material – the metaphor is significant – and poor preparation at an earlier stage of education are among the attributions used. This theory implies that all problems in teaching and learning reside outside the lecturer, the programme of study, or even the university. Increasing the standard of entering students is one typically mentioned remedy to the problem of poor learning, in addition to the technological solutions mentioned above. This is at heart an additive way of conceptualising teaching and learning.

Theory 2: Teaching as organising student activity

In theory 2, the focus moves away from the teacher towards the student. Teaching is seen as a supervision process involving the articulation of techniques designed to ensure that students learn. Authoritative subject knowledge, so salient in the first theory, recedes into the background.

Student learning is now seen as a perplexing problem. How can ideals (developing independence and critical thinking, teaching in a way that is more exciting than the teaching that oneself experienced, etc.) be translated into reality? Activity in students is regarded as the panacea. It is assumed that there is a finite set of rules which may be infallibly applied to enable them to understand; these all imply that students must learn energetically. The methods may include ways of motivating students so that they are in the right psychological frame of mind to learn dull subject matter; simple 'rewards and punishments' approaches to assessment ('If you don't learn this, you'll fail the exam; if you do, it will be useful next year'); techniques for promoting discussion in class; and processes which require students to link their theoretical knowledge to their experience, such as forms of experiential learning.

This theory represents in many ways a transitional stage between theories 1 and 3. Ms Lane (chapter 6) is probably working from this theory. Teaching is seen no longer as being mainly about telling or transmission: it is also about dealing with students, and above all about making them busy, using a set of efficient procedures to cover the ground. This theory is probably the level at which many attempts to innovate in higher education are presented, and the level at which much staff development takes place. Teachers in higher education often complain that they lack the skills to help students become more able; but they often want at the same time a set of methods that are fail-safe: tested, tried, and true for all terrains. There are many temptations to answer this plea. Improving teaching from this point of view is about extending a lecturer's repertoire of techniques rather than about changing his or her understanding. Learning teaching techniques is, in this theory, an entirely sufficient basis for improving teaching. If we learn how to do something, it is assumed that learning how to reflect on what we do and to apply our knowledge to new situations naturally follows.

The view of student learning corresponding with this theory of teaching is that there are certain conditions that will guarantee learning. If learning does not occur, something is wrong outside the learner as well as inside. Much student learning may still be seen as an additive process, and different in kind at first year and postgraduate level, but it is no longer seen simply as the individual learner's responsibility.

Theory 3: Teaching as making learning possible

If theories 1 and 2 focus respectively on the teacher and the student, theory 3 looks at teaching and learning as two sides of a coin. Theory 3 is a compound view of instruction. In this conception, teaching, students, and the subject content to be learned are linked together by an overarching framework or system. Teaching is comprehended as a process of working cooperatively with learners to help them change their understanding. It is making student learning possible. Teaching involves finding out about students' misunderstandings, inter-vening to change them, and creating a context of learning which encourages students actively to engage with the subject matter. Note that this theory is very much concerned with the *content* of what students have to learn in relation to how it should be taught. As we saw in the previous chapter, a teacher who uses this theory will recognise and focus especially on the key issues that seem to represent critical barriers to student learning. The content to be taught, and students' problems with learning it, direct the methods he or she uses.

The teacher's conception of his or her role differs radically in this theory. This is because it draws on a different epistemology from theories 1 and 2. It is recognised that knowledge of the subject content is actively constituted by the learner, and that this process of constituting reality is not qualitatively different whether the learning is of accepted fact and theory in a first year course or whether it takes place at the frontiers of knowledge in the same subject. The nature of obtaining knowledge does not differ. Learning is applying and modifying one's own ideas; it is something the student does, rather than something that is done to the student. 'Transmission' of existing knowledge is at best a half-true description of education; *all* knowledge is new and requires to be decoded if you have not met it before; all facts must be interpreted imaginatively. This is no doubt what Whitehead had in mind when he spoke of 'imaginatively imparting information' in university teaching:

> A university which fails in this respect has no reason for existence. This atmosphere of excitement, arising from imaginative consideration, transforms knowledge. A fact is no longer a bare fact: it is invested with all its possibilities. It is no longer a burden on the memory: it is energising as the poet of our dreams, and as the architect of our purposes. Imagination . . . enables men to construct an intellectual vision of a new world, and it preserves the zest of life by the suggestion of satisfying purposes.
>
> (Whitehead, 1929, p. 139)

Jerome Bruner makes a related point that neatly expresses the central idea of this theory:

> A curriculum reflects not only the nature of knowledge itself but also the nature of the knower and of the the knowledge-getting process . . . . A body of knowledge, enshrined in a university faculty and embodied in a series of authoritative volumes, is the result of much prior intellectual activity. To instruct someone in these disciplines is not a matter of getting him to commit results to mind. Rather, it is to teach him to participate in the process that makes possible the establishment of knowledge. We teach a subject not to produce little living libraries on that subject, but rather to get a student to think mathematically for himself, to consider matters as an historian does, to take part in the process of knowledge-getting. Knowing is a process, not a product.
>
> (Bruner, 1966, p. 72)

We are a long way away from surface approaches in these views of education and this theory of teaching.

Improving teaching is an integral part of theory 3, precisely because it expresses a notion of teaching as a speculative and reflexive activity. Using theory 3 means listening to students and listening to other teachers in an effort to teach better. Continuous improvement of skills through constructing increasingly elaborate professional knowledge becomes part of teaching from this perspective; puzzling practical events engender actions that entail reconceptualisations of the events (see Schön, 1983);

the teacher understands the need to identify critical obstacles to student learning for different topics and give them special attention in the curriculum. This implies a certain attitude to educational principles and research: while theories 1 and 2 typically regard these as separate from the 'real' world of classrooms and teaching strategies, theory 3 recognises a complementarity between teaching and educational thinking. Teachers working from this perspective are interested in learning from a variety of sources about how they might improve their teaching (see Marton and Ramsden, 1988).

The lecturer using this theory will realise that his or her curriculum will need to contain different ways of encouraging students to learn and different sequences of material, so that individual differences between learners can be fitted into the general goal of helping all students to change their understanding. The corresponding view of student learning is therefore clear: there are certain favourable conditions for learning which, however, need to be actively reinterpreted to fit specific circumstances, particular students, and the subject matter. The activities of teaching, in other words, are seen as context-related, uncertain, and continuously improvable. Unlike theory 2, this view of teaching does not accept that there can ever be one solution, one set of perfect rules, that will ensure learning.

The structure of the theories

These theories have a progressive, or hierarchical, structure. Thus, theory 1 assumes that content knowledge and fluent presentation are enough for good teaching. Theory 2 complements this picture with additional skills focused principally on student activity and the acquisition of extra teaching techniques. Theory 3 presupposes all these abilities and extends the understanding of teaching so that it becomes embedded in the nature of subject knowledge and the nature of how it is learned.

The most sophisticated theory therefore implies aspects of both the others: in other words, teaching does involve presenting information, motivating students, and creating opportunities for them to learn; good lecturing does imply clear and orderly presentation; and in the last analysis, only the student can do the learning – it is his or her own responsibility. But good teaching as represented in theory 3 does not stop at doing these things, nor does it place all the responsibility on the student's shoulders all the time. In contrast, theory 1 is locked into a notion of teaching as information transmission or skills exposition and it focuses on the actions of the teacher in isolation from the student. The relation between teaching and student learning is taken for granted. Formally, it implies rejection of the six principles of good teaching described in chapter 6, and it logically leads to behaviours in the classroom and elsewhere which reduce the probability of changes in students' understanding.

Theory 2 occupies an intermediate position, accepting the need to orchestrate teaching skills and to get students to carry out various exercises, as well as a requirement to present information. But it fails to integrate these activities with students' learning of subject content. Student activity does not in itself imply that learning will take place. Theory 3, which is about making learning possible, exemplifies the qualities of effective university teaching previously described. It delineates a way of thinking about teaching that is qualitatively different from, and pedagogically superior to, the others. It is associated with better quality learning: it represents the goal towards which all efforts at improving teaching in higher education should be directed. Changing lecturers' understanding of teaching is a necessary condition for improving teaching in higher education.

The theories, of course, represent 'ideal types'. They are logical constructs rather than descriptions of every individual or every course – although we shall soon see, in Part 2, how excellent and committed teachers really do teach from something close to the perspective represented by theory 3. There is a rational line of development from one theory to the next which accords with a process of an individual lecturer's learning about teaching. Each higher theory expresses a twofold and seemingly contradictory development – towards an increasingly relativistic and problematic understanding of the relations between teaching and learning, on the one hand; and towards recognising the unity between what the lecturer does and what the student learns, on the other. It is as if the development itself denotes an acceptance of the restless tension of opposites in education.

The extent to which these different ways of understanding teaching are more common among lecturers in some subject areas than in others is obviously a provocative issue. The question has yet to be satisfactorily answered. It seems likely that theories 1 and 2 may be more often represented in those subject areas which typically receive lower student ratings (such as engineering) than in those which usually receive higher ratings (such as humanities). But it would be very unwise indeed to jump to the conclusion that any differences are inherent in the nature of the subjects, or that the social organisation of disciplinary cultures determines the theory its teachers should use. It is easy to think of courses and teachers that illustrate each way of understanding in all subject areas, and variations in student perceptions of courses within the same subject area, as we saw in chapter 6, definitely confirm these impressions. It may be that good teaching is more common, and perhaps even easier to achieve, in some subject areas than others; its principles, however, apply to all of them.

A MODEL OF TEACHING IN HIGHER EDUCATION

In chapter 5 we looked at a model of student learning which linked together students' previous experiences, their approaches to studying, and the outcomes of their learning. In Figure 7.1, we see how the idea of theories of teaching might be used to understand how lecturers go about their work and how their teaching might be improved. A lecturer's general theory of teaching is actually brought into action through how he or she thinks about specific aspects of teaching, such as how to teach a particular topic in a tutorial, how to set an assignment question or mark an examination question in a specific area, or how to convince colleagues that a change in the curriculum is needed. 'Teaching in action' is a phrase used here as shorthand for the observable activities related to these ways of thinking that may be described as teaching in higher education – such as relationships with students, the time devoted to preparation and course development, marking and feedback, evaluation of one's performance, and so on.

Lecturers, like their students, work within an academic environment; this environment includes their discipline as well as the academic department (or other organisational unit) and the institution in which they work. Ways of going about teaching are the outcome of a teacher's perceptions of the conditions defined by the context of teaching. At the same time, his or her understanding of teaching is influenced by this context. (As I shall emphasise later, a lecturer's activities are not completely determined by it.) Importantly, the quality of a teacher's reflections on how his or her teaching is working affect the theories used and in turn the future actions taken. For example, Ms Ramsey in chapter 6 clearly listened to the ways in which learners tried to make sense of the ideas about light and seeing she was trying to teach them, and used that information to structure both how she thought about teaching and her interaction with the pupils.

This model enables us to make some predictions about the effects of different evaluation procedures and training programmes on the quality of lecturers' teaching, in a similar way to the projections concerning the outcomes and process of student learning that can be derived from Figure 5.1. These issues, however, are ahead of us: we need to look first at how a lecturer who understands teaching as making learning possible will carry out the activities of teaching in higher education.

Figure 7.1 A model of teaching in higher education

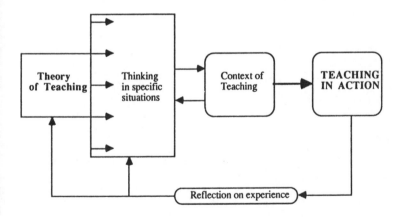

Part 2

Design for learning

Chapter 8

The goals and structure of a course

Surely, in every subject in each type of curriculum, the precise knowledge required should be determined after the most anxious inquiry . . . I am sure that one secret of a successful teacher is that he has formulated quite clearly in his mind what the pupil has got to know in precise fashion. He will then cease from half-hearted attempts to worry his pupils with memorising a lot of irrelevant stuff of inferior importance.

(A.N. Whitehead)

INTRODUCTION TO PART 2: APPLYING THEORY TO PRACTICE

This chapter begins Part 2 of the book, in which we examine some applications of the theoretical material considered in Part 1. You should by now be familiar with some principal ideas about how students learn and the relations between their approaches to learning, the quality of their learning, and the context of learning in higher education. We have seen how these concepts could be used to clarify the nature of good teaching and how they might be linked together into a way of understanding the process of instruction which explains variation in teaching quality using the simple device of different theories of teaching.

How can we use our understanding to improve the practice of teaching in higher education? There are five issues that need to be addressed:

1 What do I want my students to learn, and how can I express my goals to them and make these goals clear to myself and my colleagues? This is the problem of *goals and structure*.

2 How should I arrange teaching and learning so that students have the greatest chance of learning what I want them to learn? This is the problem of *teaching strategies*.
3 How can I find out whether they have learned what I hoped they would learn? This is the problem of *assessment*.
4 How can I estimate the effectiveness of my teaching, and use the information I gather to improve it? This is the problem of *evaluation*.
5 How should the answers to 1–4 be applied to measuring and improving the quality of higher education? These are the problems of *accountability and educational development*.

The present chapter and the two that follow it deal in turn with problems 1 to 3. In each chapter in Part 2, I illustrate the application of the principles of effective instruction by referring to case studies which show how lecturers in several subject areas have addressed these questions. Since our preferred theory of teaching maintains that evaluation is an inseparable part of the enterprise of higher education, implicit within each of these chapters is the idea that good teaching involves monitoring and improving the effectiveness of the curriculum, how it is taught, and how students are assessed. This means that we shall also be addressing the fourth question as we go along. A more general discussion of evaluation will be postponed until Part 3, where the focus widens to include the fifth problem as well. In Part 3 we shall consider measures of teaching performance, the political issues surrounding staff appraisal, and the challenge of educational development.

A word is necessary about this approach before beginning the main part of this chapter. Very few books about teaching in higher education adopt it. They focus instead on methods of teaching and assessing students (practicals, objective tests, lectures, small groups, examinations, etc.) rather than the subject matter which the methods are supposed to help students learn. Naturally there cannot be any meaningful discussion of teaching strategies without some reference to content: we always teach students something. However, the content and the students remain in the background in most treatments of this subject. The same is true for many investigations of the effectiveness of higher education teaching. They are concerned with questions such as whether lectures are more effective than independent study, or whether students prefer computer-assisted learning to textbooks.

As I think you must by now be aware, I think these are wholly mistaken approaches. This book looks at teaching from the opposite perspective. From this point of view, in the foreground is what students are expected to learn and how they go about learning it. Methods form the background. They are secondary: they are means, not ends. Decisions about which methods to use in order to teach and assess our students should be based on their effectiveness as means of encouraging high quality learning outcomes, which by definition are concerned with subject content and the people who learn that content.

If the argument that all teaching and learning is concerned with specific content and how students address it were to be carried too far, however, we would end up in the paradoxical position that we could never give any generic advice on teaching methods. Every topic is unique: every topic therefore requires a different teaching strategy. This would evidently be an impossible conclusion as far as improving teaching is concerned. There are generally applicable principles for good teaching, such as those described in chapters 6 and 7. Despite variations in the way effective learning and teaching manifests itself in different subject areas, we found that there was a core of principles, ways of thinking and activities that was common to all successful educational experiences.

But how can this be, if the content is in the foreground and the method in the background? The answer is that we were looking at principles, not techniques, in those chapters. We were not considering how to lecture: we were considering how we should help students to learn what we wanted them to learn. We were not examining whether to use multiple-choice tests or essays: we were examining the educational importance of feedback on learning and the uses of assessment as a way of helping *us* to learn how to improve teaching. Principles of good teaching do not prescribe or proscribe certain techniques, but rather point us towards or away from certain procedures in particular situations. All effective teaching methods will realise – in their different ways – the principles of student responsibility for learning, the teacher's concern for students, clear structure, cultivation of student interest in the subject matter, and so on. The choice of any particular method, and the way it is applied, should be based on positive answers to the question of whether the principles are maintained. Yet no one can predict with certainty whether a certain method will work in a particular context. The inevitable conclusion of this argument is a recognition that we, as teachers, cannot avoid the responsibility of constantly making decisions about student learning. There can never be a set of techniques that will ensure good teaching and learning.

STUDENTS' EXPECTATIONS OF COURSES IN HIGHER EDUCATION

To begin a course of higher education is for many students to begin a period of uncertainty and confusion. Whether the transition is from school or work, or even from a previous year of study in the same institution, students often have only the slightest idea of what to expect. When I became an under-graduate for the first time, while I was surprised at the extraordinary freedom the experience afforded, I happened to fall in with a group of fellow students who were extremely interested in the subjects they were studying. The experience was liberating. I was lucky. Many students find the experience utterly confusing, especially if they come from school systems where attainment in the qualifying entrance examination is seen as something close to an end in itself. We easily forget how students can experience a sense of disorientation owing to a rapid shift from an ordered and familiar environment to one of considerable freedom. Although it is apparent from several studies of transition from school to university and the early experiences of higher education that the first few weeks of a student's experiences in higher education are critical to success in the remainder of their programmes, the effects sometimes do not show themselves until the second year of a programme of study or even later (see, for example, Entwistle et al., 1989; Entwistle, 1990). It is clear that students often spend a lot of their time simply trying to discover what we want them to learn, and that many of them fail to perceive the links between the academic knowledge they have acquired in school and the work they are required to do at university (Martin, Ramsden, and Bowden, 1989). Both mature age and younger students may also be encumbered by naïve conceptions of what learning consists of, as we saw in chapters 3 and 4.

The first question in teaching anything should be 'What do I want my students to learn?' It should be closely followed by a second question: 'How can I express my requirements to my students?' It cannot be emphasised too strongly that satisfactory answers to these questions must precede attempts to address problems such as how to present a lecture, manage a tutorial, or use visual aids. To appreciate the significance attached by students to the clear expression of the pattern, content, and expectations of a course, consider again some of the items from The Course Experience Questionnaire study (see chapter 6) that differentiated the 'good' courses from the 'bad' ones:

> It's often hard to discover what's expected of you in this course.

> The aims and objectives of this course are not made very clear.

> You usually have a clear idea of where you're going and what's expected of you in this course.

> It's always easy here to know the standard of work expected of you.

> The staff here make it clear right from the start what they expect from students.

In the good courses, students tended to disagree with the first two statements listed and to agree with the rest. Additional examples that made clear the meaning attached by students to unambiguous aims and an orderly framework to the curriculum appeared in chapter 5. It is indisputable that, from the students' perspective, clear standards and goals are a vitally important element of an effective educational experience. Lack of clarity on these points is almost always associated with negative evaluations, learning difficulties, and poor performance.

Weak teaching will acquit itself of responsibility for student confusion arising from unclear structure with the kinds of excuses we dismissed in chapter 6. Some students will always do badly for reasons beyond our control. What teachers can do is to make sure that they do not falter for reasons within our control. If we intend to teach well, in accordance with a theory 3 approach to teaching, we must help students to adapt to the freedom of higher education by making plain what our requirements are, and by providing an explicit set of constraints which is gradually relaxed as students gain more experience.

Thoughtful teachers understand that highly structured initial experiences provide students with confidence and a sense of purpose; these experiences tend to make subsequent freedoms all the more fruitful and exciting. Specific examples of teaching strategies for achieving these general aims will be discussed in the next chapter.

CONTENT AND AIMS

The content of a course is traditionally communicated through its syllabus. 'Intermediate cartography', 'An introduction to clinical decision analysis', 'The developmental psychology of Jean Piaget', 'Theory of partnership and company accounting', 'Advanced topics in thermodynamics', 'Quattrocento Venice' are all examples of course content as it is frequently expressed. There is nothing wrong with them – except for what they leave unsaid.

Syllabus topics easily obscure the fact that content embraces the range of theories, ideas, processes, principles, concepts, facts, and skills that a lecturer expects students to learn. The less sophisticated theories of teaching fail to recognise that content is not identical to knowledge of a list of topics, or that the higher-level aims typically expressed by teachers in higher education must needs be incorporated in our expectations for student learning. At their most extreme, lists of topics to be 'covered' invite students to adopt narrow strategies aimed at gathering quantities of information that will permit assessments to be negotiated – to use, in other words, an essentially quantitative approach to learning. No wonder that students sometimes waste valuable time trying to discover the implicit criteria on which they will be assessed, or that they often focus on issues which the lecturer did not intend them to concentrate on.

You will remember from the studies of lecturers' expectations summarised in chapter 3 that teachers in higher education normally speak of two elements of their subject when they describe their intentions for student learning – the substantive (the key ideas) and the procedural (the typical ways of arriving at understanding in the discipline). The most important aspect of course content follows directly from a perspective on education as changing conceptions: what *changes in understanding* do we expect students to undergo as a result of experiencing the course? What will students be able to do as a result of these changes, after they complete the course, that they could not do before?

Logically, there can be no such thing as teaching if the teacher does not know what he or she wants students to learn. Few lecturers would be unable to describe the progress they expect students to make during a course. Yet many of them, as we also saw before, may be diffident about expressing the goals of their teaching in terms other than syllabus topics or general statements such as 'critical thinking' or 'independent judgement'. In answer to questions about student learning, they will often point to a series of items which lists what *they* will be teaching rather than what the *students* will be learning.

Lennart Svensson and Christian Högfors (1988) describe their experiences of trying to persuade engineering lecturers to articulate the aims of a mechanics course, and its place in an engineering programme at a Swedish university, as being of just this kind. The academic staff were able to talk in detail about the discipline of classical mechanics and its relationship to engineering, but did not link the knowledge and skills gained by students in the mechanics unit to the aims of the entire programme. They assumed that specifying the content to be taught in each specialist area, such as mechanics, automatically implied its contribution to the general aims. Specification of the content to be taught, not how the content enabled students to become engineers, was seen as 'the problem' by these lecturers. Svensson and Högfors call this view an 'administrative' conception of course design. The starting-point of this perspective is the division of the curriculum into subjects and their component parts. Mastery of the parts constitutes the aim of the whole course:

> What it means to master or know these units is considered non-problematical. How to further and control this knowledge are seen as practical problems that do not have to be treated during discussion of the goals . . . . Discussion . . . indicated that when people thought of better ways of meeting the aims, they mainly considered new courses that would fill the gaps.
>
> (Svensson and Högfors, 1988, pp. 174–5)

AIMS AND OBJECTIVES

Svensson and Högfors' experiences are ubiquitous. What can be done to change these views of course content, and thus begin to change the context of student learning? Much fruitless debate has been expended on debates about aims and objectives in education without reaching what seems to me to be the core of the problem, which is that lecturers often do not reflect on what they want students to learn and why they want them to learn it. A typical misconception is that students do not need to know about the goals of a course: the content of the syllabus plus attendance at lectures will be enough. We have seen that it is frequently not enough.

One of the central arguments of this book is that all aspects of teaching in higher education should be driven by the changes in understanding we want to see occur in our students. The purpose of expressing aims and objectives is to improve the quality of education, in two senses. The activity should enable teachers to think more critically and deliberately about student progress, and the manner of its connection with what they do in their teaching. Secondly, the results of the exercise should make clear to students exactly what they have to learn to succeed, and what they can leave aside. Aims and objectives are no magic wand, but neither are they the dangerous witchcraft that some people seem to think they are. They will not necessarily cause teachers to reflect on their teaching or improve their students' learning, but they may be a useful technique for making those ends possible.

As in so many other things about teaching in higher education, it is very unwise to be dogmatic about the techniques of using aims and objectives. The principle of being clear about the key elements of competence that students should acquire is what matters. Objectives do not have to consist of 'things that students can be observed to do', as some proponents of behavioural objectives would try to have us believe. It is quite acceptable to think directly about the concepts that a student who has successfully completed his or her course will have understood – such as 'opportunity cost' in economics, 'the Avogadro constant' in chemistry, or 'metaphor' in literature – and how they will have arrived at an understanding of them (see also Rowntree, 1981, pp. 68–85).

Aims are best thought of as general statements of educational intent, seen from the student's point of view, while objectives are more specific and concrete statements of what students are expected to learn. The medical course at the University of Melbourne, for example, includes the general aim '[To achieve] an understanding of principles in the analysis of human behaviour and functioning relevant to health and disease'; within the list of objectives for the subject of behavioural science which forms part of this programme is a specific example of what this entails: '[The student should understand] family structures and their impact on patient care, particularly in regard to primary medical care.'

The rationale for using statements of aims and objectives would seem to be based on three linked assumptions:

- That education is about changes in students' thinking and knowledge.
- That it is useful at the start of a course to inform students plainly, methodically, and accurately what they need to learn.
- That it is what students do, rather than what teachers do, that ultimately determines whether changes in their understanding actually take place.

Writing aims and objectives, and thinking systematically about the concepts that students will need to understand and how they will understand them, becomes a perplexing task if instruction is seen from the point of view of teaching theory 1 (telling or transmitting knowledge using efficient teaching skills). Looking at what the student has to do in order to learn is not part of this way of considering teaching.

Like most tasks in education, devising and articulating objectives can be done in a superficial way. It is frankly not worth the bother: it is an imitation of teaching as surely as surface approaches are an imitation of learning. It is easy when struggling with the idea of aims and objectives to fall into one of three traps. One is to attempt to restate syllabus topics using the language of aims and objectives. For example, a lecture topic in introductory economics might be 'Exchange rates and trade'. The 'objective' then becomes 'To acquire knowledge about exchange rates and trade'. Needless to say, this sort of thing provides students with no extra information about what they have to do. What does it mean to acquire knowledge about exchange rates and trade? It presumably implies an understanding of key concepts and their application to real situations; we might try, as two objectives related to this topic 'To explain the meaning and function of flexible and fixed exchange rates in relation to the concept of equilibrium' and 'To explain the significance of a current account deficit'. Students may not know what all these terms mean at first, but they will help direct their attention to what is relevant in a lecture or text, and provide them later with a useful means of reviewing their knowledge of the topic.

Almost the opposite of this error (but with an equally unhelpful effect, as far as students are concerned) is to provide another kind of imitation goal – vague, extremely general aims that are practically content-free: 'To become more critical of established theory'; 'To improve written communication skills'; 'To understand links between the practical and the theoretical'; 'To become an independent learner'. There is a place in exhaustive declarations of educational goals for very comprehensive statements like these, but they need to be combined with more precise statements related to a particular profession or discipline if they are to be useful to students and helpful in planning teaching. These general aims only gain meaning when they are actualised in specific subjects: the historian's understanding of links between theory and practice will be very different from the chemist's. It is certain that students do not acquire competences like this except in association with particular subject matter. General intellectual development arises from students' relationships with the content. In Perry's scheme of levels of thinking, for example, (chapter 3) the general categories derive entirely from students' interaction with domains of knowledge; students come 'to "realize" through the necessities of intellectual disciplines' as Perry puts it (Perry, 1988, p. 158).

The third kind of imitation objective is the one so roundly criticised by those who are against the whole idea of aims and objectives. They have a reasonable point. This type of objective describes only observable student behaviours and is extremely narrow and specific. It thus excludes, for example, statements beginning 'To understand' (understanding cannot be observed). It has also regrettably been assumed by some of those who take this approach that every valuable educational aim can be specified in advance, and that a good list of objectives only contains skills and knowledge that are 100 per cent achievable.

These assertions are highly contentious. To concentrate only on observable behaviours in writing objectives trivialises learning. It narrows courses to the things that are easily measurable rather than to the things that are educationally important. It encourages surface approaches by giving exactly the wrong message to students: that achieving the signs of learning is more important than achieving the changes in understanding that should underlie them. It is equally mistaken to think that all important objectives, particularly the less concrete ones concerning changes in attitudes, can be pre-specified. It is impossible to predict exactly what outcomes will occur from a course of study, and it is inadmissible to think, particularly in higher education, that anything that is learned that was not foreseen is worthless. The practical effect of focusing only on objectives that can be fully mastered is to concentrate on low-level changes in students' knowledge. Many important skills and understandings are infinitely improvable. Aims and objectives should rather describe *progress* towards understanding. If a minimum standard needs to be achieved (for professional practice, for example) this should be separately specified.

Try to describe concepts and relations between concepts if you write objectives for your courses. If course objectives concentrate largely on procedures and facts, students will inevitably receive the message that higher order outcomes (including both an understanding of key concepts and the development of complex skills such as a systematic approach to experimentation or historical argument) are less important than an ability to categorise and reproduce disconnected pieces of knowledge. *Imitation objectives imply surface approaches.*

Some examples of aims and objectives which avoid these mistakes, and which are likely to be useful both to students and staff by providing a methodical structure for a course of study, appear in Table 8.1. In Table 8.2 we see an example of a well thought out list of general aims for a professional programme. Note how much further the aims shown in Table 8.2 take us than the abstract aims of 'independent analysis' and 'critical thinking': they describe subject-specific intentions for student learning which resemble the kinds of general goals expressed by lecturers when they are asked to talk about what they expect from their students (see chapter 3).

While we may avoid all the errors listed earlier in this chapter, it is necessary to remember something else if we want to use the technique of writing aims and objectives to plan a curriculum. Listing aims and objectives alone, and perhaps giving out the list at the first lecture, is an entirely unsatisfactory means of describing to students what we want them to do.

Table 8.1 Some examples of aims and objectives

Aims

Students should:

- Acquire skills of economic analysis and reasoning (economics)
- Develop their ability to pose purposeful questions about the past and answer them imaginatively (history)
- Develop the capacity to think creatively and independently about new design problems and make a realistic estimate of their own potential for solving them (engineering)

Objectives

Students should:

- Recognise and explain the role of government in planning through a detailed examination of the 1947 Planning Act (environmental planning)
- Be able to explain, using graphical and algebraic methods, the meaning of elasticity in different contexts (economics)
- Appreciate the range of normality in the living human body due to age, sex, and body build, and the effects of posture, phase of respiration, and pregnancy (anatomy)
- Understand the properties of ionising radiation (physics)
- Comprehend fundamental concepts in the historical study of the French Revolution: be able to examine, for example, eighteenth-century meanings of 'bourgeoisie' and 'feudalism' and distinguish them from twentieth-century interpretations (history)
- Be able to interpret contemporary human activities in the light of the psychology of memory (psychology)

Objectives must be connected quite forcefully to the learning activities that are designed to enable students to achieve them; they must be embodied in the actions and words of the teachers who profess them; they must be continually presented to students in order to provide a clear framework in which they can work. The most compelling reason for using aims and objectives, or some similar method of describing content, is that it forces us as teachers to make our intentions for student learning explicit. There ought to be a definite educational justification for every activity, every piece of content, that is present in a course of study. Tradition and habit are not satisfactory educational reasons. This leads me naturally to consider ways of selecting the content that a list of educational goals is designed to express.

Table 8.2 The aims of a law course

Students should:

- Understand, and be able to identify, use, and evaluate rules, concepts, and principles of law, their derivation, and the various theories that attempt to systematise them
- Acquire the techniques of legal reasoning and argument, in oral and written form
- Understand the institutions of the law, and their social, economic, and political context
- Learn to find the law, to carry out independent research and analysis, and to think creatively about legal problems
- Develop a continuing interest in the law, and obtain satisfaction from its study and practice
- Develop a critical interest in the reform of the law
- Appreciate the responsibilities of lawyers to the courts, the legal profession, the community and individuals within it
- Develop a commitment to promoting justice

Source: Based on the aims of the undergraduate curriculum in Law, University of Melbourne

SELECTING CONTENT AND AIMS

How should we select appropriate content for a course of higher education? How are aims and objectives generated? Even if the syllabus has been fixed by someone else, even if you have been provided with a list of topics, it is still useful to reflect on the content using the approaches described in this chapter and to consider ways in which it might be interpreted and structured. There is nearly always room for some manoeuvre. A colleague of mine who used to be a high school physics teacher has recently been working as a part-time tutor of first year students in a university science department. There, although the content is defined by the full-time lecturers, he has been able to deploy his own knowledge of typical student misconceptions derived from his secondary school experiences to focus particularly on certain areas of the subject that students often have problems with. His *de facto* curriculum gives much more time to some topics than others. This approach is quite compatible both with the requirements of the department and with the principles of effective teaching.

It is probable that most readers will have more freedom than this in deciding the content, either in devising an entirely new course or in revising an old one. I do not propose to look at all the possible sources of content in this chapter. A good general review appears in Rowntree (1981); an excellent description related to the specific area of laboratory teaching is that of Boud *et al.* (1986). It is important to stress that different ways of devising course content will suit different subjects, different students and different lecturers. Among the numerous sources of raw material for content are:

- Recognised problems and lacunae in educating students in this particular field (reports of review bodies and external evaluators, for example)
- The requirements of a professional or licensing body
- Examinations of similar courses in other institutions or departments
- Discussions, more or less formal, among colleagues and/or practitioners and employers about key skills
- Discussion with students doing similar courses elsewhere
- Research reports and more informal studies of students' misconceptions and typical errors related to the subject matter
- Conceptual schemes devised by educators for a particular series of topics (such as Novak's 'concept maps' in biology (Novak, 1981))
- An academic department's statement of its educational values and goals
- Key texts in the subject
- Examination and assignment questions, and examiners' reports
- Reflection on the main activities students will have to undertake in order to learn the topics in question, and on the assessment methods that will be used to find out whether they have learned them
- Considering the amount of time required to achieve complete understanding of the topics
- Thinking about the relation between the particular unit or subject and a student's entire programme of study

It is all very well to collect this information: how is it to be *used?* Again it is valuable to return to first principles of good teaching in determining a curriculum based on data from any or all of these sources. Good teaching involves finding out from students and other sources about the difficulties students experience in learning the subject matter, finding out about key outcomes that are not achieved or are only partially achieved, and considering the needs of particular groups of students. High quality education cannot occur unless these activities take place. The growing numbers of students entering higher education without traditional sixth form qualifications imply that increasing attention will have to be paid to studying the variety of understandings and skills with which students begin a course of higher education. The principle of good teaching as learning about where students are in relation to where we want them to go, however, remains the same.

EXCESSIVE WORKLOADS

Much the easiest mistake to make in deciding upon content and aims is to include too much content. We should rather strive to include less, but to ensure that students learn that smaller part properly. Resisting the temptation to add more and more content is extremely difficult if a lecturer sees undergraduate student learning as an obstacle course or as a process of acquiring huge quantities of information for later development and use. Facts and details have no life outside those who interpret them. That the presence of abundant information implies neither knowledge nor wisdom is evident all around us. The idea that students must lay down a basis of fact and detail on which to build understanding is an aspect of the mythology of teaching theory 1, which tends to regard content as fixed and students as consumers and receivers of information. But more reflective teaching recognises that content is fluid, information is nothing except organised data, and that students have to make sense of it. We cannot just tell students what is right and wrong, if we expect them to understand for themselves.

We noted in chapter 5 how many courses are saturated with detail and are overdemanding on students' time, so that little space remains for the essential activities of thinking about and integrating the content. Some lecturers seem to think this approach has the effect of a kind of perverted commando training course, sharpening the powers of the strong and eliminating the weak. I hope they may grow out of this unfortunate view of student learning, for its documented effects mean that it represents the lowest possible rating on any scale of teaching quality. Anyone who has ever done any academic research will be aware of the devastating influence on the quality of output of an excessive number of small but different demands on one's time. The inevitable result of too much busy work is that many students adopt minimising strategies and complete their courses with sketchy and confused knowledge of the topics they have 'learned'. Busy work is bad for hard work – and bad news for the quality of education. A.N. Whitehead once again encapsulates the whole idea in three or four memorable sentences:

> We enunciate two educational commandments, 'Do not teach too many subjects,' and again, 'What you do teach, teach thoroughly.' The result of teaching small parts of a large number of subjects is the passive reception of disconnected ideas, not illumined with any spark of vitality. Let the main ideas which are introduced into a child's education be few and important, and let them be thrown into every combination possible. The child should make them his own, and should understand their application here and now in the circumstances of his actual life.
>
> (Whitehead, 1929, p. 2)

I appreciate how hard it is to reduce the amount of content in many courses, especially science-based ones. While it is easy to plead for increasing the quantity because of the enlarged amount of knowledge in a subject, it is a lot harder to have the courage to argue for avoiding some topics altogether. This is particularly true when resources and power in an institution are tied to contact hours with students. There is then an incentive to stuff the curriculum to bursting point in order to justify more contact time. In selecting judiciously, it is important to appreciate that a curriculum should give special attention to the important ideas in a subject that students find especially difficult to understand. We saw in chapter 6 how good teachers are typically very aware of these particular elements, and give special attention to them at the expense of 'covering' the subject matter. Keep in mind again that a lecturer's 'covering of the ground' does *not* imply that the students will cover it.

ORGANISATION AND SEQUENCE

After the broad structure and aims of a course have been decided, teachers face the question of how to arrange and sequence the content. We can deduce from our analysis of good teaching that the quality of a course's organisation can be understood in terms of its focal point. A less effective course will focus primarily on *content* (with the main emphasis on the teacher's knowledge). In contrast, a soundly structured course will focus on *aims for student learning* (with the emphasis on the relation between students and the content to be learned).

The taken-for-granted structure of the majority of courses in higher education is probably of the first type. It is consistent with the 'administrative' view of course goals described by Svensson and Högfors and summarised earlier in the chapter. It is common for courses to be structured around a series of lectures, seminars, tutorials, and practicals purely because of tradition and administrative convenience. This structure represents a teacher-dominated view of subject content. Exactly how *students* will use these opportunities to learn the content does not come into it. It is often assumed without question, for example, that lectures will be the dominant mode of teaching and that students will learn from them. An object of this book is to encourage its readers to feel uncomfortable about this kind of assumption and to acquire the knowledge that will permit a more sensible approach to be undertaken. What will a more effective course structure look like, in general terms?

Many thousands of words have been written about the rules for sequencing in education, and discussions of it are often highly theoretical. Proceeding from the simple to the complex, from the particular to the general; structuring around enquiry, the order of events in the physical or social worlds, or the use of knowledge; strategies involving linear sequences, chronological ones, or those symbolised by the relation between the core of an apple and its flesh – few of these expositions, however logical, reach the heart of the matter, which is that there are two vital principles to bear in mind whatever sequence and organisation is adopted. First, the ordering of content should be *educationally* justifiable. In other words, it must be possible to defend the particular order and structure in which material is tackled from the point of view of its favourable effects on student learning. The second, related point is that the logical ordering of topics that is 'obvious' to a subject expert is not necessarily the best way for a novice to go about learning that subject.

An 'administrative' view of course content is the enemy of an educationally sound sequence. An effective course will have its material arranged in such a way that the issues addressed generate confidence and interest in students. Developing confidence in one's ability to learn a subject is essential to success. At the start of a course, students should be given a few tasks to perform at which they can succeed quickly (this is one of the reasons why it is so important to enquire into students' understandings before teaching). They should feel they can win some new knowledge by simply linking it to what they are already confident about. It does not matter if these tasks seem quite trivial to the teacher, or even to the student three months later. Revision of what is known in a helpful environment, and successfully going a tiny bit beyond what is known, helps to give a sense of assurance of one's own capacities. Without a feeling of security that the next step will be achievable, learning anything is a trial and often a failure. It is our responsibility as professional teachers to provide that security. The same rules apply to the structure within a topic as to the relation between topics and a course.

We know from our discussion of effective instruction that any course which does not engage students' interest, especially at the start, is heading for trouble. Material should preferably be ordered in such a way that it proceeds from common-sense and everyday experiences to abstractions, and then back again to the application of the theoretical knowledge in practice. Good teaching is certainly aware of the desirability of building an understanding from basic ideas, and of getting the fundamental ideas of the subject clear in students' minds early on. But the basics do not have to be dull, as some lecturers appear to assume. Students should always feel they are doing something useful, something that they find stimulating; good teaching always makes the essentials interesting. Moreover, it recognises that in real learning one goes 'back to the basics' time after time; learning subject matter properly involves several passes through the same material. But the journey of exploration should be made different, and more difficult, each time. Nothing is more lifeless than simple 'revision' of the same material in the same way. Again, it is our task to arrange these experiences in the design of our courses.

In order to decide on which prerequisite concepts really are essential for further work, it may be useful to work backwards from each objective for student learning and to decide which operations a student would not be able to perform without a certain piece of knowledge. For example, you cannot understand calculus unless you understand algebra; you cannot understand algebra unless you have a clear knowledge of the rules of arithmetic. Yet once again this procedure requires a self-critical approach if it is not to mislead. It is easy to be deceived into confusing actual prerequisites with traditional ways of presenting a subject. Sometimes the conclusions reached from actual studies of how students learn produce findings that go completely against tradition and seem, at first sight, to contradict commonsense. It is not at all clear, for example, that students should first understand concepts, facts, and theories before applying them to actual problems. Trying to tackle a real problem may provide the motivation needed to learn the concept required to solve it. Moreover, different students prefer different routes through the same material (see Laurillard, 1987, for example). Nor is it clear that techniques and concepts are 'naturally' applied once they have been learned. They must have meaning to students before they can be used. Numerous studies have documented the enormous difficulties students have in applying scientific knowledge to professional practice in medicine and engineering. Eraut *et al.* (1975) show how discarding the traditional view that the concepts of economics should be learned before applying them to the kinds of problems economists try to solve improved students' learning. Giving them an opportunity to analyse actual problems made learning the techniques and concepts easier and more satisfying. Problem-based learning makes use of precisely these principles to encourage students to engage with the content of the subject.

CASE STUDIES OF EFFECTIVE COURSE DESIGN

What happens when these ideas are put into practice? The remainder of this chapter looks at several examples of courses which apply the principles suggested here. Surely, you may say as you read through these cases, anyone can do the kinds of things these teachers do. Precisely. Every lecturer can teach as well as this. But most do not.

A unifying theme in all these illustrations, and those in chapters 9, 10, and 11, is the particular understanding of teaching and learning which they represent. All the 'answers' are context-related, dynamic, and experimental. Not only do good courses in higher education characteristically make their expectations clear; they also permit more freedom and provide more structure than poor ones. Another important property of effective teaching shown in each of these examples is that its practitioners reveal a thoughtful rather than a taken-for-granted approach to content and aims. They see their students' understandings of the subject matter as a puzzle which students need help to unlock.

The case studies are all of real teachers and courses. They represent excellence in teaching, and yet they are imperfect: sometimes, these lecturers make mistakes. By the time you reach the end of this book, if not before, you should be able to explain this apparent paradox to yourself.

The studies which are based on unpublished material use fictitious names, and any resemblance between these names and the names of actual lecturers is accidental.

Designing a course in materials for interior designers

Elaine Atkinson teaches materials technology to design students. She describes the purpose of her third year course as helping students explore relationships between design and technology through the study of materials and through investigating how designers make decisions about interior detailing. Traditionally, the course in materials had been taught as a series of lectures describing the technical details of the strength of materials and their related characteristics. Observe here how the teacher reflects on her aims, identifies problems, and communicates the goals of her teaching to her students:

> I found that teaching the course in this way, as an information dispensing subject, bored me and failed to interest the students. I decided it was time to look at the curriculum afresh and to question the assumptions behind it. I realised that the important thing was to forget about imposing new gadgetry or just improving my presentation skills and think about what I wanted students to learn. That took me back to my own definition of interior design practice. What I wanted students to learn was how designers actually use materials. That implies something fundamentally different from just knowing about materials; I wanted students to understand the nature and technical details of materials so that they could perform as

designers and appreciate how designers think. It became important to think about what students already know about materials. It was necessary to devise a programme that really confronted their current conceptions of materials, and to make explicit the idea of 'thinking as a designer'. We are dealing with a lot of factual material and students get overwhelmed by information in the traditional way of running a course like this. I explained that this course was different, and why, and tried to underline this in the subject guide provided to students. For example, one of the objectives was a negative one [see below]. I explained that they would not be able to pass the course unless they had really started to think about how designers work with materials. You might know the tensile strength of granite, but that wouldn't be enough to pass the assessment. I also emphasise 'key understandings' and try to work from the misconceptions students have of materials. For example, a specific misunderstanding about stone is that all stones are basically the same – they're all expensive and have similar properties as materials. I use this idea to start off the presentation of details about metamorphic, sedimentary and igneous stones. Then, this is linked to a guest speaker talking about how different stones are actually used in design practice.

The objectives for Atkinson's course, as presented to students, are as follows:

At the conclusion of this course you should –
1 be able to relate design objectives to the selection of materials using appropriate performance specifications;
2 understand test methods and measurement procedures for the materials studied;
3 understand the structure of existing resources for the investigation of materials' properties and be able to evaluate the information from these sources for new or developing materials;
4 be familiar with custom design services and procedures and be able to identify appropriate design situations for these services;
5 detail competently with the materials studied;
6 NOTE: The specific objectives do not include the memorisation of large bodies of factual information about materials.

We shall look at how this lecturer teaches and assesses this course in chapters 9 and 10.

The aims and content of an anatomy course for medical students

Eizenberg (1988) has described an orchestrated set of interventions in curriculum based on recent research into higher education students' learning and his own experience as a teacher. An understanding of the anatomical structure of the human body is regarded as an essential basis for the subsequent study of pathology and many of the clinical disciplines, and in traditional medical curricula it forms a necessary preliminary to both these areas of study. Students often see anatomy as a mass of factual material that must be committed to memory; they frequently use the approaches to learning it which we now know will lead to poor retention of detail and to the inability to apply the knowledge that is remembered to realistic medical problems. But anatomy is actually a highly structured subject with many important concepts which link the details together. It explains how the structure of the body developed, uncovers patterns of distribution, and develops an appreciation of the basis of variation (Eizenberg, 1988, p. 187).

The purposes of the revised course are to encourage students to comprehend this structure, to display to students and teachers the importance of understanding key concepts rather than memorising details, to clarify goals and standards by matching the aims and their assessment, and to reduce the sheer volume of knowledge to be understood by selecting those parts of the discipline which are crucially important to medicine. These purposes, of course, are congruent with our theoretical understanding of good teaching and our knowledge derived from the experiences of students in higher education.

Students are encouraged to view the subject as an integrated whole, and to use deep-holistic approaches, by means of careful sequencing and explicit frameworks for study. The previous course encouraged students to see the subject as the accumulation of isolated facts. The revised course begins with the basic principles of general similarities of each type of anatomical structure (such as the arteries). Students are required to construct organisational frameworks to help make sense of the information about each structure. A study guide is used to describe each set of learning tasks, in which the relative importance of each topic is clearly shown. The sequence of presentation enables students to coordinate their study of anatomy with other subjects studied at the same time. This allows students to focus on the same organ systems simultaneously.

Making the aims of a humanities course explicit

How important are aims and objectives in arts subjects? Whether we use the formal language of aims and objectives or not, making clear to students what is required of them and showing that teachers care about student learning is just as important in history or English as in chemistry or engineering.

When Hazel Lybeck and Barbara Yencken revised a course in fifteenth-century Italian art, they made changes to the subject matter and to the structure of seminars which they connected explicitly to their aims for student learning. They wanted to overcome some common misconceptions of, and negative attitudes to, the subject – specifically, the uncritical acceptance of the positions and methodologies represented in authoritative historical texts; the related belief that there were right and wrong answers about Renaissance art that had to be discovered and repeated in assessments; and students' passivity and lack of initiative in researching and presenting their ideas. All these problems, we know from our analysis of students' experiences in Part 1, are predictable responses to teaching which is perceived to be inadequate. As we shall see in the next chapter, specific instructional strategies quite different from the usual tutorial or seminar were used to address them.

Lybeck and Yencken represented their aims to students both in a study guide and in the structure of the teaching programme. The guide clearly stated their expectations, and what they did not intend, using concrete examples:

> The course is designed to overcome what is seen to be problematic in the teaching of Renaissance art, namely that can produce an uncritical acceptance of received texts and methods, and that it can produce a nervousness about looking at the art independently because of what is perceived as its remoteness from our present culture. Hence we will encourage students to think about the issues presented by art historians and theorists in relation to visual material and to *examine their worth*. The ability to read texts critically and to work towards

freedom from the 'dogma of the written text' will be stressed. For example, in Week Two we examine Michael Baxandall's concept of the 'period eye' (*Painting and Experience in Fifteenth Century Italy*, chapter 2) in relation to a range of fifteenth century paintings, as well as in relation to other theories of visual interpretation, for example those of Leo Steinberg and John Berger (*Ways of Seeing*). While understanding of scholarship in the area of study is essential, the course emphasis will be on developing the student's intellectual independence within the context of traditional Renaissance art theory/history. The ability to *ask questions intelligently* will be stressed, rather than providing 'correct' answers. For example, the emphasis of the class cited above will be on understanding the assumptions that underlie Baxandall's thesis, the selection of material he provides and the use he makes of it, rather than assuming that the categories and analyses he provides for visual experience are correct and can be used uncritically in other studies.

I shall show how these expectations were linked to teaching and assessment in the next two chapters.

A basic statistics course for planners

The aims and sequence of John Dunn's statistics course are geared to his knowledge of his students. They are preparing to be environmental (town and country) planners; most have studied mathematics (including some statistics) to a high level at school, yet he knows from pre-tests that three-quarters of them are unable to remember most of what they have learned, far less apply it to the analysis of planning problems:

> I asked them to write down what a standard deviation *meant*. Nobody, nobody was able to hazard a guess as to how to define a standard deviation! They had learned the techniques, the formulae, of each isolated statistic, but they had no idea of how to put it together, how they were derived, or how they are used in real contexts. It is possible to go on learning quantitative subjects like that in higher education, without properly understanding the meaning. That is exactly what was lacking in my own education [in physics and mathematics] and I have reacted to that in planning this course. I've tried to design it with that problem in mind.

Before I came, the course was taught by the statistics department in first and second semesters. I changed that, spreading it over two years and four parts. The first part is now about descriptive statistics; the second part is about measures of association; the third involves students in doing a survey; the final part is inferential statistics. That has less emphasis than in most courses, for a special reason. It is important to gear the statistics to the needs of the students. Ninety per cent of them won't need inferential statistics; 8 percent will need to read material with inferential statistics in; only 2 percent will need to do it. Of those, most will learn quite quickly given a context for it at work. So the emphasis is on building up basic skills, numeracy skills, and coping with those students who come in without maths, so that by the end they can all handle the sophisticated thinking needed, such as an intuitive understanding of the nature of probabilistic statements. A thorough understanding of descriptive statistics plus that intuitive sense is more important than half-understood powerful statistics.

Another idea of structuring it this way is to encourage repeated bites at the same topics so that students can develop an understanding gradually. One of the principles was to make it a circular thing, so that I'd do standard deviation in the first semester, but of course I'll keep on talking about standard deviation all the way through; correlation also, once initially introduced will then be gone through again in terms of various problems that they meet at a later stage. So the idea was that, having some control over the course, I would spread it out and encourage recurrent attempts at the same concept in order to develop understanding.

Here we see the application of several principles of designing an effective course: unambiguous specification, for the benefit of both teacher and students, of what will and what will not be learned; learning from students about their current understanding; careful pacing; and a sequence where the curriculum returns to consider the same concept on more than one occasion.

A problem-based engineering course

Problem-based learning is a form of education which embodies several key principles of effective teaching and is particularly relevant to professional training. Such courses focus on problems of the type that are typically met in professional life, and students are required to identify the nature of the problem, collect the information needed to tackle it, and synthesise a solution. In conventional professional courses, discipline knowledge is taught separately from its application to actual problems. In problem-based courses, knowledge, skills, and professional attitudes are simultaneously addressed. There is evidence that such courses increase the use of deep approaches (see chapter 5, p. 81), improve the retention of information, and develop student independence and motivation. All these outcomes are to be expected from our previous analyses of student learning and its relation to teaching in higher education. Unfortunately, most problem-based courses require the comprehensive redesign of whole programmes of study, entailing in their turn massive shifts of conceptions of teaching on the part of departments and institutions; the application of such curricula has so far been limited.

Peter Cawley (1989) has described the use of such a course as part of a conventional engineering programme. The stimulus for changing the format of this third year course on vibration analysis was that Cawley, its teacher, 'was concerned that there was too much emphasis on technical theory and too little on the application of the material to real engineering problems. It was noticeable that in the examination, the students tended to avoid questions requiring the type of diagnostic and problem-solving skills which are essential to engineering practice' (Cawley, 1989, p. 84).

The course's aims were therefore broadened, away from simply transmitting content towards developing professional skills of using the content to solve problems and communicate the solutions. The aims became:

1 To develop skills of modelling, analysing, and proposing practical solutions to vibration problems in engineering
2 To develop skills in criticising proposed solution to problems
3 To develop an appreciation of how systems vibrate
4 To be introduced to several standard methods of analysis
5 To develop independent study skills
6 To develop oral and written presentation skills

A list of detailed objectives related to these aims was also drawn up to help both teachers and students understand the requirements of the course. Knowledge, technical, problem-solving, and attitudinal objectives were included (see Cawley, 1989, p. 86). How the teaching and assessment were organised to help students achieve the aims and objectives, and demonstrate their achievement, will be described in chapters 9 and 10.

Chapter 9

Teaching strategies for effective learning

> I would be content if we began, all of us, by recognizing . . . that discovering how to make something comprehensible to the young is only a continuation of making something comprehensible to ourselves in the first place – that understanding and aiding others to understand are all of a piece.
>
> (Jerome Bruner)

At the beginning of Part 2 I argued that applying an understanding of education to improving the practice of teaching involved addressing several related issues. These were summarised in terms of five groups of problems: defining goals and structure, using appropriate teaching strategies, assessing students, evaluating teaching, and educational development and accountability.

In this chapter we are concerned mainly with the second of these issues. Most of us probably think of teaching strategies in terms of the different teaching methods that are used in higher education, such as the lecture, the practical, and the seminar. I have already argued that this is an unhelpful way of conceptualising the problem: it locks us into an 'administrative' way of looking at learning and teaching. However, I shall start this examination of teaching strategies using this framework, precisely because it is a good way of highlighting the problems which it raises.

As the chapter proceeds I shall try to show how in good teaching the method used is always secondary to the teacher's aims for student learning and the extent to which the particular strategy actualises the principles of effective instruction within a certain context. The chief object is not to provide solutions to the problems of selecting and using teaching strategies; such absolute remedies do not exist, and anyone who offers them is open to an accusation of deception. It is rather to help readers to understand what the problems are, so that they may find their own solutions.

TEACHING FOR UNDERSTANDING: SOME PROBLEMS WITH CURRENT METHODS

From the theory of learning and teaching described earlier in the book, it is no large step to the proposition that sound teaching strategies encourage students to *relate to the subject matter* they are studying in a purposeful way. As we saw in Part 1, the lecturer in higher education who would succeed in making this kind of relationship possible is faced with two main tasks. The first of these is to discourage students from using surface approaches: this implies avoiding excessive workloads, busywork, and unnecessary time pressures; shunning assessment practices that require recall or rehearsal of trivial detail; abandoning all attempts to devalue students' tentative steps towards understanding; avoiding cynical comments (explicit or implicit) about the subject matter and students' grasp of it.

To do these things is never easy, especially if the departmental or institutional context is one where surface approaches are seen as a normal way of learning and where students' learning difficulties are not seen to be teachers' problems. Actively encouraging deep approaches through engaging students responsibly and actively with the subject matter is, however, very much harder. There are several ways in which we can try: helping students to become aware of their current conceptions, so that they become conscious of the fact that there *are* different conceptions of the phenomenon in question; highlighting inconsistencies in learners' conceptions and their consequences in real situations; focusing on central issues that are most problematic for students; finding ways of integrating the 'knowing how' of a subject (such as how scientists approach experimental enquiry; how political scientists analyse information) with the 'knowing what' (such as Newton's laws of motion, Weber's concept of authority), and so on (see Marton and Ramsden, 1988). The impact of each of these strategies will be conditioned by the ability of the teacher to reflect on its effectiveness and its limitations.

If we now put together these general comments about teaching strategies for understanding with the principles of good teaching articulated in chapter 6, we find that the focus on intensive student interaction with content, clear curriculum structure, engagement of interest, cooperative student endeavour, responsible choice, the lecturer's concern for students, and his or her commitment to developing professional competence as a teacher, fit rather tidily into the picture. The entire system can be seen to point inexorably in the direction of certain teaching methods. Thus while there are no 'best' teaching methods, some methods and combinations of methods are indisputably better than others at realising the sort of constructive engagement with learning activities that leads to changes in understanding (see also Biggs, 1990). Such methods involve students in actively finding knowledge, interpreting results, and testing hypotheses against reality (often in a spirit of cooperation as well as individual effort) as a route to understanding and the secure retention of factual knowledge. These methods are in sharp contrast to those which concentrate on placing authoritative information before individual students and leaving the rest up to them.

The reader will now I hope be able to see one step ahead in the argument and confront the inevitable truth that many popular methods, such as the traditional lecture–tutorial–discussion–laboratory–class method of teaching science and social science courses, do not emerge from this analytical process unscathed. In fact, not to put too fine a point on it, many teaching methods in higher education would seem, in terms of our theory, to be actually detrimental to the quality of student learning. How accurately does the theory represent reality?

Problems with lectures

Some temerity is necessary for anyone who would enter the conflict between the proponents and the detractors of lecturing. It is hardly an overstatement to say that lecturing remains the pre-eminent method of teaching in most subjects in on-campus institutions. The majority of university teachers seem to favour it; many timetables are organised around it; lecturers will argue that students, especially first year students, are unable to learn without it; most students arrange their studying lives around lectures, and are indeed dependent on it (in some courses it is impossible to determine the content to be learned unless one attends lectures); numerous books have attempted to justify it, to improve it, to change it. Arguments against lecturing are likely to meet the same withering replies that other arguments which cut across tradition in higher education meet: it is not realistic to abandon or even substantially to modify it; it is not economical to change it; it might reduce standards if we tampered with it.

We take lecturing in higher education so much for granted that we easily forget just how powerful its hold is. The conventional one-hour lecture represents a rigidly quantitative conception of teaching and learning. It is seen by many of its adherents as a way of transmitting information at relatively low cost. Knowledge is information; information is a product 'sold' by the producer to the consumer. The producer is the source of wisdom: the teacher is an authority by virtue of the quantity of knowledge he or she possesses. The information transmitted and the learning that takes place are simply unproblematical; they cancel out of the calculation, so to speak. This is about as far away as one can get from the outlook of the present book.

It is all too simple to identify naïve beliefs, sometimes thinly veiled by quasi-scientific jargon, in advice that is supposed to represent expert opinion on the subject of lecturing. One respected work on improving university teaching defends the lecture in terms that seem like a parody of a model of teaching as transmitting information:

> One aspect of lecturing that is rarely, if ever, mentioned by its critics is its efficiency. With the aid of microphones and closed-circuit television it is possible to teach large audiences within one building . . . . Had there been little else to say in their favour, these advantages of economy and availability would certainly ensure their continuation, but, even without television, lecturing is still an economical method.
>
> (Beard and Hartley, 1984, p.154)

Economical for what, exactly? In a similar vein, another recent book for lecturers in higher education argues that student learning in a lecture demands that the lecturer should 'get accurate information into [students'] short-term memory' and that this process can be helped by increasing the students' level of arousal ('a general state of readiness of the brain to accept new information').

'Getting information into students' memories' discloses an interesting theory of teaching and learning. Learning, in this view, plainly stands in a direct relation to teaching, is measurable on a single quantitative scale, and consists in portions of information transferred from the lecturer's mind to the students'. This is a complex of ideas about teaching that is congruent with Roger Säljö's description of the lowest level conception of knowledge and learning demonstrated by students. We will recall that learning is seen by these students as an increase in the amount of knowledge the learner possesses; it is equated with information or facts that are learned through memorisation (Säljö, 1984, p. 85). The research into student learning in higher education leaves no room for doubt about the effects of this view of learning on the quality of learning outcomes. Are we really defending a teaching method that leads to poor learning?

These, then, are some of the pitfalls into which a belief in the inevitability of lecturing can lead even specialists. What are the facts about lecturing's effectiveness? A comprehensive critique of lecturing appeared in Gibbs (1982); rather than go over the arguments again, it may be useful to summarise some of Gibbs's conclusions here and to add some others.

1 Lectures are no more economical than other methods as a way of teaching students. There are efficient courses, and even institutions, that have no lectures, or very few. There are alternative methods that involve less preparation time and less contact time, or which apportion the same total time differently.

2 Lectures are no more effective than other methods at conveying information to students. Discussion and reading are as effective. Methods other than lecturing are better for helping students to apply knowledge and use it to analyse problems (see also 5 below).

3 The idea that lectures ensure that 'the ground is covered' is false. The ground is covered for the lecturer, perhaps, but not by the students. Few, if any, modern philosophical, educational, and psychological theories accept that there is any direct relation between what is taught and what is learned. Most learning in higher education goes on outside the lecture room, even in high contact-hour subjects such as engineering and medicine. Information transmission is a meaningless

metaphor as far as teaching and learning are concerned. Students have to make sense of information for themselves if they are to learn anything.

4 Some lecturers are seen by students to be inspirational and stimulating. But more often students complain of poor structure, overloading, and confusion (see chapter 5). Perhaps the most compelling argument against lecturing is that few lecturers do it well, many do it just about passably, and quite a lot do it very badly indeed. This is true in spite of the fact that it is one of the easiest forms of 'teaching'; that many books have been written about how to do it; and that countless hours have been spent by educational development personnel in trying to help lecturers to lecture better. Nor is there any evidence at all that the lectures of today are better than the lectures of 50 years ago, despite a general improvement in teaching technologies. Is it an economical use of resources to try to improve the techniques of lecturers when we have failed for so long?

5 Students are usually very passive and dependent during lectures. Passivity and dependence on the teacher, grading into wool-gathering and even somnolence after 30 minutes or so, provide an excellent basis for surface approaches. We have seen how deep approaches are associated with activity and responsibility in learning – exactly the opposite conditions to those obtained in most lectures.

We continue to lecture so much in higher education for three related reasons: because we are unaware of alternatives, because we work with undeveloped theories of teaching, and because we enjoy the sense of power that lecturing gives us. Defying the norm that lecturers are supposed to lecture may also lead to trouble with students – particularly more experienced students. After a year or so in higher education, students expect teaching to be a passive experience where something is done to them, and they object to having to be active, especially if the activity concerns creating explanations of uncertain phenomena. Pirsig (1974) highlights this type of reaction in his description of the first class he takes after giving the students an assignment on 'What is quality in thought and statement?':

The atmosphere was explosive. Almost everyone seemed as frustrated and angered as he had been by the question.

'How are *we* supposed to know what quality is?' they said. 'You're supposed to tell *us!*'

Then he told them he couldn't figure it out either and really wanted to know. He has assigned it in the hope that somebody would come up with a good answer. That ignited it. A roar of indignation shook the room. Before the commotion had settled down another teacher had stuck his head in the door to see what the trouble was.

'It's all right,' Phaedrus said. 'We just accidentally stumbled over a genuine question, and the shock is hard to recover from.' Some students looked curious at this, and the noise simmered down.

He then used the occasion for a short return to his theme of 'Corruption and Decay in the Church of Reason'. It was a measure of this corruption, he said, that students should be outraged by someone trying to *use* them to seek the truth. You were supposed to *fake* the search for truth, to *imitate* it. To actually *search* for it was a damned imposition.

(Pirsig, 1974, p. 199)

It is better to lecture well than to lecture badly. I would not want to leave anyone with the impression that it is impossible to deliver a good lecture, or that I think good teachers should not lecture (though I do think they should do less of it, and for shorter periods). Lectures can be a useful way to introduce a new topic and to provide an overview of the relation between topics. It *is* possible to give a traditional lecture well, to engage the audience's interest, to stimulate their thinking and their desire to find out more about the subject, to pass on knowledge to a large group, to explain phenomena at the audience's level, to select illustrations that are memorable, to restrict the amount of material contained in a single lecture, and to show respect for and sensitivity to one's students in so doing. It is a rare occurrence to see these things combined, though the examples of how students respond positively to effective lecturing that appeared in chapter 5 show that it is not out of the question.

Problems with small groups

It is highly revealing of prevailing theories of instruction in higher education that small group work, by which I mean any teaching strategy involving up to 30 students where student participation is expected, is normally seen as a supplement to lecturing. When I was a part-time tutor in a university department 15 years ago, I was provided with a list of lecture topics and a series of questions written by the lecturer for weekly tutorial discussion with a group of 12 students. The dominant and highly valued part of the teaching was the lecture programme (undertaken by the tenured lecturers); the tutorials (taken by both the tenured staff and a mixed bunch of research students, research assistants, and contract lecturers) were a convenient extension of the 'real' teaching. The general view was that tutorials were much less time-consuming and challenging than lectures. Some of them could safely be left to the apprentices.

Studies of lecturers' attitudes to group discussion methods (see Beard and Hartley, 1984), not to mention repeated moves to save money by abandoning tutorial support altogether in some Australian undergraduate programmes, indicate that these experiences are still both common and relevant. Many lecturers regard discussion as a luxury item designed to reinforce information transmitted in lectures. The authority of the lecture and the lecturer, epitomising the overarching command of the discipline over those who would learn it, remains paramount.

We need search no further for the causes of the most typical problems in small group teaching, identified by both lecturers and students, and addressed in virtually every educational development workshop on small group teaching and every book about teaching and learning in higher education. The difficulties, all interrelated, are thoroughly predictable outcomes of a learning context created by a theory 1 approach to teaching:

- The teacher gives a lecture rather than conducting a dialogue.
- The teacher talks too much.
- Students cannot be encouraged to talk except with difficulty; they will not talk to each other, but will only respond to questions from the tutor.
- Students do not prepare for the sessions.
- One student dominates the discussion, or blocks it.
- The students want to be given the solutions to problems rather than discussing them.

The ideal and the reality of small group work are exemplified in two descriptions, one on the art of questioning pupils (published in 1879), and the other from an article on university seminars of more recent date:

[The teacher] must not attempt, even for the sake of logical consistency, to adhere too rigidly to a series of formal questions, nor refuse to notice any new fact or inquiry which seems to spring naturally out of the subject . . . . For indeed, the whole sum of what may be said about questioning is comprised in this: It ought to set the learners thinking, to promote activity and energy on their part, and to arouse the whole mental faculty into action, instead of blindly cultivating the memory at the expense of the higher intellectual powers. That is the best questioning which best stimulates action on the part of the learner; which gives him a habit of thinking and inquiring for himself; which tends in a great measure to render him independent of his teacher; which makes him, in fact, rather a skillful finder than a patient receiver of truth.

(Fitch, 1879; quoted in Eble, 1988, p. 91)

The average seminar runs like this. There are two types. In the first, the seminar is related directly to the course of lectures. It is conceived as a way of giving students the opportunity of discussing problems that they have confronted in the lectures. The tutor meets the class. 'Have you any questions?' he asks. Silence. The tutor says, 'These *are* dim students', while the students sit embarrassed and anxious and, thus, less ready to join in discussion . . . .

The tutor may try another tack: 'Did you understand what Professor X said about social structure?' But students often don't know what they don't understand: or if they do, find the atmosphere of the seminar not conducive to admitting their ignorance. Hence: silence, embarrassment and anxiety!

The second type of seminar begins with one student reading a paper. The others relax, it's *his* worry, not theirs, and it is doubtful if they will be pushed to make a contribution. So, the paper is read and the tutor poses questions to the student who has read it and discusses it with him, while the rest sit quietly and undisturbed by the tutor. Finally the *viva voce* ends: and once again, silence, embarrassment and anxiety.

So, the tutor is now 'on the spot'. He, accordingly, begins to talk and frequently feels compelled to fill the gap of silence by giving a mini-lecture.

(Broady, 1970, p. 274)

At this point it is usual to provide a list of recipes designed to overcome these all-too-familiar problems. There are many effective techniques (among the best compilations being Habeshaw *et al.*, 1984, which readers should consult for specific advice on technique), but none of them will succeed for long unless the reason why the problems exist is clearly understood. Just for now, forget about detailed solutions: think about what effective teaching consists of and how you would try to implement its prescriptions in the situation described in the second extract above. If you can work out one or two things that might follow from what you know about teaching, they will be worth as much as ten books full of recipes you have not arrived at for yourself.

Problems with computers and other media

The adaptation of technology in various forms to the task of teaching has been going on in higher education at least since Gutenberg's time – and some would say, given the continuing predominance in many courses of oral instruction over print, at a painfully slow rate. Computers should in theory provide a learning environment that permits intensive and relevant engagement with the subject matter, being individualised and self-paced, allowing immediate access to large amounts of data, asking questions to test student understanding, and providing guidance when errors or misconceptions are noted (Laurillard, 1987; 1988). It may be the potential for interaction and for encouraging deep approaches, or less charitably it may be the vision of an easier and cheaper form of information-transmission that looks up to date, that has led some authors to predict the imminent arrival of the 'completely electronic classroom'.

Whatever the reason for the prediction, it has yet to be realised. Computers and video in higher education have so far rarely lived up to the promises made for them. The fruits of their effectiveness remain to be harvested. The most serious inadequacies are closely associated; they concern the failure to articulate principles for designing teaching materials of these types, naïve technological determinism, and the use of potentially interactive media in a passive way that takes no account of the individual learner. Videodisc, for example, in spite of its enormous potential for requiring the student to participate in active knowledge-seeking, may simply be used as an expensive way of illustrating a lecture. At their worst, views of media technology as a determinant of change have led to a reinforcement of the message that education is passive reception of quantities of (entertaining) information. It is unnecessary to provide numerous examples of this perspective here; they are ubiquitous. I have personally seen examples of computer-assisted learning (CAL) programs in higher education which do no more than present the information to be found in a book and test whether the student has memorised it; the computer becomes an electronic page-turner that rewards surface approaches to learning. We are back in the realm of a theory 1 perspective on university teaching as an activity separate from learning, where the benefits of educational technology are seen in terms of making the traditional lecture a better form of passing on larger and larger amounts of data in less time.

> We risk, therefore, becoming rich in information but poor in knowledge. The spread of information is dangerously entropic. It may lead to uncertainty and insecurity rather than confidence and self-assurance. What we need from educational technology is forms of knowledge which may lead to under-standing, rather than information overload and confusion.
>
> (Hart, 1987, p. 172)

Computers and other interactive media should offer students an opportunity for a *conversation* involving listening as well as talking on both sides (see Bork, 1987). Good programmes, like good teachers, are designed to listen and learn from students as part of the process of instructing them. This implies a measure of student control. Poor CAL programs offer the learner no control over decisions about the sequencing of content and learning activities, or the manipulation of the content, nor do they allow the student to create his or her own perspective on the subject. Rigidly controlled programmes provide the student with no challenge and little motivation to understand the subject matter. Some teachers, having discovered a marvellous machine that can solve the 'problem' of controlling student learning completely, have been unable to resist the temptation to exert this power. Coupled with the use of multiple-choice questions as an easy way of interacting with students via the computer, CAL is often used in a way that *reduces* the quality of learning.

Although some writers have suggested that student control leads to inefficient learning, research into CAL and interactive video quite clearly demonstrates that learner control may be more effective than programme control. Diana Laurillard, one of the very few researchers to have investigated the educational effectiveness of an interactive video programme in higher education, shows how when students are given freedom to work through the learning material (in this case on the technology of materials) in their preferred way, they exhibit a wide range of routes. Some begin by looking at what they already know; others start with the least familiar topics. Some work through systematically; others leave an exercise to look at another section, then return to the first exercise. Some take a test before an exercise to check how well they know the material before going on to do only those exercises on which they perform badly; others take the test after the exercise. A single path imposed by the programme designer, thinking perhaps that he or she knew best about how students should learn, would seriously inhibit students' access to the content and the potential for understanding it (Laurillard, 1987).

Several of the problems identified above may easily be extrapolated to other media. No medium, however useful, can solve fundamental educational problems. Media cannot alter the way teachers understand teaching. In using media sensibly the least we can do is to try not to reinforce existing pedagogical errors.

Problems with textbooks

Few discussions of media, and few books about teaching in higher education, say much about the medium through which many students will continue to learn for the foreseeable future – the book. The book is a remarkably flexible learning resource. Reading printed materials of various sorts occupies varying amounts of time for students in different institutions and disciplines, but the time is always substantial, even in laboratory-based subjects.

When advice is given, what is said tends to focus on strategies for helping students to read better. Two of the most worrying problems – the quality of the reading materials themselves and their selection – are usually left untouched. Works on teaching and learning which include discussions of distance learning (such as Rowntree, 1981) are among the few exceptions. It is often the case that reading lists underline the view of a subject presented in lectures that every fact, every interpretation is of equal and great importance, and that nothing must be left out. This approach has the expected effect of excessive workload: it invites students to neglect material indiscriminately and to adopt a superficial approach to what they do read (and of course to receive the lecturer's criticism that students can't be trusted to read anything properly). Selecting a major text for a course also presents problems; it is often not made clear why a particular text or texts has been chosen, or what the student is expected to learn from it (is it a supplement to the lectures? A substitute? Is every chapter important? Which parts are mandatory and which inessential?).

The dense and formal nature of the language of many textbooks in science and social science is an added difficulty. The problem is well defined in Black and his colleagues' label of 'Scientish' for the special language used in scientific writing which has spilled over into undergraduate texts (Black *et al.*, 1977). The use of the terms of formal argument ('let', 'assume', 'consider'); the highly economical use of specialist terminology and explanation; the fact that things are said in one way, and once, rather than in several different ways and more than once (as in speech); the tendency to use many concepts at once, some of which have only recently been introduced to the reader; the fact that the abstract is regarded as normal and the concrete as unusual; the habit of making the reader feel that all is unarguably true and correct, and never tentative and uncertain. Rowntree (1981, p. 166) gives an example from an economics text, and Black *et al.* have one from a physics text; they are by no means unusual:

> Let us now consider what will be the shape of the supply curve of the industry where entrepreneurs are heterogeneous, but all other factors are homogeneous. So far as the short-run supply curve is concerned, the fact that entrepreneurs are heterogeneous will make little difference. It will still represent a lateral summation of the short-run marginal cost curves of the individual firms . . .
>
> If a vertical line is drawn at some arbitrary chosen pressure, it will intersect the isenthalpic curves at a number of points at which μ may be obtained by measuring the slopes of the isenthalps at these points.

These ways of writing may conduce to a feeling of inadequacy in the student who is not made of stern stuff. A great deal is assumed about the reader's knowledge, not only of the subject matter but also of how its textbook writers write. Because everything is apparently true and clear and correct and not in doubt, students are led to feel that any lack of understanding on their part must be their fault. Neither can the student ask for guidance: the flow of information is one-way and the experience is frequently passive. No wonder some students develop a negative attitude to the subject and to their own abilities as learners of it through studying textbooks. In brief, textbooks are often poor teachers.

Problems with practical and clinical work

How far does practical work – including clinical experience, projects, fieldwork, and laboratory work – actually fulfil the expectations which lecturers have for it? Laboratory teaching, in particular, is extremely expensive of resources; its existence goes a long way towards accounting for the fact that engineering, science, and medical courses are several times as expensive per student as humanities ones. The main aims of practicals are generally agreed upon; most lists would include:

- Developing an understanding of the process of scientific enquiry, or its equivalent in other subjects (such as the process of design in architecture)
- Learning relevant manipulative and technical skills (examining a patient, for example)
- Learning information and scientific concepts
- Learning relevant procedural and observational skills
- Developing a capacity for independent problem solving and learning
- Understanding the connections between the theoretical and the practical
- Developing relevant professional values and attitudes
- Learning how to interpret and present experimental data
- Learning how to work cooperatively with colleagues.

This is already a formidable list of aims, though many more could be added. It is clear from many investigations (see, for example, those summarised in Boud *et al.*, 1986) that practical work often does not help the student to achieve them. Moreover, several aims whose achievement is thought to require laboratory classes could be addressed in different ways. For example, learning how to interpret data and present reports does not require any expensive apparatus; science students can and do pass science courses *without doing any laboratory work at all*; students report highly negative attitudes to practical work in science until the final year of their undergraduate programme (Bliss and Ogborn, 1977); conventional laboratory classes are probably no better than other methods (including lectures) at teaching problem-solving skills (Hegarty, 1982); laboratory work is not a cost-effective way of teaching factual information and concepts (Boud *et al.*, 1986). Beard and Hartley (1984) summarise several studies which are critical of the tendency of practical work in science to emphasise low-grade skills, to reduce student responsibility, and to foster a superficial and mechanistic approach to the relations between theory and practice. Balla (1990a) describes a rather similar situation in medical education, where the knowledge taught in the pre-clinical years is often not integrated into the practical methods learned during the clinical ones; students perceive the two areas to be unrelated, and have difficulty in applying their scientific understanding to clinical problems. These effects are all familiar concomitants of surface-atomistic approaches.

The chief problem with practicals, apart from their expense, is similar to the problem with lectures and some CAL. Just as in lectures, it is taken for granted that students will learn if they are presented with information, so in practicals it is taken for granted that students will learn if they do things. This is somewhat reminiscent of Ms Lane's approach to teaching (see chapter 6), and of the theory 2 approach to teaching described in chapter 7. But doing things does not imply understanding processes of enquiry or relating practice to theoretical knowledge. Just as it is possible to reproduce ideas and facts without understanding them, so it is possible to learn how to do things without understanding the reasons for doing them. The key to the problem is to appreciate that the traditional practical, like the lecture, is a teacher-dominated form of instruction. It leaves too little room for students to engage with the content in a way that will help them to understand it. Too much of the real work, such as deciding what procedure should be used to test a hypothesis, how to relate the basic skills together to tell a story, or what a client or patient requires in a particular case, has often already been done by the lecturer.

TOWARDS MORE EFFECTIVE TEACHING STRATEGIES

The weaknesses in teaching described above represent the inverse of the principles of good teaching described in chapter 6 and the theory 3 approach to instruction outlined in chapter 7. Small groups should be encouraging active confrontation between students and with ideas, and feedback on a student's progress towards grasping those ideas – all within a clear and supportive structure. However, they regularly create passivity, anxiety, and silence. Practicals should serve to integrate, interest, and challenge. But they are frequently dull exercises that involve students minimally. Computers ought to foster interaction, excitement, independence, and choice in learning. Yet they are often used non-interactively as an expensive way of presenting more information. The conventional lecture rarely stimulates thinking; it is more likely to promote a view of learning as remembering masses of isolated detail and to underline an impression of the lecturer as an unapproachably remote authority concerned with 'getting information into students' memories'. Far too infrequently does it imply clear explanations of key concepts pitched at the right level for students' present knowledge.

In many ways, these problems in teaching also reinforce the comments on ineffective experiences of learning made by students in chapter 5. It is worth looking once more at students' responses to some of the teaching performance indicator questions (see also chapter 6) to re-emphasise the characteristics of courses where poor quality teaching is the norm:

- Lecturers here frequently give the impression that they haven't anything to learn from students (agree)
- To do well on this course all you really need is a good memory (agree)
- Staff here show no real interest in what students have to say (agree)
- The staff make a real effort to understand difficulties students may be having with their work (disagree)
- Our lecturers are extremely good at explaining things to us (disagree)
- Teaching staff here work hard to make their subjects interesting to students (disagree)
- This course really tries to get the best out of all its students (disagree)

- We often discuss with our lecturers or tutors how we are going to learn in this course (disagree)
- The course seems to encourage us to develop our own academic interests as far as possible (disagree)
- We are generally given enough time to understand the things we have to learn (disagree).

It is certain from the results of numerous investigations of teaching in higher education that students in all subject areas express deep dissatisfaction with, and learn less from, teaching strategies which involve the impersonal, repetitive transfer of information, paralyse responsible attitudes to studying, and push learners into working passively at low levels of intellectual endeavour. How could it be otherwise? And yet a great deal of our teaching is like this. Only when the message gets home that higher education teaching must encourage active and responsible student learning, within a cooperative, clearly structured and considerate environment, can we hope for improvement.

Some lecturers seem to have a natural sense of the necessary coherence between teaching and learning that renders the kind of advice given in this book superfluous. The vast majority of us have to operate at a more terrestrial level. We need to stipulate in some detail how and why our proposed pedagogical changes will improve student learning. To put this in another way, we ought to be able to see through to an end point and keep it clearly in mind as we try out different strategies. At this point you may find it valuable to consider the implications of the resemblance between this focus in teaching on the parts in relation to the whole and the characteristics of a deep-holistic approach to learning (see chapter 4).

In the remainder of this chapter I shall first look at some general advice, derived from our theoretical knowledge of teaching and learning, on how to improve some current methods. The practical application of the advice will be illustrated by means of several examples of actual teaching strategies which embody the principles of good teaching and an understanding of teaching as the nurturing of student learning. Working from the perspective I have adopted in this book, it is neither necessary nor practicable to consider every teaching technique separately. Excellence in teaching implies that what students are expected to learn and how they go about learning come first, and the techniques second. The examples focus especially on small group and large group teaching, and readers should be able, with the help of the suggestions on further reading, to apply the same ideas to other methods – including the choice of textbooks. The basic elements of effective teaching illustrated below concern clarity in structure, methods of sustaining interest and involvement (including the use of a variety of different learning methods to reduce tedium and link theoretical ideas to practice), engagement and responsibility, and the use of knowledge about students' approaches and current understandings in teaching.

Despite the firmness of the lecture's foothold, the best general advice to the teacher who wants to improve his or her lecturing is still 'Don't lecture' (Eble, 1988, p. 68). Many objectives can be achieved more efficiently and effectively by variations on traditional methods or new methods altogether. This is true for large groups of 100 or more as well as for smaller ones. The task the lecturer faces in both cases is paradoxically how to make 'lecturing' less like a lecture (passive, rigid, routine knowledge transmission) and more like an active communication between teacher and students. In other words, we should be thinking about teaching rather than lecturing. Lecturers ought to provide very clear signals to help students appreciate the links and points of separation between parts of the content, and to enable them to disentangle principles from examples. They should explain what they are doing and why. Talk should pass *between* teacher and students, not just from teacher to students. Students should have to do something more energetic than just listening and note-taking, preferably in cooperation with each other, and they should be required to work with the content as soon as possible after the class. There should be opportunities for the teacher to monitor the effects of his or her instruction on student learning in order to see whether students are understanding.

In short, a teacher faced with a series of classes with a large group of students should plan to do things that encourage deep approaches to learning; these things imply dialogue, structured goals, and activity. Such advice will of course be resisted by some academics and departments (as well as second year and later students); it seems too much like school teaching and not enough like traditional views of university lecturing. But it is entirely realistic advice. An example of how one teacher has successfully applied it appears later in this chapter.

Similar advice may be applied to improving teaching in small groups, practicals, and other classes. Everyone can provide the answers to the problems in small group teaching described on p. 157 if they will look at the problems with a fresh eye for a moment. For example, the reason why students do not talk in tutorials and seminars is to be found by asking: who do *we* like to talk to? (see Black *et al.*, 1977). The answer? We like to talk to people who are responsive and inquisitive about our ideas. We do not feel like talking freely to people who dismiss them or who seem unsympathetic to us. Tradition in university teaching, it seems, may have temporarily blinded us to an obvious truth.

The solutions also follow immediately from the principles of good teaching and its relation to deep approaches. The supreme purpose of small group work is to encourage students to confront different conceptions and to practise making sense for themselves – 'to promote activity and energy on their part' – whether this involves learning through cooperating with other students or in direct contact with the teacher. Teaching is a sort of conversation. In a conversation, listening and talking are equally important. Teaching properly in a small group implies listening to students and using the information we gather to help them understand. Helping understanding does not mean correcting every mistake. Often it is better to say nothing at all; time and reflection, or discussion with peers, may serve the purpose of correcting errors much better, as well as fostering the independence of thought that every teacher in higher education desires. Knowing when to intervene and when to let it go is one of the great arts of small group teaching.

Above all, students must feel that they are part of the interaction and they must not be made to experience a sense of inadequacy. This requires the tutor to show true interest in all student responses, not just the 'right' ones; to ask questions that are genuine questions (which move students towards understanding rather than just eliciting right answers – however trivial they may appear to an expert in the discipline); to have a nice sense of the social climate of the group; to know each member's predilections; to get students to do things; to provide absolutely clear expectations and standards without inhibiting freedom. Desultory chit-chat results from unclear work expectations. Without a very explicit structure and agreed goals, effective discussion in groups is usually doomed. This is why books about the techniques of running small groups place a lot of emphasis on setting ground rules and agreeing contracts between students and teachers.

Because the answers appear simple from this analysis does not mean that they are simple to apply. This is an exceptionally difficult collection of teaching skills to master. Whatever else small group work is, it is hard work, and most of us will make many mistakes and have our share of disasters, however experienced we are. Anyone who has ever given both lectures and tutorials, and who has reflected a little on teaching, will know that small group work is many times harder than ordinary lecturing.

The extent to which the cultures of different subject areas influence typical patterns of group work is a topic which has not been thoroughly explored. Science lecturers are usually more likely to see tutorials as ancillary to lectures than humanities teachers; physical scientists are more likely to define their role as authorities who answer student questions; social scientists are somewhat more likely to expect a more free-ranging discussion; and so on. These generalisations would not be very helpful in themselves, except that they point up an important source of misunderstanding about improving teaching in different subject areas. As I have been at pains to stress the key role of subject content in deciding teaching strategies, it may be useful to clear up this source of confusion now. It is sometimes asserted that existing practices are in some way determined by the nature of the subject matter – for example, because physical sciences are generally more paradigmatic and cumulative than social sciences, then didactic teaching in tutorials is inherently more appropriate. I am sure that this argument, though very convenient to lecturers who do not want to modify their existing routines, is entirely wrong. It confuses the existence of different approaches to teaching in different disciplines with their inevitability. The typical culture of teaching in a discipline, as I argued in chapter 6, cannot fairly be used as an excuse for not improving instruction within it. The principles of good small group work do not change, even though the way they are actualised in different subjects must differ.

One excellent study of tutorial teaching in science to which I have already referred several times (Black *et al.*, 1977) articulates clearly this distinction between the need to focus on content (the tasks carried out in a physics tutorial will include ones not usually found in a history one, for example) and the requirement to suspend belief in 'necessary' discipline differences (there is usually too much teacher talk and teacher–student question and answer talk, and not enough open discussion between students, in science tutorials).

CASE STUDIES OF EFFECTIVE TEACHING IN ACTION

We are now ready to consider some specific instructional strategies which higher education teachers in several different subject areas have used to help their students learn. We begin by returning to the experiences of the teachers whose courses were described in chapter 8. Most books about teaching in higher education present an idealised picture of how it should be done in an unblemished world. But teaching in the real world is always messy, unpredictable, and sensitive to context.

Remember, as I mentioned in the last chapter, that these 'solutions' are examples of real teaching, problems and imperfections and all. They demonstrate the application of the principles of good teaching and the ways in which lecturers who use developed theories of instruction teach, but they are not examples to be slavishly copied. I intend them to be used as sources of ideas, and hope that you will be able to learn from them.

Structure and cooperation in a humanities course

In the preceding chapter we saw how two fine-arts teachers reflected on their aims for student learning and devised a new set of goals which helped their second year students understand exactly what was required of them in a course on Italian art in the fifteenth century (see pp. 145–6). How did they help students to achieve these goals? The changes to teaching involved different approaches to the subject matter and alterations to the seminar structure, each of which was systematically linked to the intention to encourage students to develop a critical and questioning attitude to texts and images. The two teachers came to discover through this process the integration between how a class could be run and the sort of material that could be taught and learned in it.

The main change instituted was the use of collaborative class papers. Two students cooperated in research and presentation for these papers, although the paper each subsequently produced for assessment purposes was written independently (it emerged that each student often took a quite different viewpoint in the written paper). This was not the usual presentation of seminar papers; students were given entire responsibility for 'teaching' the topic to the rest of the group, under the guidance of their lecturers. Thus, the role of the student leaders was not to deliver a formal paper, but to explore a range of ideas about a topic, to give necessary information, and to inaugurate questions and group discussion related to the key ideas.

Students were placed in a challenging situation where they were accountable to their peers as well as their teachers for the quality of their work. It was therefore essential to provide a good deal of support. The teachers structured each class carefully in terms of material to be covered and aims to be achieved, and spent time with each pair of students prior to the class discussing how the material could be arranged and the seminar run. Techniques for initiating group work – such as having students discuss questions in pairs and fours, or having one half of the group work on an article or painting and the other on another article or painting, prior to sharing information – were considered in these pre-class sessions. The aim was to have work actually done in class by all class members, and to put the responsibility on to students for ensuring that it was done; the teacher intervened only minimally once the class was under way. The first two seminars were led by the teacher in order to give students a model of how to proceed, and to establish a sense of group commitment and identity.

A critical approach was built into the teaching programme by exacting selection of content. The material for each class was chosen to develop wide reading and to ensure that the viewpoint of any particular writer under discussion would be critically questioned. Twentieth-century images were used to explain the unfamiliar by way of the familiar and to break down the isolation of the Renaissance both in its images and the theories applied to them.

The effects on students' attitudes to the subject and on their learning were extremely favourable. Although some students found themselves unsure and anxious about the structure of the course at first, comments at the end of the course were extremely positive; there was also evidence of changes in students' understanding of important concepts related to the critical study of Renaissance art.

Teaching strategies in a materials technology course

Atkinson's course (see pp. 142–4) uses a range of different methods to achieve its goals, each carefully chosen to help students towards more sophisticated understanding of key ideas. These methods are intended to stimulate students to change their view of materials technology from one that focuses on 'getting information that might be useful in the future' to one that emphasises the application of facts and concepts about materials to professional practice. In teaching this course, Atkinson gives a great deal of her time individually to her students, a strategy which is made easier since the group is quite small (about 30).

The programme reduces the amount of class time devoted to transferring information (in what has previously been regarded as a dry and factual subject that could be taught in no other way; compare Eizenberg's course below) and increases the amount of time devoted to the active use of ideas to make sense of, apply, and remember the information. It thus reflects a theory of teaching close to the preferred one described in chapter 7.

A particularly important and innovative strategy to note is the use of the 'User's Guide' as a form of teaching and assessment. Students are placed under an obligation to produce a guide to the advantages and disadvantages of a particular material that would answer the kind of questions a young, practising interior designer would be likely to want answers to. The format for the guides was decided on collaboratively by the class under the supervision of the teacher. Also of interest is the use of practical exercises (see below) that involve the study of actual design problems and their solutions as undertaken by practitioners. These strategies address well the problems of the traditional practical and laboratory class, helping students to understand the nature and the links between practice and basic knowledge.

This teacher's experiences also exemplify aspects of the process of evaluation in relation to teaching, an issue we return to in chapter 11:

> Improving the course proved to be interesting and not at all easy. It is a continuous process of development which I never

expect to end. There are still problems in fitting everything in. There are three strands to the teaching: one involves looking at key concepts in different areas, such as textiles, stone, ceramics and glass. This is a whole class session and involves some presentation and discussion. The details related to these concepts are not dealt with in this part, but in a piece of cooperative work done by students. Groups of students are required to produce 'User's Guides' to particular materials: this encourages them to think about the information, make sense of the details, and consider how the data might be used in the process of design. For example, it is very helpful to understand how far marble can be cantilevered in construction. These guides provide resources for other students and practitioners.

The next part involves students in studying the actual process of design by professional interior designers. I have lined up 15 different practices. Pairs of students look at one product and the whole process from conception to production of that assignment. These case studies are then presented to the whole class. This strategy entirely removes students' naïve belief that there is a simple sequence from working drawings to final product: they realise how messy the real process of design is. The third strand involves talks, followed by discussion, by guest speakers who are experts in particular materials. These are experts in industry. This introduces students to a group of people they will be working with and the kinds of thinking they will have to understand.

It should be possible for you to trace each of the principles of good teaching through these comments, and it would be helpful to consider how these ideas might be applied to a course which was not aimed at developing professional skills, but rather at the mastery of a specific discipline.

Improving student learning in anatomy

Norman Eizenberg's aims for his pre-clinical medical course were also described in chapter 8. Through studying his students' experiences of learning, he has been able to restructure the teaching of this course so that it encourages them to appreciate the relevance of anatomy to clinical work and enhances their ability to integrate basic science knowledge with medical practice.

Eizenberg found that many students were using surface-atomistic approaches to learning anatomy. They saw the subject as a mass of facts which had to be rote-learned; they failed to see its relevance to clinical work. This approach seemed to be reinforced by an academic culture which regarded the subject as being one where no alternative existed to learning factual information prior to understanding its application, and by a teaching programme that followed the most expedient order for dissection, rather than the most appropriate order for learning the subject. This made it difficult for students to distinguish underlying principles from details and led to them being unable to relate the various parts of the same structure. Eizenberg changed this by linking his aims and objectives directly to the teaching programme. His object was to encourage students to view anatomy as an organised whole, rather than as a collection of discrete parts. He therefore analysed the derivation of new terms in lectures, actively engaged students in problem-solving, continually stressed the importance and efficiency of learning concepts and principles, and altered the sequence in which the material was presented in order to give students repeated opportunities to develop an understanding of key concepts. Each major section of the body (thorax, neck, head, and so on) was considered in four stages:

1 The structures forming the musculo-skeletal framework (*what* they are, and *how* they are interlocked together)
2 An analysis of the structures contained within the musculo-skeletal framework (each structure's position and how it relates to its neighbours)
3 The vessels and nerves supplying the region and how they are laid out are examined
4 The focus returns to structures which are supplied by the vessels and nerves, and how effective, exclusive, and variable the supply to each is.

The deliberate manipulation of the content of the subject to make it relevant to the practice of medicine was described in chapter 8. Readers should refer to Eizenberg's own description of his teaching programme (Eizenberg, 1988) for further details and evaluative data concerning this important example of how reflection on and analysis of students' experiences of learning can be used to improve instruction.

Linking goals to methods: problem-based learning in a conventional programme

Cawley (1989) relates how the benefits of problem-based learning can be derived from a course introduced into an existing programme. As we saw in chapter 8, he wanted to develop third year mechanical engineering students' skills in applying technical theory to real engineering problems in vibration analysis. Diagnostic and problem-solving skills essential to engineering practice were not being properly understood in the old course, which focused on technical content; the new course sought to develop students' understanding of how systems vibrate, at the same time as enhancing their analytical and critical skills and their ability to communicate solutions to clients.

Six problems are required to be solved in this course: they are typical of those that a practising engineer would meet and they provide the necessary motivation, interest, and challenge for students to cover the technical content as well as acting as vehicles for developing the professional attitudes and skills described in the objectives. Notice carefully how the teaching strategy mirrors the goals (it is driven by the aims for student learning) and reflects also our principles of good teaching:

- The students tackle the problems in groups of three or four, providing an opportunity for cooperative learning and simulating more accurately than the more typical individual learning task the joint responsibility for problem-solving that characterises much professional life. The problems encourage students to connect knowledge, attitude, and skill objectives.
- The six problems form three pairs. Each group solves three problems only, acting as a client group which prepares a critique of the solutions to the other three problems in the pairs: this emphasises checking and critical analysis of proposed solutions.
- Introductory sessions set out in detail the structure and requirements of the course and include a compulsory tutorial designed to monitor the degree to which the students are using deep approaches to the first problem. The teacher probes the group's grasp of the subject of the problem and their understanding of what will constitute a satisfactory solution.
- There is a gradual shift of emphasis away from dependence to independence; there are no compulsory tutorials afterwards,

but students are encouraged to seek advice during the tutorial periods shown in the timetable; in these sessions, the teacher acts as adviser and facilitator, not as an authority dispensing right answers. Students are treated with concern and expected to be responsible and mature.

- There is a variety of teaching techniques used: as well as the above methods, printed notes and bibliographies are provided and four mini-lectures/demonstrations are given to illustrate how systems vibrate.

- The assessment is directly linked to the objectives, giving a clear message to students about what is required from them: the reports of the consultant and client groups, both oral and written, are the main assessed material, supplemented by an assessed example and a test (see chapter 10).

- The course does not remain stable: it is continually evaluated by examining the quality of students' work and their comments on their experiences; it has been improved as a result, through amendments to the assessment, for example (for more details, see chapter 11).

A myth has grown up that innovative courses, especially problem-based ones, are very expensive. So it is worth adding that Cawley reports that the course is not only more effective in terms of the quality of student learning, but that it costs little more to run than a conventional engineering course. It is also more enjoyable for both staff and students.

Using variety and improvisation in teaching statistics

I have argued that all good teaching recognises the primacy of content over method, engages students actively, is responsive to their needs, and requires the teacher to live with uncertainty. John Dunn's teaching expresses these principles very well. The aims of his statistics course for environmental planners (see pp. 146–8) are made real through a variety of different methods. As he said in an interview:

> I basically treat every week differently according to the topic. I put a programme on my door at the beginning of the week which says whether it will be a lecture followed by tutorials, or two tutorials, or perhaps a three-hour problem class. I literally design the three- or four-hour block in a way that suits the

topic; there is no model that I adopt every week. On occasions I start with a lecture, or I might start with exercises in groups. For example, I'm talking about crosstabulations tomorrow. What I'll be doing is using a small questionnaire that I handed out to the class at the beginning of the last semester, which was a little survey on travel and place of residence. I'll present the results and explain ways of reporting them separately, but then say that you're really interested in issues of causation and relationships. They will then be asked to work out some crosstabulations individually, based on the raw data they supplied. After a suitable time I'll ask for some examples, put them on the board, and start talking about measures of association, giving a short lecture. In a follow up on a later day in small groups, we'll tackle some more rigorous problems and get them working together on them. That's a combined workshop-lecture-tutorial. But I might do a lecture first followed by tutorials when there's something like regression analysis, which is fairly hard conceptually to understand – they'll need to know some basics which this group may not have such as X-Y coordinates on graphs before tackling this topic – the style then will be delivery followed by exercises . . . I'm constantly reappraising how I did it last year, changing it and I hope improving it. I'll vary it. I'm neither highly rigid like some of my colleagues, nor so flexible that the students don't know where they're going. If it doesn't work, I'll write down at the end of the day the lessons I've learned from it.

Dunn summarises the various strategies he uses to teach basic statistics in the example that follows. Notice how formal presentation, discussion, student activity, and different ways of addressing the same material are used to help students engage with the subject matter and understand the relations between theory, procedures, and applications:

The following activities will typically proceed through several two-hour sessions:

1 *Class exercise*: run a small sample survey in class
2 *Prompted discussion* exploring with the class ideas for analysing the data
3 *Discuss* the type of questions asked (level of measurement) and the purpose of the analysis
4 *Lecture* on appropriate techniques for basic analysis (for

example: graphing, stem and leaf plots, means, medians, and modes)

5 *Class exercises* to help students grasp basic skills in producing plots and calculating means and medians

6 *Lecture* to emphasise the formal steps of calculation; subsequently explain the meaning and value of the statistics that have been covered, using examples

7 *Exercises* to take home; these are then studied in tutorials

8 *Computer packages* to practise skills further

9 *Formative test* (not counting towards final marks) is used as a learning tool and to provide guidance to the teacher concerning material that is not understood and needs additional or different teaching (see chapter 10 for further details).

A computer-based simulation in a politics course

Higher education teachers are often unadventurous in their choice of teaching strategies. The experiences of a lecturer in middle eastern politics whom I interviewed for this book illustrate how things can be done differently. He decided that students' understanding of the intricacy of middle eastern diplomacy and the impossibility of arriving at any simple solutions could not be sufficiently developed unless they could grasp the connections between practical action and ideology.

He therefore devised a simulation in which students played the roles of important characters in an imaginary middle eastern crisis – George Bush, Yasser Arafat, Yitzhak Shamir, and so on. The 'game' was played by electronic mail with another group of politics students in Texas. It forced students to work cooperatively, to apply and test the theory presented in classes and texts in practice, to do research into the background of the people and their countries, to learn about the relation between character and action in the political world, and to receive feedback from their peers on their performance. The students became enthralled by the simulation, spending large amounts of time at the computer terminals; their evaluative comments and the quality of their subsequent assessed work indicated that not only did they enjoy themselves, but that their understanding of the details and the complexity of middle eastern politics had developed substantially.

Encouraging active learning in large groups

Alan Jenkins (see Gibbs and Jenkins, 1984; Gibbs, 1990) is an example of a teacher who has gradually introduced more active learning methods into his lectures. Students in his undergraduate geography classes are now expected to obtain much of the information previously presented in lectures from detailed course guides and reading materials. Less material is 'covered' in the actual classes, but it is engaged with in a way that requires the application of ideas to new situations so that the quality of understanding is greatly improved. The method also allows the lecturer to obtain evaluative information on how well students are understanding the content and allows him to give immediate feedback on learning. Jenkins describes the subtle and skilful art of devising questions and problems that really do involve students, and other difficulties likely to be encountered in introducing this type of innovation, such as the need to proceed gradually and to develop good relationships between students outside the lectures.

It is important to stress that, as is the case with all teaching, the method cannot always be expected to work perfectly. Good, responsive teaching cannot avoid making mistakes. The example which follows, adapted from Gibbs (1990, p. 13) is an account of one 'lecture' on Christaller's central place theory given to a first year human geography class of about 100 students.

An example of a geography class designed to encourage active learning

Stage 1 A revision overhead transparency is displayed, summarising previous work related to the topic of the lecture (5 minutes).

Stage 2 Revision talk on previous lecture, including handouts. Material from earlier parts of the course is provided to form a background for the new material (9 minutes).

Stage 3 Student task: What aspects of central place theory can be used to analyse the number and location of shopping facilities in towns? Students are asked to discuss the question in twos and threes (5 minutes).

Stage 4 The lecturer gives a short lecture, answering the question and introducing new material (7 minutes).

Stage 5 Student task (in pairs) involving applying the new theoretical concepts to data presented on the screen (4 minutes).

Stage 6   The lecturer summarises some of the students' answers, commenting and giving feedback on students' learning (6 minutes).

Stage 7   Students are then set a harder task involving interpreting change over time in the location of towns. The task is to explain the changes shown in four simplified maps using the theory. Students work in pairs (6 minutes).

Stage 8   The lecturer answers part of the question and leads students into a more advanced issue (1 minute).

Stage 9   Students work on in small groups (2 minutes).

Stage 10   The lecturer completes the analysis and moves on to apply the concepts to various other situations in a short lecture (3 minutes).

Stage 11   The class is set an open question which involves applying the theory to a completely new context. Not enough time is allowed (1 minute).

Stage 12   The lecturer goes over material in the handout which has not been covered so far (6 minutes).

Stage 13   Students are asked to write a brief summary of the lecture (2 minutes).

Chapter 10

Assessing for understanding

I was examined in Hebrew and History: 'What is the Hebrew for the Place of a Skull?' said the Examiner. 'Golgotha', I replied. 'Who founded University College?' I answered, 'King Alfred'. 'Very well, Sir', said the Examiner, 'then you are competent for your degree.'

(Lord Eldon, quoted in James Woodforde's Diary of a Country Parson)

The assessment of students is a serious and often tragic enterprise. Less pomposity and defensiveness and more levity about the whole business would be an excellent starting point for improving the process of evaluating and judging our students' learning. Some lecturers in higher education become stuffy and formal when the talk turns to student assessment. It is as if they measure their own worth as teachers in terms of the difficulty of the questions and the complexity of the procedures they can devise to test and grade their students and to deter cheating. Assessment is all hedged around with a thick bureaucratic mystique designed to form an effective barrier against the inquisitive. The mystique often lightly clothes a profound ignorance about measurement and testing and their relation to teaching and learning.

Assessment, as Derek Rowntree has defined it in the best of all books on the subject (Rowntree, 1977) is about getting to know our students and the quality of their learning. We can get to know people in different ways. One way is to label and categorise them – women, men, clever, ignorant, English, German, weight 60 kilos, weight 80 kilos. Another way is to understand them in all their complexity, considering how their various strengths and weaknesses contribute to what they know, and what these strengths and weaknesses imply for their potential as learners of the subject.

The proper assessment of student learning requires teachers to combine these forms of knowing. We shall nearly always have to grade students in some way so that a summary of progress in an area of learning can be provided both for the student and for others who may wish to know something about the student's general level of performance; grading and categorising is not in itself a 'bad thing', as some people seem to believe. And yet we should also recognise that assessment is a way of teaching more effectively through understanding exactly what students know and do not know. *Assessment is about several things at once.* It is not about simple dualities such as grading versus diagnosis. It is about reporting on students' achievements and about teaching them better through expressing to them more clearly the goals of our curricula. It is about measuring student learning and it is about diagnosing specific misunderstandings in order to help students to learn more effectively. It concerns the quality of teaching as well as the quality of learning: it involves us in learning from our students' experiences, and is about changing ourselves as well as our students. It is not only about what a student can *do*; it is also about what it *means* he or she can do. This relativistic perspective on assessment is compatible with the view of teaching and learning permeating this book.

SIMPLE MODELS OF ASSESSMENT

I now want to try and unpack this rather complicated-sounding way of thinking about assessment by contrasting it with simpler ones. We have seen repeatedly (especially in chapter 5) how assessment plays a key role in determining the quality of student learning. If students perceive that their learning will be measured in terms of reproducing facts or implementing memorised procedures and formulae, they will adopt approaches that prevent understanding from being reached. The widespread use of surface approaches to learning, and the related fact that students may successfully complete their courses while never gaining an understanding of fundamental ideas which the teachers of those courses themselves desire their students to gain, together indicate beyond reasonable doubt that much assessment in higher education is flawed.

The main source of the deficiency is our own ignorance about how to do the job properly. Teachers in higher education frequently assess as amateurs when the task demands grave professionalism. The majority of courses and lecturers in higher education do not operate from the understanding of assessment outlined above, in which assessment is fundamentally about helping students to learn and teachers to learn about how best to teach them. Using a theory 1 or theory 2 understanding of teaching, they subordinate the task of comprehending the quality of student learning to the requirement to define, select, classify, motivate, and report on students. Assessment is regarded as an addition to teaching, rather than an essential part of it. It is symptomatic of this view that assessment techniques come to be regarded as being more important than the subject matter that the methods are assessing and whether they are assessing that subject matter properly. Questions such as 'How can I write a multiple-choice item?' become more important than 'What effect on the outcomes of student learning is my use of multiple-choice tests having?'

A view of teaching as the transmission of authoritative knowledge by a subject specialist has little space to accommodate the idea that different methods of assessment may be appropriate for the evaluation of different parts of the subject matter, or that assessment techniques themselves should be the subject of serious study and reflection. In such a conception, teaching, learning, and assessment are seen to be tenuously related in a simple linear sequence; assessment is something that follows learning, so there is no need to consider its function as a means of helping students to learn through diagnosing their errors and misconceptions and reinforcing their correct understandings. Assessment, like teaching, is something done *to* students. As teaching tells information and procedures, so assessment classifies the students on the criterion of how well they have absorbed the data thus transmitted. What could be simpler?

In this view, because most students are fundamentally lazy, and the bright ones few and far between, assessment performs a vital secondary function of motivating students; the threat of failure in a competitive situation is required to stimulate them to attend lectures and practicals and to do at least some private study. From this perspective, it is believed that whatever assessment method is used, the clever students are likely to come out on top, as long as opportunities for cheating (including plagiarism, copying, and collusion) are minimised. Whether the questions are tests of understanding or of basic facts, the same thing will happen. From this perspective, it is in any case necessary to test students' knowledge of facts and details to ensure that they have a foundation upon which they can proceed to relate them to the actual problems in the discipline that they will confront later in the course. (This 'building block' conception of curriculum, as we noted in chapter 8, makes use of an assumed identity between the established structure of knowledge in a subject as it is represented in textbooks and the best way to teach and learn that knowledge).

'Learning', from this perspective, is adding quanta of knowledge to one's store of knowledge: thus, assessment is seen as an activity that should test how much has been added. From this point of view, good assessment will provide objective data about the amount of a student's knowledge relative to that of other students in the class. It is valuable to describe this knowledge in terms of a single grade or number. Because students are always basically out to subvert the system by doing as little work as possible, an apparatus of security and privacy must be erected against fraud. Highly controlled assessments, typically unseen closed-book examinations, measure how much knowledge has been acquired, while at the same time ensuring that cheating is kept to a minimum and reducing the subjectivity attached to attempts to grade essays, reports, and project work.

Although the above description may appear to some readers to be a parody of bad practice, I meet plenty of lecturers in higher education who would assent to most of these propositions. It is still common to see courses assessed entirely by final examinations, which in some subject areas consist chiefly of multiple-choice and true/false items. It is quite usual for lecturers to regard assessment as having a purely 'summative' function (serving to report on students) and as having nothing to do with *teaching* them at all. And no unbiased study of the written machinery of assessment procedures could fail to conclude that we think students are at heart plagiarists and cheats.

It is sometimes argued that the feedback function of assessment – its teaching aspect – and the process of making judgements about students' ability should be kept strictly separate from each other. Similarly, it is occasionally asserted that grades based on comparisons between students (known as 'norm-referenced assessment' in measurement jargon) should be seen as distinct from grades based on whether a student has achieved a particular standard ('criterion-referenced assessment'). What is happening in these cases is that their protagonists (including several writers on teaching in higher education) are seeing the world of assessment in terms of absolutes: diagnosis vs. judging, or teaching vs. reporting, or comparison vs. categorical standards. It is helpful for us as teachers to be aware that many educators tend towards these rather dogmatic views on assessment. The open-minded and more complex understanding represented so well in Rowntree's book (Rowntree, 1977) is unusual.

These conceptions of assessment run, in their different ways, almost exactly counter to the principles of good teaching that were considered in chapter 6. They often ignore the disastrous effect of threatening assessment procedures on approaches to learning. They consider the different aspects of teaching and assessment as independently selectable, unrelated pieces, not bound together by any concept of educational quality. Nothing is said about evaluating teaching through assessment; about using assessment to encourage interest, commitment, and intellectual challenge; about using it to make our expectations unequivocal; or about using it to enhance independence and responsibility. They often focus on the divisive and competitive elements of grading, and instead of showing respect for learners as partners on a road to understanding, treat them as unworthy of trust; they may reveal an obsessive interest in security and cheating and exalt techniques for reducing the incidence of fraud. They seem to maintain that some kind of absolute standard of validity in assessment is possible, as if every measure and its interpretation could be set free of its errors – in student assessment if not in any other field of human endeavour. Instead of seeing feedback on learning as a primary task of all teaching, they either ignore it altogether or place it in a rigidly separate category from making a judgement about a student's achievement relative to other students.

Seen from the point of view of our understanding of good teaching, these are upside-down views of teaching and learning, administratively convenient perhaps, but educationally impotent. They ignore what is known about students' perceptions of effective instruction in higher education, and they demonstrate a conspicuous disregard of our knowledge of the relation between educational practice and high quality learning.

MORE DEVELOPED MODELS OF ASSESSMENT

There is evidently a connection between different ways of thinking about assessment and the quality of student learning. A view of assessment as being primarily about the allocation of rewards and punishments to students through the grading process is part of an undeveloped theory of teaching. These ideas are reflected in students' cynical and negative attitudes towards the subject matter and in superficial approaches to studying it. Seeing assessment as an external imposition to be negotiated in order to earn a grade, rather than a way of learning and of demonstrating understanding, is an optimal recipe for surface approaches.

Assessment which is the servant rather than the master of the educational process will necessarily be viewed as an integral part of teaching and the practice of improving teaching. A sophisticated theory of teaching leads directly to the proposition that the assessment of students is above all about *understanding the processes and outcomes of student learning, and understanding the students who have done the learning*. In the application of these understandings, we aim to make both student learning and our teaching better.

Now this implies that assessment is happening continually, both formally and informally. Listening to what students say in a tutorial is as much assessment as reading their exam scripts and assigning marks to them. Assessment always involves making fallible human judgements, whether its chief purpose is to report on students or to give them feedback, whether we are considering the design of a practical test in surveying or marking a history essay. There are no error-free tests. Assessment does not just occur at the end of a course, whether we use continuous assessment methods or not; judgements are being made by students and teachers about progress all the time. By no means does this view of assessment exclude the use of complex measurement procedures to evaluate what students learn; but these quantitative techniques are seen as media through which fuller and more useful descriptions of these different outcomes can be achieved.

Assessment is not a world of right or wrong ways to judge or diagnose, of standards versus improvement, of feedback versus certification: it is in reality a human and uncertain process where these functions generally have to be combined in some way. For example, although we may say that we wish to assess only whether a student has achieved the objectives of a course, rather than how well he or she does compared with others, in practice we consolidate the two functions. It is impossible to decide on which test to use or how to interpret the student's performance unless we compare it against a standard of some kind. The standard is inevitably, and quite validly, derived from what we know about other students at a similar stage of their progress – ideally, the whole population of other students at a particular stage of learning a particular subject.

Unless we understand assessment in this essentially relativistic sense, as a series of relations between the person whose work we are assessing, the quality of the outcomes he or she demonstrates in comparison with others, and our own understanding of what students know and do not know, there is little hope of using it to improve teaching. How will a teacher who understands assessment in this way go about defining what he or she will assess, and selecting and using assessment techniques? What help is available to teachers? In the remainder of this chapter I want to examine aspects of this desirable understanding of assessment, by means of a general discussion of the connections between underlying principles and their realisation, and through considering some examples of good practice.

ASSESSMENT AND THE CONTENT OF A COURSE

What is worth assessing? It is tempting to take a nonchalant approach to this question, and simply to answer that assessment should test knowledge of the content of the syllabus. But if we operate with a well-developed understanding of assessment we will remember one of the principal lessons that we learned from looking at students' experiences of the context of learning. It cannot be repeated too often. From our students' point of view, assessment always defines the actual curriculum. In the last analysis, that is where the content resides for them, not in lists of topics or objectives. Assessment sends messages about the standard and amount of work required, and what aspects of the syllabus are most important. Too much assessed work leads to superficial approaches; clear indications of priorities in what has to be learned, and why it has to be learned, provide fertile ground for deep approaches.

Good teaching thus implies a considered selection among the content of the subject area of which aspects will be formally and informally assessed, together with explanation of their relative importance. The aims and objectives of the course should be devised at the same time as the teacher thinks about their assessment (see the advice and examples in chapter 8); the central purposes of the course (those key concepts and skills, and vital procedures and attitudes that define competence in the subject at this stage of progress) will have been carefully articulated and linked to the assessment methods used. Every effort will have been made to make the criteria for assessment explicit and public rather than hidden and vague.

A great deal has been written about different levels of cognitive activity in relation to assessment, much of it based on the work of Benjamin Bloom and his associates (Bloom *et al.*, 1956). The scheme most often discussed contains 6 levels, ranging from knowledge, through comprehension, application and analysis, to synthesis and evaluation. What is often not understood is that in Bloom's scheme the levels are strictly hierarchical; being able to work at what he calls the 'transformational' levels (that is, at the level of analysis and above) implies an ability to operate at the lower ones. It is often not necessary – and it may be detrimental to student learning – to have separate assessments at each level.

Unfortunately, it is much easier to set assessment questions at the lower levels of recall of knowledge than at the higher ones of its analysis and evaluation, especially in subjects which involve mastering quantitative procedures. Sometimes we deceive ourselves into thinking that these sorts of questions really do test understanding. Naïvely, we frequently infer higher level skills from lower level ones. Writing and marking questions that require understanding is like all good teaching: it is challenging, tricky, and time-consuming. It is scarcely surprising to find numerous examples of university examination questions – generally in science and social science subjects – that can actually be answered without any understanding at all of the fundamental principles that the lecturer says he or she is testing. Many lecturers will deny that this happens, yet the facts could not be plainer. Beard and Hartley (1984) and Elton (1982), for example, quote several studies over the past thirty years which have analysed the content of examinations in university science and medicine courses. These analyses show how the majority of questions test no more than the isolated recall of factual knowledge or the straightforward application of principles to familiar problems.

A primary danger avoided by the teacher who thinks about assessment in terms of what essential understandings he or she wants students to acquire is this tendency to focus on assessing isolated parts of the curriculum at the expense of the higher-order principles that link the parts together. Although it may well be important to know whether a student can remember a formula and substitute correctly it in chemistry, or identify the effect of a specific drug on an animal in pharmacology, or connect an artist's name and dates to a painting in art history, it is generally preferably to assess these matters as part of the measurement of broader, more integrative concepts and skills. This is mainly because the separate assessment of basic skills and knowledge, unless clearly flagged as a relatively unimportant part of the whole assessment process, leads to a focus by students on these activities rather than on more complex ones that are related to understanding.

The teacher with a well-developed understanding of assessment will strive to connect his or her goals for learning firmly with the assessment strategies he or she uses. Questions in every formal examination will be carefully reviewed to ensure that they cannot be answered merely by recall; the proportion of questions which involve elementary applications of principles to problems will be kept small.

This teacher will also be thinking carefully about the related need to assess students' values and commitments to the subject area (see Rowntree, 1981, pp. 188–90). These aspects of competence, whether implicit in other objectives or explicitly stated in the curriculum, are too rarely addressed in formal assessments. Their achievement is generally revealed in how a student applies knowledge to unfamiliar situations – an experiment that refuses to work, an author that has not previously been read, a new problem in the analysis of an economy's performance. Commitment to and interest in the subject, the extent to which the student values ideas and procedures in it, and the progressive development of independent thinking in relation to it, will all be assessed by teachers who teach from this perspective. This implies that attitudinal aspects of subject competence must be included in a course's aims and objectives; courses operating with a well-developed conception of teaching include such goals, and assess them systematically. Among the original objectives of the Newcastle problem-based medical course, for example, were requirements such as being prepared to invest time in the further development of medical knowledge and skills over and above the pursuit of higher qualifications, having a positive attitude to preventing illness, and having an awareness of how one's own anxiety and prejudices may alter patient attitudes and behaviour. The assessment methods were designed so that they explicitly tested each of these objectives (see Engel and Clarke, 1979).

The application of these principles will be considered in more detail when we look later in the chapter at several examples of how teachers have gone about assessing their students.

CHOICE OF ASSESSMENT METHODS

Just as our choice of teaching methods should be informed by the nature of the subject matter we are teaching, so our choice of assessment methods should be conditioned by our goals for student learning. The foremost thing to remember in selecting methods of assessment for any course is that there will rarely be one method which satisfies all educational objectives. A willingness to experiment with a variety of methods and to monitor the effectiveness of each method in helping students to learn, and in helping the teacher to measure their progress in an area of learning, is highly characteristic of a thoughtful approach to teaching.

If assessment is seen as being about finding out what students have failed to learn, or as a way of comparing the weakest against the brightest, variety in assessment has decided disadvantages. It is so much more difficult to combine the results from different methods than to add up the marks from one method; students have an awkward habit of performing inconsistently on different tasks. It is by no means unusual to find that the marks from practical assignments and project reports correlate poorly with examination results, for example.

Our understanding of the way students learn leads us to see that these are not educational problems at all. They are actually desirable outcomes: any one-dimensional measure of a person's achievement in many different tasks is almost certainly inadequate, and may be entirely misleading. Uniformity of methods makes comparisons superficially easy but forces students into a situation where they may not be able to display what they have learned, and where there are often hidden rewards for conformity rather than originality. Thus we observe a well-known phenomenon in assessment: the marks come out in a handily consistent and easily comparable way, but judgements made about student ability on the basis of these marks are frequently invalid. The measuring instrument is perfect, but it is measuring a trivial or irrelevant thing.

Generally, the more predictable, more narrow, and the more conventional the learning outcome which is measured is, the more likely it is that assessment will produce consistent results. This consistency is known in measurement terminology as the 'reliability' of a test. Tests of simple recall are usually highly reliable (see Elton, 1982, p. 115). An additional incentive for lecturers to test like this is the fact that, as we have seen above, it is rather easy to think up hard questions about specific information, procedures, and details. It is infinitely more difficult to construct questions that demand and reward an understanding of concepts, disciplinary or professional processes of thinking, and their related evidence and procedures. It also takes more time to mark such questions. No wonder we sometimes beguile ourselves into thinking that imitation assessment is the real thing, especially in large undergraduate classes.

The alternative approach is to think about assessment less as a way of getting a single score for comparative purposes, and more as a means of providing opportunities for students to demonstrate how much they understand. A conception of assessment for learning first and grading second implies the use of a spectrum of methods. A greater variety of methods may be administratively inconvenient, but it offers more latitude for students to display their knowledge, and it has the potential to provide a more accurate – though more complex – depiction of each student's achievement. We have seen how students' perceptions of the degree of choice and independence offered in a course are associated with positive evaluations and deep approaches to learning. An important way in which students' preferences can be accommodated is through providing a variety of assessment methods. Variety in method, which may usefully be combined with a degree of student choice over the methods themselves (such as examination versus essay) encourages greater responsibility for self-direction in learning.

Yet variety in methods is insufficient in itself; how does one decide which methods, and in what proportions? These answers will partly be determined by contextual features such as the number of students being assessed. But the most important criterion which a competent lecturer will use in the choice of method concerns its relevance to the aims and objectives (including attitudes as well as procedural and conceptual skills) it is supposed to test. No rules can be given for applying this criterion, any more than rules can be given that will avoid subjective decisions about students' achievement; we have to exercise professional judgement to decide whether a project report, an examination, an observation of a practical activity, or any combination of the dozens of possible methods is the most applicable to a particular situation. This is not the place to give a detailed description of different methods themselves; Gibbs *et al.* (1988a) provide one of the most comprehensive sources of ideas. At the very least, all teachers should be aware of the existence of an assortment of methods in all subject areas, ranging from multiple-choice questions, short-answer examinations, essays and lab reports, through to quizzes in class, student presentations, simulations, clinical exercises, self-assessment, and assessments based on the products of groups.

We should think carefully about the possible dangers of using some methods rather than others. Ease and tradition are no more likely than innovatory methods to be efficient and effective. Many conventional practical tests, and traditional assessments that occur regularly throughout a course, consume prodigious amounts of staff resources in marking and student time in preparation. Much wider use could be made, with educational as well as economic benefits, of methods which emphasise students' cooperative work, rather than competition against each other; of self-assessment techniques; and of short-answer questions which are geared to measuring understanding (in preference to multiple-choice tests). Rowntree (1977), Gibbs *et al.* (1988a) and Crooks (1988) are three important sources of further information about these techniques. Boud (1989) has given a particularly useful overview of the problems and possibilities of student self-assessment.

FEEDBACK TO STUDENTS

Entwistle's investigation of first year engineering students in Scottish higher education (Entwistle *et al.*, 1989; see also chapter 8) showed that an important contributory cause of student failure was an almost complete absence of feedback on progress during the first term of their studies. Some students only realised they were in danger of failure after receiving the results of the first end-of-term examinations; even then, they were usually not given information that would enable them to improve. They simply suffered a sense of demoralisation and their problems became compounded by an ever greater reluctance to seek help (Entwistle, 1990, p. 10).

It is impossible to overstate the role of effective feedback on students' progress in any discussion of effective teaching and assessment. Students are understandably angry when they receive feedback on an assignment that consists only of a mark or grade. I believe that reporting results in this way, whatever the form of assessment, is cheating students. It is unprofessional teaching behaviour and ought not to be tolerated. We will recollect that the most important question on the teaching performance indicator questionnaire was 'Teaching staff here normally give helpful feedback on how you are going': it seems that beneficial information about progress is valued even more by students than qualities such as clear explanations and the stimulation of interest. What directs the actions of lecturers who give no information to students about their progress? It is probably a mixture of motives. Fear of losing one's authority by revealing the reasons for low marks; a mistaken notion that providing students with feedback is somehow helping the dull ones more than they deserve; sheer laziness about making the effort to compose model answers or meet students – these are among the reasons.

As we saw in our discussion of teaching strategies, there is no sharp dividing line between assessment and teaching in the area of giving feedback on learning. A lecturer or course applying a sophisticated understanding of teaching is aware that every evaluation of a student should be valuable to the student as well as to the lecturer. Among the features of such assessment will typically be formal, timetabled opportunities for students to discuss their assignments, reports, or examination answers with academic staff; repeated informal assessments of students in class, designed with the intention of understanding their achievements and informing them about their progress in a way that is readily comprehended; and written comments on work which are genuinely useful to students. No assignment should be set unless the lecturer who sets it is prepared to discuss with students what an appropriate answer to it would have consisted of. The prudent use of model answers, taken either from students' work or specially written by the lecturer, is an excellent form of feedback.

As we have previously seen, this way of looking at teaching conceptualises the relationship between student and teacher as an interaction or *dialogue* rather than a one-way communication. The teacher shows that he or she is interested in what the student is saying; he or she seeks evidence or clarification, or tries to persuade the student to think about the issue in a different way, perhaps by asking provocative questions. Negative comments will be carefully balanced by positive ones; great delicacy is needed if critical feedback is to have the effect of helping students, especially inexperienced ones, to learn something rather than to become defensive or disheartened. Sarcasm comes too easily to many teachers. Learning how to find the right tone and level of specificity of feedback is another of the particularly difficult arts of teaching that has to be mastered if high quality instruction is to be achieved.

In large classes, lecturers find it difficult to provide this level of individual feedback quickly on practical reports or essays. As students generally find timely feedback far more useful than delayed comment, a possible alternative in this case is to examine the assignments for typical misunderstandings and to list these errors, together with brief explanations and recommended further reading, on a numbered feedback sheet, a copy of which is returned with every assignment. Most errors can then be simply identified by numbers on the student's script. Specificity of comment to the subject matter and the particular errors in understanding is very important indeed in this case: generalised comments ('Rambling construction, lacking continuity', 'Superficial treatment', 'Figure not necessary,' and the like) are quite useless. Multiple-choice questions provide another excellent opportunity to offer feedback in an efficient form. Feedback on multiple-choice tests – if it is given at all – is usually limited to a score indicating the proportion of right answers obtained. Students do not know which questions they have got wrong, why they are wrong, or what the correct answers would be. Yet it is a relatively simple matter to provide students with the marking key for such a test and to provide short explanations of the basis for the correct answer.

Gibbs *et al.* (1988a) have described a computer-based testing system of this type. The student takes the test at the computer, which is programmed to supply printed tutorial comments, written by the test author, for all the items which the student has answered incorrectly, as in the following example:

Student Progress Report
Student   A.N. Other
Survey No.   1
Biochemistry Test No.   3

You correctly answered 23 out of the 25 questions in this survey.

Amides are generally neutral. The carbonyl removes the basic properties from the adjacent $-NH_2$ or $-NHR$.

Oxidation of a mercapton (thiol), RSH, causes two molecules to link to give a disulphide $RSSR$ and water is eliminated.

(Gibbs *et al.*, 1988a, pp. 77–8)

An understanding of assessment as part of teaching will lead to the design of opportunities for students to make mistakes and advance their understanding through making these mistakes. Effective CAL programs of the simulation or intelligent tutorial type, some of whose characteristics were briefly discussed in the previous chapter, incorporate exactly this type of teaching; so do the various forms of testing associated with individualised learning systems that require mastery of skills and ideas before proceeding to a subsequent stage.

It is worth emphasising that it is not always necessary for academic staff to give feedback: students can often learn more from formal or informal assessment by their peers or by themselves. Giving feedback on another student's work, or being required to determine and defend one's own, not only increases a student's sense of responsibility and control over the subject matter, it often reveals the extent of one's misunderstandings more vividly than any other method. It is therefore an important form of cooperative teaching. Svensson and Högfors (1988; see also chapter 8) have described how students' ways of thinking about physics concepts can be improved through this strategy. Svensson and Högfors recognised that telling someone else what you know about a concept is an excellent means of teaching yourself about it. We can all understand our mistakes better through having to put our ideas into words for the benefit of another learner.

Assessment should also serve a feedback function for teachers. I shall have more to say about the way in which assessment can be used to enable us to refine our teaching practices through telling us about our students' learning later in this chapter and in Part 3.

MAKING EXPECTATIONS CLEAR AND ENCOURAGING STUDENT AUTONOMY

Discussing assessment expectations with students is a principal means by which a lecturer can reinforce the view he or she has expressed in the description and teaching of a course that understanding rather than recall of isolated detail is required and will be rewarded. Underlining this requirement cannot be done too often; students will have had many experiences of being told that a course is about comprehension, synthesis, and application and of finding out that the assessment actually tests reproduction of material presented in lectures (see chapter 5). They will need some convincing that your course is different. If several methods are used, you will also need to explain the purpose of each method and how each relates to the rest. If a particular assessment is to serve multiple functions, the precise arrangements should be made clear as well.

It is possible to help students to learn how to use assessments to display as much of their understanding as possible, and to develop a self-critical, independent approach to their work. For example, I – in common with many other teachers – have used assignments to encourage students to develop a self-critical attitude to their work through using feedback constructively. The same assignment is the basis both for feedback and a final mark that counts towards the course grade. Thus there are two deadlines: students get fairly detailed oral and written feedback on the first draft and return an improved version which gets a mark. A similar approach involves students in being critics of their own work. They are provided with a grade, but no comments, in the first instance. They are then invited to write about the assignment or lab report's strengths and weaknesses and how they would improve it. In the second stage, complete feedback is provided and the grade may be improved (but never worsened) depending on the quality of the student's self-assessment.

Discussion of sample answers in class (see p. 194) or a dialogue focused on your meaning of such terms as 'discuss', 'evaluate', and 'express your answer quantitatively' are useful means of making expectations clear, helping students to learn how to do their best in assessments, encouraging independence, and reducing the debilitating anxiety that assessment too often imposes. There need be no apprehension of reducing a student's anxiety too much: if a learner desires to understand, that inner pressure will always provide enough tension. The main point bears restating: good teaching helps students to become aware that educationally valid assessment is an opportunity to learn and to reveal the depth of one's knowledge.

CASE STUDIES OF EFFECTIVE PRACTICE

We can now look at how some of these ideas have been applied to improving assessment in higher education. The first set of illustrations returns us to the experiences of teachers whose instructional methods have been considered in earlier chapters. The remaining examples concern the use of new ideas about measuring learning to improve the diagnosis of misunderstandings and to make more valid judgements of achievement.

Assessment in an anatomy course

Eizenberg's assessment methods are explicitly designed to encourage and permit students to demonstrate their understanding of anatomical concepts; at the same time, they actively discourage surface approaches. He appreciates that the wording of a question (for example, asking for a description or 'brief notes') may restrict the opportunity to show understanding;

similarly, asking closed questions in oral examinations ('What is this structure?') dismays students who have struggled to understand. He does not use multiple-choice questions, citing evidence from his own students that, whatever their other merits, their negative effect in reinforcing the idea that learning anatomy involves the indiscriminate recall of bits of information is unacceptable. If multiple-choice tests are used, students soon gain the impression from previous cohorts that the test is 'really about' remembering facts, however well it is constructed; this inevitably directs their learning strategies.

The assessment in Eizenberg's course is tightly linked to the goals of the programme and the associated learning tasks. Knowledge and skills requirements for each component are displayed in the course handbook. The requirement to understand is continually restated. A variety of methods is used. Open-ended written questions in examinations are used to provide students with an opportunity to give explanations, subsuming descriptive information, of important principles. Other written tests involve describing characteristics of specimens. In oral tests, he attempts to establish a dialogue with students and to help explain their answers; if they get a wrong answer, he tries to help them retrace their steps to the source of the mistake.

In these ways, instruction and assessment are closely connected, with the teaching function of assessment taking first priority. Eizenberg uses assessment deliberately to learn about students' conceptions and misunderstandings, and as we have seen, his entire course has been structured around the important problems he has learned that students experience in understanding the key concepts in the subject. He explained in an interview that he was still learning, however:

> It's one thing to read the answers in order to give a mark and quite another to really read what they have written to see how much they understand. It's amazing from reading answers to what you might have felt was an absolutely watertight question that you felt could only be interpreted in a particular way, to find a whole range of levels of understanding. To see the ways students interpret these ideas is incredibly illuminating too: it helps me to help them. We can return to some misunderstanding whose origins might be quite subtle, but absolutely fundamental to their future comprehension.

Assessment in materials technology for interior designers

The interior design students in Atkinson's course receive plenty of feedback on their work through personal consultations and other types of assessment. Notice how assessment is seen basically as a way of helping students to identify important concepts and perform to their maximum capability, while at the same time the information gathered through assessment is used by the teacher to revise the course:

> At various points in the course I have tried to build in ways of checking on how they are learning. With the development of the User's Guide we went through in class the process of identifying key objectives and meeting performance criteria; I later saw them in pairs and we considered together what they had developed. That enabled me to get some idea of how they were thinking and to suggest directions they hadn't thought of pursuing. It helped them to understand more about the professional process. The individual tutorial type classes, where you actually have a chance to have a conversation with the student over a piece of work, seem to provide me with valuable feedback on students' understanding in the way more formal assessments don't. I actually feel quite comfortable with that sort of interaction: I enjoy it, and I don't find it difficult to relate to students in that way. My students are very used to that – sitting down with a piece of work and having a chat about it. I try and provide opportunities where that can happen, and I find it helpful to learn about the problems they experience from their perspective. The information is useful for improving the teaching next time round. Outside class time, students do come and talk to me quite a bit, though there is always a problem of time.

I have suggested that variety in assessment methods, and the close articulation of objectives to the different methods, is characteristic of many effective higher education courses. The formal assessment in this course comprises four parts: the User's Guide to a particular material, described in chapter 9; a case study of the process of design of an existing interior; a take-home exam consisting of several problems in detail design; and an assessment of the effectiveness of a student's critique of another case study. Each method offers an opportunity to test different aspects of student performance, and each is justified and explained to students in terms of the particular outcomes it is intended to test, so that students are left in no doubt about the goals of their study. All these goals, we have seen, involve understanding and application, surface approaches being explicitly penalised. To complete the user's guide successfully, for example, students are told that they must identify the information necessary to translate designs into reality, establish an accessible format, evaluate the information, and present it concisely so that the information forms part of a coherent argument. These objectives imply the exercise of diverse skills, including understanding the limitations and advantages of a material and being able to communicate effectively with tradespeople.

For the assessment of their ability to provide their peers with feedback, the main criterion is the quality and constructiveness of the information presented in relation to criteria for a successful case study which are established cooperatively in class. Note in this instance how students are involved in assessing their own work indirectly – that is, through the device of assessing their ability to assess their colleagues.

As an additional aid to students, the teacher provides them with a model answer to a sample question similar to those presented in the take-home examination. This model answer is handed out *after* students have attempted the sample question in order to encourage them to learn from their mistakes and assess their own performance.

Assessment in a problem-based engineering course

Cawley's engineering course (Cawley, 1989; see also chapters 8 and 9) illustrates the use of a variety of methods dependent on the main goals and strongly linked to the teaching programme. The aims of the course, as we have already seen, are related to the development of a deep understanding of the application of engineering principles, increased professional responsibility and independence in learning, the ability to solve engineering problems, and the ability to criticise constructively the work of colleagues. The assessment directly measures these main goals. The three consultant reports and the three critiques of these (see p. 175) are written up and submitted by the groups concerned; the oral presentations of these reports are also assessed by the tutor; a worked example on a particular topic that previous students are known to have had difficulty in understanding is required; and a one-hour test of understanding was introduced on the second time the course was run. This test was designed to check on students' grasp of basic technical ideas; students could use notes in it and were not expected to revise analytical details; it included questions of the form 'A junior member of your department suggests that the problem may be solved by . . . . Is this likely to be feasible?' (Cawley, 1989, p. 92). The consultant and client presentations clearly offer many opportunities for fruitful discussion and feedback on learning, from fellow students as well as from teachers:

> As a tutor on the course, I observed that the students enjoyed it and seemed to develop their skills as the year progressed. I found that the discussions with the students at tutorials were more productive and generally at a higher level than those on conventional courses, probably because the students were well motivated and had dealt with many of the basic issues by themselves. The oral presentation sessions turned into important learning forums: on many occasions a consultant group would make an incorrect statement which was seized upon by the clients, or failing this, by the tutor, and in the ensuing debate the issue was clarified. Subsequent conversations with students suggested that their retention of points raised in this way was high.
>
> (Cawley, 1989, p. 91)

The reports combine summative and formative functions in a rational way. More weight is given to the later reports than the earlier ones, so that students can focus in the early stages on getting practice at tackling problems and on improving their skills by learning from critical comments.

Table 10.1 shows a checklist used in Cawley's course to help markers focus on relevant issues. This kind of list is a very useful means of increasing the consistency of grading when the outcomes of learning cannot be pre-specified in great detail.

Assessing the content of a humanities course

The revised course in fifteenth-century Italian art for second year undergraduates, constructed by Hazel Lybeck and Barbara

Table 10.1 A marking checklist for students' written presentations in a problem-based engineering (vibration analysis) course

Element	Checklist	Grade (5 = high)
Development of appropriate model	Criteria for appropriate solution correctly identified and interpreted?	1 2 3 4 5
	Ways in which system vibrates correctly identified?	1 2 3 4 5
	Appropriate model chosen and developed?	1 2 3 4 5
	Assumptions made in model justified correctly?	1 2 3 4 5
Analysis of model	Method of analysis correct?	1 2 3 4 5
	Answer reasonable?	1 2 3 4 5
	Answer completely correct?	1 2 3 4 5
	Check using simple analysis and/or reference to behaviour of similar systems?	1 2 3 4 5
Conclusion and recommendations	Conclusion and recommendations justified in relation to needs of client?	1 2 3 4 5
	All relevant factors taken into account?	1 2 3 4 5
Quality of presentation	Clearly laid out and structured?	1 2 3 4 5
	Sufficient information, but without unnecessary padding?	1 2 3 4 5
	Appropriate to audience?	1 2 3 4 5

Source: Based on Cawley (1989), Table V

Yencken, abandoned one of the traditional methods of assessment in their department – the 'visual test', in which students were required to identify works of art presented under examination conditions (slides shown once for a few seconds). These teachers were aware that students disliked this type of assessment: the students had argued that it emphasised recall of trivial details and that they also found it very threatening. The teachers reached the conclusion that the test would, in addition to encouraging activities that were not aims of the amended course (memorising the names of the creators of visual images, for instance), discourage the achievement of several of its main objectives: learning how to look at diverse works of art with confidence and independence; relating reading and personal experience to the examination of works of art; understanding the assumptions underlying particular concepts (such as Michael Baxandall's concept of the 'period eye' (Baxandall, 1972)); encouraging a questioning and critical approach to art history authorities and texts in general; active involvement, cooperation and responsible criticism in class; and capacity to give a mature response to critical comment. The staff also reasoned that if students acquired these skills and understandings, they would be able to recognise the works of art on which they were based.

The new assessment regime incorporated tasks connected to the aims:

1 One paper based on the joint class presentation (see p. 170), in which students were required to discuss the processes whereby they arrived at their conclusions and to include material that arose from the class discussions (worth 35 per cent). These sessions, we will remember, involved learning about the material through having to explain it to other students;

2 One long essay, designed to test students' ability to research a topic independently and present an argument clearly and convincingly (worth 40 per cent);

3 A take-home exam, designed to provide an opportunity to engage freely with a work of art in a limited time, but without the necessity of lengthy research, or bibliographic apparatus (worth 25 per cent).

Observe how this course uses student assessment in a quite simple way to realise the principle of encouraging student independence and choice, and advocates in its methods the view that the programme will be both an enjoyable and a challenging experience for students. The students are treated as responsible participants in a search for understanding, answerable both to one another and to their teachers for the quality of their learning.

Assessment for learning in a statistics course

Assessment in Dunn's statistics course (see pp. 176–8) is connected to learning and teaching by means of diagnostic exercises of different kinds. For example, students are required to carry out a small social survey and present its results; they then receive feedback on this exercise prior to submitting a report on a major survey which counts towards their final grade. Tests on statistical methods, whose marks do not count towards the student's final grade, are used both to make clear the teacher's requirements for understanding and to provide extensive feedback on performance.

There are deliberate attempts in this assessment regime to encourage and reward deep approaches. Note how, in the example shown (Table 10.2), students are required to explain the meaning of a concept, and interpret an equation, as well as perform calculations. Such questions cannot be answered fully without a thorough understanding of the material. At the same time, they provide the lecturer with valuable information about typical misunderstandings, which can then be used to modify teaching, and work with individual students who continue to experience difficulties. In order to reinforce the application of statistical methods to professional practice, students are told that extra marks (as many as 10 out of a problem marked out of 20) can only be gained if they show how the principles involved can be related to practice.

Table 10.2 A question designed to test understanding of some concepts in statistics

Last year a paper was published which reported a study of pedestrian behaviour in Sydney. The author looked at the relationship between pedestrian walking speed and shopping centre size (the latter being measured by number of shops). He got the following result:

Speed = 1.27 + 0.05 log *Size*

r = +0.60

(r is statistically significant at 'the 1% probability of error')

(a) Briefly explain this result in non-technical words. (7 marks)
(b) Explain clearly the *meaning* of the phrase 'Statistically . . . error'. (10 marks)
(c) What is the null hypothesis in this case? (4 marks)
(d) What is the standard error under the assumption of the null hypothesis? (4 marks)

Source: Walmsley, D.J. (1989) 'Pedestrian behaviour in Sydney', *Australian Planner* 27: 26–9.

Passing end-of-semester tests is made compulsory to ensure that students cannot pass the whole course without achieving a minimum level of competence in statistical technique. To encourage students to cooperate with each other and work responsibly together, Dunn often requires students to learn from each other in problem classes: they have to explain their answers and how they arrive at them to each other, prior to the teacher going around the class and checking and correcting answers.

Assessment as learning from students about their understanding: an emerging methodology

The lecturer who would teach from a conception of assessment as understanding the process and outcome of his or her students' learning has until recently been faced with the problem that a view of learning as the passive absorption of quantities of provided knowledge is implicit in most accepted theories of educational measurement. The theory of learning underlying traditional testing regards the acquisition of facts, skills, and techniques as an additive process, rather like progressively building a wall by adding extra bricks. Competence becomes defined as the ability to reproduce these facts, skills, and techniques.

This effect is particularly noticeable in disciplines such as the physical sciences where the achievement of quantitative skills and understanding of mathematical models needs to be tested. In this kind of assessment, students' answers are typically compared with a single right answer (or narrowly circumscribed set of right answers) in order to establish whether a particular piece of knowledge is present. Diagnosis of errors is seen as the identification of gaps in the student's knowledge. The idea that variation in the *kinds* of wrong answer given by students might be pedagogically valuable information, or that studying the process of learning these wrong answers from the learner's own perspective could be a useful part of teaching, has been absent in conventional test methodologies (Masters, 1989, p. 153).

The last few years have seen the development of a different way of looking at measurement in education. This has grown from an increased awareness of the importance of the active nature of most human learning and from an understanding of the way in which students' conceptions of subject matter and approaches to learning are related to achievement. This perspective draws on the ideas presented in earlier chapters and is perfectly harmonious with the conception of teaching advocated throughout the book. It accepts that students are engaged in an active search for meaning and that even novice learners begin from a point where they display some understanding of the phenomenon being assessed. Understanding is neither 'right' nor 'wrong': 'wrong' answers usually reveal partial competence. The problem-solving methods from which they are derived are applied rationally and consistently by students. Moreover, insights into the nature of these wrong conceptions can be gained from the qualities of the answers provided, and these insights can then be used systematically to help students appreciate the differences between the desired conceptions and the ones they currently display (examples of this process may be found in Ramsden, 1988b).

Assessment considered from this perspective becomes the servant of good teaching as I have defined it, helping lecturers to intervene to change students' conceptions through a greater awareness of their place in a hierarchy of understanding, and at the same time representing to students a conception of learning as being about moving from one way of seeing the world to another. This approach to measurement also helps teachers to use the diagnostic information to provide summative reports on students' progress which more truly represent whether a student understands the subject matter.

This form of assessment can describe, in a more human and individual way than any grade or mark (especially if it includes some narrative comment), the complexity of a particular student's achievement (see also Rowntree, 1981, p. 237). It can encourage a more responsible and self-critical view of one's own achievement: rather than assessment being 'something that is done to you' by a band of external experts, it becomes 'something that you have to make sense of'. The results are relativistic rather than dualistic: they require interpretation to fit the particular requirement they are to be used for. Assessment of this type provides a highly informative record of a person's or a group's achievement, and is less likely to fragment and trivialise learning than methods based on long checklists of skills to be mastered or facts to be remembered.

The two examples of this kind of work summarised below employ sophisticated statistical models to describe progress and to help teachers understand their students better. The details of this methodology do not need to be presented here; it is enough to recognise that if a lecturer understands assessment in the way I have proposed, he or she will neither fight shy of quantitative techniques nor believe that they will in themselves solve the problems of assessing students.

Using SOLO to assess medical students' understandings of key concepts

John Balla has used the SOLO taxonomy (see chapter 4, especially Table 4.4) to assess medical students' performance in elementary statistics and behavioural science (Balla *et al.*, in preparation). SOLO, you will remember, places students' responses into predetermined, hierarchical categories according to the quality of their answers. The categories range from simple unstructured responses, which use irrelevant information, through to high level abstractions that use available information to form hypotheses based on general principles.

Balla and his colleagues begin from the propositions that medical education should aim to produce graduates who understand the scientific basis of their discipline and that assessment should help teachers towards knowledge of their students' developing conceptualisations so that they can develop appropriate teaching strategies. But most tests of students' knowledge in medical science either lack reliability or fail to measure understanding: thus their results are of limited use both for formative and summative purposes. He then goes on to show how SOLO items can be written which assess increasingly complex understandings of a key concept (see Table 10.3 for an example from clinical decision analysis). The responses to the questions are graded pass/fail, and it is assumed that success at each higher level implies success at all those beneath it. (The validity of this assumption is tested using the probabilistic Rasch Partial Credit Model, which is also used to combine scores on the different questions. The technical details of the model are described in Masters, 1988 and Wright, 1988.)

Balla states that the computer software which allows the Partial Credit Model analysis to be run is easy to operate and produces almost instantaneous results. A lecturer can thus obtain much-needed insights into the conceptual development of his or her students. The Partial Credit Model analysis additionally shows how difficult the students find each step from one interval of conceptual development to the next, and which aspects of a topic are hardest for students. This information from students helps

Table 10.3 Example of an item used to test understanding of clinical
             decision analysis concepts in Balla's study

In a population of 100 in a village, 20 people have TB. All of them have
a chest Xray.
Nineteen Xrays show abnormalities that look like TB.
Further tests reveal that 18 of these abnormal Xrays are in people with
TB.

1 What is the TPR (true positive rate) of Xray chest for TB?	(Level: Unistructural)
2 What is the FPR (false positive rate) of Xray chest for TB?	(Level: Unistructural)
3 What is the prevalence of TB in that population?	(Level: Unistructural)
4 What is the PV+ (predictive value positive) of Xray chest for TB?	(Level: Multistructural)
5 Give a formula to work out PV+	(Level: Relational)

Note: students were provided with definitions of the technical terms TPR,
prevalence, predictive value, etc. on the question sheet.

teachers to devise a curriculum which focuses on students' difficulties in learning this particular content; and the methodology
allows the effects of changes to the curriculum to be evaluated in
the same way.

*Using knowledge of students' conceptions to assess understanding in
physics*

The second example is from our work in Melbourne[1] on identifying
the key principles and concepts that underlie, and are necessary for,
a complete understanding of important principles in mechanics
such as Newton's laws, relative speed, frames of reference, and
independent components of motion. Traditional physics tests
require students to recall appropriate formulae and apply them to
particular examples; we are concerned with exploring what these
concepts mean to students, and then describing the hierarchical
nature of the different ways of understanding in a way that is useful
to teachers. The different conceptions are organised into a limited
number of ordered outcome categories for a particular problem.
While in the example above, the SOLO categories were used to write
items, the categories in this study are derived from the responses to
the questions. The research team includes subject specialists who are

Table 10.4 A test of understanding in physics, showing assessment categories derived from qualitative analysis of first year students' responses

Problem:
Martha and Arthur are running along a straight road at a constant speed. Arthur is ahead of Martha. Arthur's speed is less than Martha's speed. How far must Martha run before she catches up to Arthur, and how long will this take her?

Response category 3
Students who take this approach solve the problem by focusing on relative speed and relative distance. They focus on the 'gap' as the distance that Martha must run. She closes this gap at the 'catching speed'. The ground is automatically conditioned out of consideration in this approach. This suggests a sophisticated understanding of speed as a relative quantity. Most students in this category will solve the problem using:

$$\text{time to close gap} \quad = \quad \frac{\text{size of gap}}{\text{catching speed}}$$

Response category 2
Students who take this approach consider the motion of each runner separately with respect to the ground. Typically, they set up two separate equations simultaneously; or they may attempt to solve the problem graphically. Almost all students taking this approach understand that Martha and Arthur run for the same time, t, and use this fact in the answer. Some arrive at a solution:

distance Martha runs	=	distance Arthur runs	+	gap
Vm x t	=	Va x t	+	gap

Others fail to solve the problem because they do not incorporate the initial distance between Martha and Arthur.

Response category 1
Students who take this approach focus on the motions of Martha and Arthur separately and, rather than trying to derive a general algebraic or graphical solution, adopt a 'trial-and-error' approach. Typically, they divide the continuous motion into discrete pieces and consider the relative locations of the two runners after a fixed interval of time or after one of them has run a particular distance (Zeno's paradox). This may or may not lead to a solution to the problem; usually, it does not.

Response category 0
Some students display a very unsophisticated understanding of the problem. They may produce one or more equations of motion and attempt to substitute into these equations. They may confuse acceleration and speed, believing that Martha must be accelerating if she is to catch Arthur. They always become lost and are unable to arrive at a solution.

able to verify the hierarchies produced from the point of view of teaching the subject matter.

Some of the tasks we have used involve algebraic and/or numerical manipulations; others involve drawing graphs or pictures. In each case, students have been asked to discuss their answers at length and to justify their conclusions to an interviewer. The discussions are then transcribed and analysed using the approach developed in Gothenburg by Ference Marton to explore students' qualitatively different understandings of a wide variety of phenomena, from elementary number facts to concepts in economics and chemistry. We have also been asking students to complete written versions of the questions, since this will be the form used by teachers when they use the questions to diagnose their students' understandings.

One example of this type of question, and the associated categories, is given in Table 10.4. This study will lead to a collection of different response categories for each question which we will then be able to present to teachers to assist them in examining misunderstandings in their first year physics classes. (The record of inferred levels of conceptual understanding will then be analysed using the Rasch Partial Credit Model mentioned above.) We shall also make suggestions, based on the practices of experienced lecturers, for teaching strategies which might be used to help students to change their conceptions, as well as for ways of combining the responses to produce an estimate of a student's progress for summative purposes.

Readers with a background in this subject might note how, in the example given in Table 10.4, a particularly difficult step in physics teaching seems to be typified in the problem of helping students to change their understanding from seeing relative speed in terms of two separate motions (conceptions 1 and 2) and the more elegant view of conception 3, where the independent motions are subsumed under a general system (see also Ramsden *et al.*, 1991).

FOURTEEN RULES FOR BETTER ASSESSMENT IN HIGHER EDUCATION

1 Link assessment to learning: focus first on learning, second on encouraging effort, and third on grading; assess during the experience of learning as well as at the end of it; set tasks

that mimic realistic problems whenever possible; reward integration and application.

2 Never assess without giving comments to students about how they might improve.

3 Learn from your students' mistakes. Use assessment to discover their misunderstandings, then modify teaching to address them.

4 Deploy a variety of assessment methods.

5 Try to get students participating in the assessment process, through:

- discussions of appropriate methods and how the methods relate to the course goals
- joint staff-student design of assessment questions and negotiation of criteria for success and failure
- self and peer assessment activities
- offering students responsible choice among different methods.

6 Give lucid and frequent messages, both in the assessment questions you set and in your course goals, that memorisation, reproduction, and imitation will be penalised and that success in your courses will only be achieved through decisive demonstrations of understanding.

7 Think about the relation between reporting and feedback; justify on educational grounds either the separation or the combination of the diagnostic and summative functions of a particular test, rather than blindly applying an algorithm such as 'No assessment for feedback should count for a mark' or 'Every assessment should count or students won't bother with it.'

8 Use multiple-choice and other 'objective' tests very cautiously, preferably in combination with other methods. When numbers of students and time permit alternative techniques (see 6 above), use these.

9 In subjects involving quantitative manipulations, always include questions requiring explanations in prose (such as 'What does it mean in this case to say that the standard deviation is 1.8?') as well as numerical examples.

10 Focus on validity (is what you are measuring important?) before reliability (is your test consistent?). Try to avoid the temptation to test trifling aspects because they are easier to measure than important ones.

11 Do everything in your power to lessen the anxiety raised by assessments.

12 'Examinations are formidable even to the best prepared, for the greatest fool may ask more than the wisest man can answer' (Colton). Never set an assignment or examination question you are not ready to answer yourself. Practise the habit of writing model answers to your questions and using them to help students appreciate what you want.

13 Reduce the between-student competitive aspects of assessment while simultaneously providing inducements to succeed against a standard (through using assessments of group products and deriving standards from several cohorts of students, for example).

14 Be suspicious of the objectivity and accuracy of all measures of student ability and conscious that human judgement is the most important element in every indicator of achievement.

CONCLUSION

I hope that the reader will by now appreciate more fully the benefits as well as the problems of the processes by which we assess our students in higher education. Assessment's educational value depends on our understanding of its multiple purposes and how they are related, on our willingness to accept that all judgements about people's performance must involve human error, and on how successfully we integrate the process of making judgements into the job of teaching.

No other aspect of instruction reveals more starkly the essential conception of teaching inherent in a course or in a lecturer's view of the educational process. Much assessment in higher education proceeds from an ingenuous conception focused on methods of collecting information and comparing the relative worth of different students. The other extreme, much less common (but equally naïve) is to think that there should be no attempt to combine the process of teaching with the process of making decisions about progress in an area of learning.

I have been arguing for a view of assessment as being (a) a means of helping students to learn, (b) a way of reporting on student progress, and (c) a way of making decisions about teaching. Functions (a) and (b) are inextricably linked: the two separate worlds of assessment called 'formative' and 'summative' in the assessment manuals do not exist in actuality. There is only one world: in that world, candid diagnosis implies valid judgements about student achievement and appropriate changes to teaching. The connection between diagnosis and judgement is like a one-way street. There can be no truthful reporting or effective changes to teaching in the absence of faithful diagnosis of students' understandings. The belief that getting to know about our students' learning and sharing those findings with them must take priority is an inescapable consequence of a view of teaching as a highly interventionist process whose cardinal aim is to change students' understandings of the world around them.

These reflections on assessment and teaching take us conveniently to the point where the final section of the book, whose concern is with how to evaluate and arrange for the improvement of teaching, can begin. Evaluation of teaching, like the assessment of students, is about learning; while improving teaching, like the improvement of students' learning, is about changes in understanding. Much of what we have learned about assessment is therefore applicable to evaluating teaching.

Part 3

Evaluating and improving the quality of teaching and learning

Chapter 11

Evaluating the quality of higher education

> The sole question is, What sort of conditions will produce the type of faculty which will run a successful university? The danger is that it is quite easy to produce a faculty entirely unfit – a faculty of very efficient pedants and dullards.
>
> (A.N. Whitehead)

In a sense, all this book is about evaluating the quality of education. Evaluation is a means of understanding the effects of our teaching on students' learning. It implies collecting information about our work, interpreting the information, and making judgements about which actions should be taken to improve practice. To reflect on what helps students to understand a concept or argument, and to apply the results to teaching, is to engage in evaluation. To experiment with a new way of assessing students, and to monitor its effects on the quality of their learning, is to engage in evaluation. To listen to a student describing his or her approach to learning a topic is to engage in evaluation. Evaluation is an analytical process that is intrinsic to good teaching.

The case studies of lecturers describing their experiences of teaching in Part 2 showed that good teachers are always evaluating themselves. Later in this chapter we shall look in more detail at some of the evaluation methods that four of these teachers used. Their experiences demonstrate that evaluation is best conceptualised not as something that is done *to* teachers by experts wielding questionnaires and computers, but as something that is done *by* teachers for the benefit of their professional competence and their students' understanding. Evaluating teaching concerns learning to teach better and exercising control over the process of learning to teach better. It is about imaginatively testing out educational ideas in practice. To understand and practise these principles is to put into action our preferred theory of teaching as the cultivation of student learning.

In the first part of the book I tried to show how we might come to understand effective teaching through an exploration of students' experiences of learning in higher education. Good teaching helps students move towards the achievement of high quality learning – the learning that embraces changes in conceptions of subject content, confident facility with the subject's syntax and methods, solid knowledge of its specific details, and a sense of ownership and delight in its practice. We saw how the students' perceptions served to highlight the properties of good teaching and how the quality of teaching itself could be understood in terms of different theories of instruction. The second part of the book attempted to apply the idea of different conceptions of teaching to the improvement of our courses, teaching strategies, and assessment of students. Both these parts were addressed directly to practising individual lecturers and course teams; I hope that some of the practical examples given will encourage others to change their teaching methods so that they more nearly reflect the aim of promoting excellent student learning.

The remaining two chapters take us into a broader and more politically sensitive arena. There are three main issues to bear in mind in any consideration of the evaluation or assessment of teaching in higher education: the nature of good teaching; its measurement; and its promotion. Few discussions of educational quality and the appraisal of academic staff have engaged with these issues other than at the most superficial level. Policies have been formed and are being implemented in apparent ignorance of the accumulated educational knowledge that enables them to be rationally addressed.

We can all agree that teaching should be better, but matters related to the measurement of teaching performance in higher education and the general application of our understanding of teaching to the improvement of its quality rather quickly lead to disagreement and defensiveness. The solution is not for teachers in higher education to hide away from these issues, but to try to understand them in order to take charge of them. We need to know about evaluation both in order to improve our teaching and in order to deal with the politics of being evaluated. Accountability, appraisal, rewards, and performance are topics that are inseparable from learning to teach better.

What I want to try and establish in the last part of the book is simply that the lessons learned about effective teaching from an examination of how students perceive it should be applied to the process of evaluating and improving instruction. Much of what is presently being done to appraise and train academic staff, and to change institutional and departmental contexts in British and Australian higher education, is a long way from this ideal.

EVALUATION AND THE NATURE OF GOOD TEACHING

If we look at what is being said about teacher evaluation and accountability in higher education from the perspective of this book, we see a collection of curious paradoxes. On the one hand, there are constant reminders that higher education is expensive and that the quality of teaching and academic standards needs to be evaluated and improved. Both the United Kingdom and the Australian White Papers on higher education argued that accountability demanded the development of systematic procedures for evaluating the quality of higher education, including arrangements for appraising academic staff, obtaining feedback from students, and monitoring student achievements. Yet on the other hand, few of the public pronouncements and hardly any of the schemes for evaluating teaching performance that have actually been instituted make any reference to the fundamental characteristics underpinning the measurement of the quality of teaching, courses, and institutions. While the criteria sometimes include imprecise references to the maintenance of academic standards and to students' 'skills in communication and numeracy' and 'employment patterns' (see, for example, DES, 1987), the concept of good teaching and descriptions of the mechanisms by which it might improve student learning are often left quite unexamined. Much more space and effort is devoted to measures and exhortations to measure than to what is being measured. The goals of improvement have to be guessed from the tests that purport to indicate their achievement.

There is an exact parallel between this approach to measuring teaching quality and unsatisfactory ways of assessing students.

Methods of student assessment should always be secondary to the vital preliminary question: What do we want our students to know (about the subject)? The equivalent question in the case of academic staff is: What do we want our teachers to know (about teaching their subjects)? Evaluation which will really improve teaching quality must follow similar principles to assessment which will genuinely help students to learn. The potential of the present approach to encourage mediocrity, foster brooding resentment, and dampen the desire to excel will be apparent to readers who have followed my arguments about the relation between educational goals, assessment, and learning.

At the other extreme, many academic staff still appear convinced that the quality of higher education teaching cannot be gauged. As we saw in chapter 6, there is a widely held myth that teaching quality is a many-sided, elusive, and ultimately indefinable phenomenon. The dogma runs along the lines that teaching varies too much across different subject areas to be tied down, is too dependent on fallible human judgement, is too quirky for meaningful quality comparisons, alters in standard depending on the ability of the students, is too subjective, and is ambiguous in its definition (is helping students good or is it 'spoon feeding' and therefore bad?). Beliefs of this kind, which form part of traditional academic orthodoxy, have led several commentators to doubt whether unambiguous measures of teaching performance in higher education could ever be devised (see, for example, Smith, 1988; Cave *et al.*, 1988).

The myth that university teaching is so idiosyncratic a matter that its nature cannot be defined may be a mistaken one, but it serves a useful function. If a function cannot be specified, it is easier to resist pressures to judge whether it is being adequately performed. Stripped down, this argument against measuring teaching is based on little more than the idea that you cannot hit a moving target. It is about as reasonable. In the light of what was said in previous chapters, we can see that it rests on a convenient misunderstanding, based on lack of background knowledge, about learning and teaching in higher education. We know what good university teaching is. We know that staff and students agree on what it is (see chapter 6). We know how it helps students to learn, in many different subject areas. It is certain that good teaching is complicated and that it is a very individual, content-related, and delicately balanced matter. It would be improper to inflict on academic staff a narrow definition, based on certain standard criteria, that left no room for the many different ways in which teachers can teach well. We nevertheless know enough to distinguish the existence of good teaching *within* these individual styles and subject variations. This means it is possible to evaluate the extent to which effective teaching is going on, and to use the results to help improve the quality of instruction. This is true especially at the level of the department (or course) but it also applies, with a wider margin of possible error, at the level of the individual member of staff.

In summary, there are degrees of freedom in good teaching; but it exists, nevertheless. To reach the goal of useful evaluation – evaluation that actually helps teachers to do their jobs better – involves some careful steering. One trap comes in thinking that defining it will remove our autonomy. The other trap comes in thinking that even if we are not really sure what we are trying to measure, we ought to grade it anyway. I hope to show how we can shape a course past both pitfalls.

WAYS OF UNDERSTANDING EVALUATION IN HIGHER EDUCATION

Every recommendation about teaching evaluation and performance measurement made in this chapter can be derived from the propositions about successful course aims, teaching strategies, and student assessment that were contained in previous parts of the book.

A highly developed understanding of evaluation corresponds to what I have previously called a theory 3 way of looking at teaching. It maintains that changes in our understanding of teaching are fundamental, and that the achievement of high standards of instruction requires a self-critical attitude, one which regards constant improvement as both natural and necessary. Skilled teaching involves the application of understanding in real situations, and embraces a variety of carefully chosen and constantly updated techniques. The ultimate guardians of excellence are not external forces, but internal professional responsibilities. This is an optimistic and relativistic theory of evaluation.

Simpler theories, in contrast, are based on ideas of absolute standards, knowledge as a quantity, and a more pessimistic view of the human potential for change. They start from the premise that teachers and courses are deficient. Academic staff lack some essential components of instructional effectiveness; and they should be placed under close supervision until they have acquired these missing parts. Hierarchy, competition, and external control will lead them to become motivated to add the skills and the knowledge to their repertoires.

The central issue to be faced now can be seen to be similar to those considered in Part 2: how can we apply a complex theory of evaluation to the processes of measuring academic performance, both for diagnostic and for summative purposes? Can we show that we are accountable while at the same time not reducing the quality of teaching?

Figure 11.1 summarises some of the important theoretical distinctions that need to be understood in order to grasp the rather complicated arguments of this chapter. Evaluation may be conceptualised along two dimensions. The first concerns levels of aggregation, shading from the evaluation of an individual lecturer's teaching through to the evaluation of courses, departments, programmes of study, and institutions. The second dimension is to do with the major purpose and the originator of the evaluation, ranging from the idea of evaluation as driven by the teacher who wants to improve his or her teaching to the idea of evaluation as the external assessment of teaching performance (with or without the underlying intention of improvement). This scheme may be illustrated by four examples: the evaluation of teaching by teachers; the evaluation of courses by teachers; the performance appraisal of individual staff; and the measurement of a department's teaching performance. These distinctions should be useful in following the discussion, even though the lines between them are permeable.

I now wish to look in turn at the assessment of teaching performance (with special reference to appraisal and performance indicators) and at the process of evaluation by teachers. For reasons to do with the politics of performance assessment it will be appropriate to consider these processes separately, although, as I have suggested in the previous paragraph, there are numerous points of contact between them. As with student assessment, the issue is not a simple one of reporting versus diagnosis. A crucial difference to bear in mind is between priorities in ways of thinking about evaluation – either as

Figure 11.1 Two dimensions of evaluation in higher education

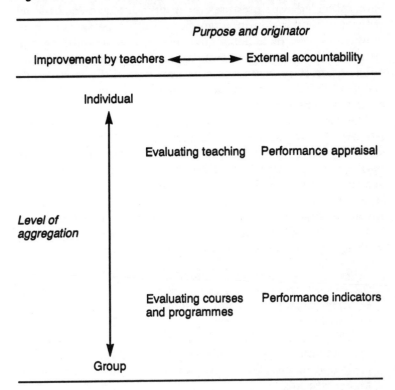

a means first and foremost of assisting the professional process of improvement, and secondarily about making decisions concerning worth, or the other way around. It is equally essential to realise that the measurement of teaching performance takes on a very different aspect when it is focused on competition for a small number of prizes than when it is seen in the light of a cooperative search for excellence.

ACCOUNTABILITY AND THE MEASUREMENT OF TEACHING PERFORMANCE

Performance appraisal of academic staff: the theory

The requirement for institutions of higher education in Australia and the United Kingdom to give a formal account of themselves to the governments that pay for them is a fairly recent phenomenon. Demands for increased efficiency and effectiveness have coincided with pressures on institutions to meet national goals of economic growth, a significant shift in power away from universities towards national government, and diminishing real resources. Attempts to redirect higher education towards more public types of evaluation have become one of the more visible features of the higher education scene in Britain and Australia during the past few years.

The profound effects of these changes on research and scholarship have been widely discussed, but their influence on teaching, though less publicised, has been prodigious. One of the ways in which institutions have responded to accountability demands is the introduction of formal systems of performance appraisal and staff training. Appraisal systems were enthusiastically endorsed in both the UK and Australian White Papers of 1987 and 1988 as preferred methods for enhancing the quality of teaching. In the confident words of the UK document:

> Systematic staff appraisal . . . makes it possible to identify both the success of individuals in contributing to the achievement of these [departmental and institutional] goals and the needs of individuals for guidance and training. Such appraisal is widely accepted in the public and private sectors, both for its contributions to personal development and for its usefulness to management. The principles are equally applicable to higher education.
>
> (DES, 1987)

It is important to understand that two quite different goals are enshrined in the rhetoric of performance appraisal of teaching in higher education. The first is the idea of evaluation as development: the positive and constructive identification of a person's needs in the area of improving teaching, the provision of feedback on teaching performance, and assistance with improvement so that effectiveness is increased. The second goal is the control of the system's personnel so that they become accountable for increased efficiency and effectiveness. Both national governments' strong belief in the idea of competitive market forces as vectors of change is evident in the supporting argument that the incentives for good teaching which follow from systematic appraisal will lead to healthy rivalry between individual members of staff and, in turn, to a higher quality teaching product. (Teachers who understand the principles of effective student assessment will immediately see the flaw in this argument.)

The combination of these goals has an irresistible political appeal. There is a public perception that much money is being expended on systems of education – at all levels – and that no checking or review of how that money is being used exists. In this context, the letters to an MP from a disgruntled constituent or two complaining about the standard of their children's university lectures take on immense and disproportionate importance. Few politicians will be able to resist an opportunity to argue for more efficient use of resources by penalising the indolent lecturer and rewarding the diligent one. This, it is asserted, will motivate all academic staff to try harder, to produce more excellence, so that our scarce resources are better spent.

So entrenched in popular thinking have these assertions become that lecturers who would discuss the *principles* of staff appraisal are considered to be brave men and women. The discussion is now entirely about *method*. Back in 1986, John Nisbet maintained that in the United Kingdom:

> To question the principle of staff appraisal in the present climate of opinion is likely to be seen as unrealistic. The common attitude is that appraisal is coming whether we like it or not; it is only a question of how and how soon, not whether or why. Consequently, so the argument runs, let us introduce our own scheme before a worse one is forced upon us.
>
> (Nisbet, 1986, p. 91).

People who wear an astonished air to greet criticisms of performance appraisal are right, up to a point. There is no rational defence against the accountability argument. The position that public support will depend on demonstrating accountability is unassailable. But the argument that appraisal will improve the effectiveness of teaching and enhance learning can be addressed logically.

The proposition that appraisal will improve university and polytechnic teaching is exactly analogous to the argument that a statutory curriculum and national testing of school students' performance will lead to higher standards of student attainment. It is a hypothesis to be tested; it is one proposition among many (Hartnett and Naish, 1990, p. 5). The effectiveness of performance appraisal as a method of enhancing teaching quality in higher education has not, however, been presented as a hypothesis to be tested. It has simply been asserted as a self-evident truth.

The validity of the proposition is by no means indisputable. The two goals of improved quality and greater accountability are not as effortlessly compatible as the publicity for appraisal would have us believe. The first is in practice being completely ousted by the second, for reasons which are predictable from theories of unintended consequences in social systems (see Elton, 1988). The desired primary change, greater political accountability, has led to a reverberation through the system which has actually made the achievement of the other goal, improved quality, more difficult.

Why is this happening? The main reason concerns perceptions of reward and support systems. Once again, the mechanism in question corresponds to the effect of certain teaching and assessment methods on student learning. We find ourselves returning full circle to Sawyer's idea of imitation subjects, which we met earlier in the book. This time, though, it applies to us as lecturers and to the improvement of our teaching. In other words, academic staff are likely to act as their students do when they perceive an assessment system to be inappropriate: they will learn to perform certain tricks in order to pass examinations in subjects they do not understand. They will not become qualified to teach better, but to hide their inefficiencies better. If scoring well is important in either performance appraisal of teaching or the assessment of learning, both staff and students understandably shift their attention towards activities that tend to maximise their scores. Unless the measure is highly accurate, and is so perceived, we soon reach the paradoxical situation where 'success' is bought at the cost of doing *without* the very thing that success is supposed to measure. As we shall see, there is no room for confidence that the measures of teaching being used in performance appraisal are highly accurate; quite the contrary, in fact.

Many institutions have moved towards appraisal methods that focus on institutional productivity and administrative convenience, express the role of academic staff in terms of standard criteria, and define the key problem as being the identification and remediation of deficiencies in teaching performance. This approach enables organisations to demonstrate apparent accountability ('We have instituted formal procedures for monitoring staff performance and deal with performance problems') at the lowest cost and with the least administrative inconvenience to themselves, but it is inconsistent with the ways academics improve their skills and knowledge (see Lonsdale, 1990). Most of our motivation to improve comes from within, and we have a healthy disdain for bureaucratic fiat.

Appraisal, like the assessment of students, can become a ritual which divides academic staff and prevents them from learning from each other. It diminishes their desire to cooperate in increasing the effectiveness of teaching through collegial procedures. This is especially likely in conditions where rivalry and incentives are built into appraisal systems. The price of rewarding 'high performers' (and punishing the poor performers) is likely to be a decrease in mutual support and openness to admitting failure, and a consequent net decrease in teaching quality. Academic staff motivation in particular is increased only to a limited extent by competition, and beyond a certain point external rewards and punishments create strong adverse reactions among teachers in higher education. Extrinsic incentive schemes (bonuses, prizes, and so on) are nevertheless attractive to management because they appear to maximise their control over staff (see Pollitt, 1987).

Performance appraisal of academic staff: the reality

So much for the theory. What of the demonstrated effectiveness of performance appraisal? There is no empirical evidence of a positive link between academic staff appraisal and better teaching in higher education. It is not that evidence of the connections is inconclusive; there is none, at least not in Britain and Australia. There is empirical evidence that performance appraisal in other organisations which is perceived to be punitive and associated with extrinsic rewards leads to lower outputs and dissatisfied staff (Pollitt, 1987). Blackburn and Pitney's review of appraisal in American institutions, undertaken for the National Center for Research to Improve Postsecondary Teaching and Learning at Michigan State University, came to a similar conclusion:

> The literature shows that most current systems of performance appraisal or evaluation do not lead to improved performance. It does show, however, that performance appraisals *can be*

dysfunctional, lead to reduced productivity, and create morale problems. The outcomes of performance appraisal have a significant, often negative impact on the climate of the organisation and the commitment of its employees.

(Blackburn and Pitney, 1988, quoted in Lonsdale, 1990, p. 94)

Perceptions of appraisal as a restrictive and time-wasting administrative procedure, essentially punitive in character, are probably the most common ones among staff in higher education institutions, at any rate in the ones I have had recent contact with. Many people feel genuinely threatened, even when efforts are made to present the process as a benign and non-judgemental one. Often these are more junior staff, on probation, who are easier targets for heads of departments who have been told to wield the big stick about teaching. They feel they are being required to compete against others in a zero-sum game whose rules change to fit the prejudices of the referee. In Australian universities, several acrimonious disputes between staff associations and institutional management over the introduction of appraisal have done nothing to reduce the sense of anxiety.

I hope that the reason why I have been hard on teacher appraisal in higher education is clear. It is chiefly because it embodies a seriously flawed understanding of the essentials of teaching and learning. Improving teaching, as I have asserted several times, implies that lecturers must learn. To help people learn, we must try to arouse their imagination. The advocates of academic performance appraisal seem to be saying that teachers who know they are going to be appraised will feel an obligation to acquire teaching skills. The theory of learning underlying this position is precisely the one that informs so much bad teaching: that motivational sticks and carrots should be employed to force people to learn things which appear to them as a series of meaningless signs and rules. The logical outcome of this process of imitation teacher learning, entirely predictable from the studies of student learning we have met in earlier chapters, will be to reinforce naïve theories of teaching – in particular the view that teaching in higher education essentially involves no more than the acquisition and deployment of rules of instruction that will enable the lecturer's knowledge to be transferred to students.

It is important that we should realise that the valid assessment of teaching performance, like the measurement of *anything*, requires the interpretation of information that has been collected in a way that minimises mistakes. It is then necessary to understand something else – that there will still be a margin of error surrounding the measure, however carefully the data are collected. Moreover, expressing results in a numerical form can in no circumstances reduce the need to interpret the data and to appreciate the implications of this area of uncertainty. Ignoring these basic rules has led to some extraordinarily inappropriate uses of methods of assessing lecturers' teaching performance – especially student rating questionnaires.

For this reason, I now want to look carefully at the idea of using student ratings as a means of measuring staff performance. They have taken on a sort of magical objectivity in teacher appraisal in higher education, presumably due to their administrative convenience. Unlike most measures of teaching quality, they provide numbers which apparently enable different teachers to be compared with each other, and they thus have a superficial resemblance to familiar research output criteria such as numbers of refereed articles published and research grants awarded.

The strange lure of the student rating instrument

The theory of teaching and learning underlying performance appraisal of teaching is nowhere better represented than in the extraordinary belief it professes in the powers of student rating questionnaires. The strength of this entirely misplaced belief vies for educational naïvety with the conception of assessment as a process of discovering the absolute truth about a student's ability through a three-hour examination at the end of a programme of study. I say this from a personal position of commitment to student feedback as the most vital source of information about how to improve teaching, as someone who believes that student ratings can be used both for judgemental and diagnostic purposes, and after having been involved in developing and testing a student rating instrument (the CEQ, described in earlier chapters) that might be used nationally for measuring the performance of academic departments. Students are in an excellent position to provide information about the quality of instruction. Valid methods of collecting such data exist; these methods should be used. It is wise to be circumspect about using student ratings to make judgements on teaching quality and to recognise their complications as well as their virtues.

These views seem unremarkable enough. They make no claim

to originality, and they are consistent with research findings and with the best practice in North America. Why, then, do they have to be restated here? Because, unfortunately, they cut right across common-sense perceptions of evaluation and staff appraisal in the United Kingdom and Australia. The use of questionnaires to assess staff performance is taking on an importance altogether surprising. Student rating questionnaires are seen to fulfil an irresistibly attractive combination of purposes. They have become the heaven-sent gadget that will improve teaching performance. Importantly, they are perceived to be a talisman that will guard against accusations that universities are not accountable; they provide the outside world with evidence that we are doing something about teaching. For some senior staff, it would appear that they *are* appraisal. Questionnaires are thought to be attractive for their objectivity; they are seen to be easy to distribute, collect, and process (and therefore cheap); they are perceived to be an opportunity to sort out the academic wheat from the chaff.

That these perceptions are incorrect or at best misleading would soon be seen by anyone who took the trouble to study the student ratings literature. The uses and misuses of student rating questionnaires have been described in detail elsewhere (Ramsden and Dodds, 1989). As most of what was said in that book was based on easily accessible published information anyway, there seems little hope of convincing the doubters by repeating it all over again. The present remarks refer to the excellent reviews by Centra (1980) and McKeachie (1983), among other things. It should be clearly understood from the beginning that there is no fair way of using student ratings for appraisal or performance measurement of teachers without going in for a sizeable investment. There is no short-cut; once in, rigorous standards must be applied and maintained.

Validity and objectivity

There is nothing intrinsically valid about something that has numbers attached to it. An apple with a price tag on it is not necessarily a better apple, nor does it provide a less subjective eating experience. It sometimes seems as if members of academic staff trained in (for example) the exact sciences or the precision of legal argument instantly forget their knowledge when it comes to applying measurement in educational settings. Maybe education is thought to be too soft a subject to require the strictures of scientific method. Or perhaps they simply have a misplaced notion of what constitutes objectivity in education. Many of the student questionnaire advocates could do worse than to read and digest Peter Medawar's eloquently expressed views on the contrast between the natural sciences and the 'unnatural sciences':

> It will at once be recognized as a distinguishing mark of the latter that their practitioners try most painstakingly to imitate what they believe – quite wrongly, alas for them – to be the distinctive manners and observances of the natural sciences. Among these are:
> (a) the belief that measurement and numeration are intrinsically praiseworthy activities (the worship, indeed, of what Ernst Gombrich calls *idola quantitatis*);
> (b) the whole discredited farrago of inductivism – especially the belief that *facts* are prior to ideas and that a sufficiently voluminous compilation of facts can be processed by a calculus of discovery in such a way as to yield general principles and natural-seeming laws;
> (c) another distinguishing mark of unnatural scientists is their faith in the efficacy of statistical formulas, particularly when processed by a computer – the use of which is in itself interpreted as a mark of scientific manhood. There is no need to cause offense by specifying the unnatural sciences, for their practitioners will recognize themselves easily; the shoe belongs where it fits.
>
> (Medawar, 1977)

Using student ratings for appraisal requires special controls

The best short description of the validity standards that must be met is by Scriven (1987). They are stringent. There can certainly be no question of using results collected by lecturers themselves, which form of collection is the best way of using questionnaires for diagnostic purposes. A sufficient and representative sample of students from each class must respond, the forms must be distributed and collected under specially prescribed conditions at particular times, ratings over several courses over a period of time are required, and ratings must be collected on every member of staff. As far as I am aware, none of the Australian and British systems conform to these criteria.

Using student ratings for appraisal will cost money

For the reasons given above, a special corps of evaluators will be needed to collect and process the data, to guard against the potential invalidity introduced by the incentive to fake good results, to collect data from other sources, and to correlate these sets of data. Whatever else it may be, any appraisal system has to be fair and be seen to be fair. Student ratings alone must never be used for appraisal: as Centra puts it, 'The evidence clearly indicates that no one method of evaluating teaching is infallible for making personnel decisions. Each source is subject to contamination, whether it be possible bias, poor reliability or limited objectives' (Centra, 1980).

Using student ratings to identify the worst teachers is probably a waste of time and money

We know the answer to the question of who the worst teachers are. Although there may be some circumstances when it is advisable to use student opinion to test whether a teacher is meeting minimum standards of responsible professional behaviour, this is not in fact how ratings are currently being used. They are being used as a way of bullying people. No one is going to be frightened into becoming a better teacher by the threat of student-ratings (most of the lecturers I have seen who have been subjected to this technique have become less confident of their ability to improve). Typically, the numbers from student questionnaires are used by heads of departments to clothe with mystique and ceremony decisions they have already made. Their time would more profitably be spent in counselling and in working out redeployment strategies. This time will still have to be spent anyway.

Collecting data isn't the same thing as improving or judging teaching

This may seem the most obvious point of all, but it is very generally ignored. There is no way to process data to yield decisions about teaching, or anything else (see Medawar, point (b) above). The evidence on improvement (Centra, 1980, p. 176) clearly indicates that teachers who change as a result of student ratings are those who already place a fairly high value on student opinion. This is not surprising; but its implications are important. It cuts away one of the main supports of the argument for institution-wide systems of student rating questionnaires. Voluntary, quasi-voluntary, or compulsory use of diagnostic questionnaires is unlikely to encourage change in teachers who do not take student views seriously. Lecturers who feel anxious about their teaching – perhaps because they feel under pressure to do it better, perhaps because they know they do it badly – are the least likely to change. Evaluation of teaching is often seen as an end in itself by administrators; this is consistent with the accountability rationale for appraisal. But no amount of measurement of teaching will make teaching better. If the aim of evaluation really is the improvement of teaching, then in some cases less evaluation would lead to better student learning (McKeachie, 1983).

Staff development personnel aren't necessarily able to distinguish valid questionnaires (and methods of data collection) from invalid ones

Most institutions now possess at least one person, and often several people, whose task is to help staff improve their teaching. I shall say more about their role in the next chapter. This problem is a delicate issue of professional standards. There are many invalid questionnaires and questionnaire items devised by, or issued with the knowledge of, educational development staff in regular use for making personnel decisions. It would be invidious to quote instances here; Medawar's final sentence in the extract on p. 231 is apposite. The most common errors are to ask face-invalid questions (such as those that students do not have the information to answer, or which are irrelevant to teaching performance); to conflate stylistic and quality measures; to equate the collection of student ratings for personnel purposes with their use for diagnostic feedback (different questions are appropriate for each purpose); to become seduced by the illusory power that databanks and numbers offer; and simply to forget that the primary purpose of using questionnaires is to improve teaching. They are a means, not an end.

Measuring performance

Staff appraisal in higher education is impelled by a perception among certain administrators that individual academics are slow to change and will not change unless they are required to face formal sanctions and are tempted by explicit incentives. As Pollitt (1987, p. 94) so accurately describes it, this conception implicitly emphasises hierarchy, competition for rewards, and the 'right to manage'; it assumes that there are dormant aspirations for higher performance that will be evoked through the extrinsic pressures that management strives to create. Most teachers in higher education will regard this model, which evidently informs the 1987 White Paper's attitude to appraisal, as impractical and disagreeable. It is also faintly risible, despite the seriousness of the issue. The vision of scholars working harder to win cash bonuses at the end of the term has a surreal, Monty Pythonesque quality.

Now there is no reason in theory why individuals' teaching performance cannot be assessed in a way that avoids these objectionable ideological overtones. We might start with minimum standards of acceptable professional behaviour; failure to reach these would invoke sanctions beginning with a requirement to seek assistance and ending, if necessary, with dismissal. These duties-based standards (cf. Scriven, 1987; Andreson, Powell, and Smith, 1987) would comprise satisfactory answers to such questions as:

1 Is the teacher *ever* available to see students out of class?
2 Are his/her assessment procedures (a) fair and (b) valid?
3 Does he/she skip teaching duties without an excuse?
4 Does he/she *ever* explain the requirements of his/her courses and their assessment to students?
5 Does he/she provide *any* feedback on assessment?
6 Is the academic quality of the content satisfactory?
7 Does the teacher adopt a professional attitude to teaching (e.g. regular attendance, efforts to improve, responses to negative feedback)?
8 Does he/she *ever* assist in course development, examining, taking other academic's duties if instructed to do so?

The danger with all minimum standards is that they become the average standard, through the by-now-familiar mechanism of the perceptions of those who are being assessed. Why strive to do better if you are already meeting these criteria? Why not ease up a little, putting more time into research, perhaps, if you are exceeding them? Thus the aggregate standard of performance may be depressed at the same time as its variability is reduced. So a second tier of assessment, for more than minimum standards (for promotion, say), has to be established. Criteria such as student perceptions of a teacher's concern for them and the quality of his or her comments on their work might be assessed using properly controlled summative ratings. Self-assessment of teaching innovations, courses designed, commitment to teaching, interest in finding out about students' understanding and applying the results, and willingness to act on the results of student feedback are other appropriate sources of evidence, as are annual reports by superiors. Reports on classroom teaching performance by highly skilled educators (not peers or superiors, even if they are trained) might also be included. Judgements based on this information would need to be formed by committees who had educated themselves very thoroughly in the fundamentals of good teaching in several disciplines. This process of learning would be greatly helped if we, as teachers, became more informed about the nature of good teaching and presented information to promotion committees which focused on our efforts to actualise these principles.

All this is fine in theory: the problem is that, as far as I am aware, no UK or Australian institution is doing it, though some are experimenting with the minimum standards approach as a way of showing accountability, and some are trying to encourage staff to apply for promotion on the grounds of teaching excellence. But many have fallen back on invalid criteria and/or sources of data, in particular defective student rating systems whose use has negative side-effects on the majority of teaching staff. It would seem that institutions do not think it worth the expense and effort to adopt more than a token approach to the business of assessing a teacher's performance. Practical considerations are on their side: first, as I have indicated, it would certainly be expensive to run defensible student rating schemes; second, there are very few times in a lecturer's career when promotion is in sight; third, few promotions committees are likely to be persuaded that they need to learn a lot about the nature of good teaching; and fourth, as long as research and scholarship remain dominant pursuits in all higher education institutions – which seems inevitable unless a much more rigidly stratified system such as that of the US is adopted – the reality will always be that teaching performance as a means of gaining promotion will take a subsidiary role.

All things considered, valid and fair teacher assessment beyond minimum standards seems at present too remote to be a realistic option for improving teaching in Australian and UK higher education. Whether minimum standards will reduce or enhance aggregate performance remains to be seen. But it is worth reminding ourselves of the ungenerous limits of any approach to enhancing the quality of teaching and learning that is based on extrinsic rewards and punishments. Evaluation should be focused on good teaching – not on assessing teachers. Ultimately, effective teaching is not about promotions and salary increases, but about the pleasures associated with helping students to learn. The effects of reward systems on teaching quality will be considered in chapter 12.

Performance indicators of teaching

So far I have talked about performance appraisal and measuring the teaching ability of members of academic staff. There is however another side to the accountability, efficiency, and effectiveness issue, which is concerned with the performance of institutions and their component units (such as academic departments) (see Figure 11.1). It is useful to understand this distinction between performance indicators (PIs), which are quantitative measures at aggregate level typically associated with decisions about resource allocation (e.g. the UGC and UFC research selectivity exercises); and staff performance appraisal, which is focused on individual academics. One starts from an economic paradigm; the other from a managerial one. PIs derive from the same pressures for accountability as staff appraisal, and, like appraisal, share many of the same potentially dysfunctional consequences. As we have seen, the single most serious negative consequence of the use of any method for assessing quality in higher education is that the measure may become the definition of success. People search for ways of getting high scores on the index of quality and neglect underlying educational goals. Particularly if the index is invalid or partial, this process tends to trivialise the process of improvement, damage morale, and lead to a distortion of the educational system.

Something like this has already happened with the use of PIs in the UK university system. Most discussions, and most applications, of PIs to higher education have been concerned with research performance. The stress on research to the exclusion of teaching (and related functions of higher education, such as the maintenance of values associated with tolerance and diversity, and service to the community) appears to be leading to the predictable consequence of a shift in effort from teaching to research (see Elton, 1988, p. 382). It is of great importance that all PIs, like any other measure of teaching standards, should be derived from clear statements about the nature of the quality they are supposed to measure, and that they express the broad range of goals of the institutions and departments to which they are applied.

Unfortunately the proposed measures of teaching quality at aggregate level mostly do not fulfil these criteria; they possess quite significant problems, including potentially undesirable side-effects, technical difficulties, narrowness, and logical inconsistencies. 'Value added', for instance (a measure of the difference between students' achievement at the beginning of a programme of study and their achievement at the end), appears at first sight to be an elegant solution, but it faces severe practical and moral difficulties. The practical problems relate to the lack of uniformity between institutions in measures of student achievement at entry and exit. The consequent need for special tests leads to further obstacles: the ethical and resource implications of requiring students to sit examinations whose ultimate purpose is to measure their teachers' performance, not their own achievement (Warnock, 1989; Pollitt, 1990); and the possible distortion of the curriculum due to the incentives for manipulation ('teaching to the test') that such value-added tests would offer. The oversimplified view of the teaching and learning relationship that this input–output model implies is also a cause of difficulty. Is it possible to assess every important educational outcome by measuring the final product of the process? Changing people's understanding is qualitatively different from changing malt into beer or collections of metal and plastic into computers. And to what extent is it just to blame or praise teachers for something which is ultimately their students' responsibility?

'Wastage' and completion rates have also been suggested as PIs; yet while they are superficially simple and easy to collect, they are determined by many factors other than teaching performance. Moreover, using them as PIs might detract from educational quality through imposing irresistible pressures on departments to lower standards. Student employment destinations, another putative measure, would require politically sensitive judgements about the comparative social value of different courses. Peer ratings of teaching performance, perhaps? They are highly susceptible to prejudice and are often inaccurate. Academics typically have scanty and biased knowledge of the teaching abilities of their colleagues in other institutions; they are likely to rate a department's teaching effectiveness using their knowledge of its research standards.

Judged against these difficulties with other measures of teaching quality, a PI based on students' evaluations of the quality of teaching – a direct measure of consumer satisfaction with higher education – appears to be an appealing option. It is neither practicable nor necessary to use student ratings of individual teachers, although many discussions of measures of satisfaction have assumed that it is. Because PIs are essentially about the performance of aggregates (departments rather than their individual members), an instrument designed to yield valid data at aggregate level is required.

The Course Experience Questionnaire, to which I have already referred several times in this book (see especially chapter 6), was intended to fulfil this function. Its national trial in Australian institutions (Ramsden, 1991b) showed that it was quite successful in its coverage, general applicability, freedom from manipulation, and economy of administration. The CEQ yielded results that clearly differentiated between student perceptions of academic units at several levels of aggregation (departments, faculties, and broad fields of study). Different departments teaching the same subject could be distinguished from each other in terms of student perceptions of the effectiveness of their teaching, and the results correlated well with other measures, such as interviews and graduates' perceptions. The questionnaire used is shown in the Appendix. It is certainly an imperfect way of measuring teaching performance (it is, for example, so designed that it takes no account of differences in teaching methods in different disciplines; and it ignores aspects of teaching not observed by students) but it has advantages over the existing alternatives.

This PI is by no means free from technical problems, especially of ensuring a sufficiently representative response from students in particular courses and programmes, of dealing with service courses, and generally of linking course-level data to academic departments. It is doubtful whether its results could be used fairly for resource allocation purposes, especially in the absence of other valid teaching PI data, but there are other important functions which it seems it could adequately fulfil – as long as we remember the maxim that evaluation ought to be about better learning and teaching, not assessing teachers. These functions are not about management of the system through incentives and sanctions but about professional improvement and better consumer choice. First, the CEQ results could provide feedback to institutions on the performance of its departments, in terms of the several dimensions of effective teaching included in the CEQ, relative to equivalent departments in other institutions. Absolute scores, in the form of percentage agreements with the scale items, could also be given; the knowledge that only 5 per cent of students in a programme of study agreed with a statement such as 'Our lecturers are extremely good at explaining things to us' (an item from the CEQ's 'Good Teaching' scale) might be regarded as worth having. Each institution could then examine the reasons why particular units are poorly or highly rated, and consider through normal collegial processes the remedial action that would be required to remedy perceived imperfections in teaching.

The second use of the results would be to help potential clients – intending students – to make informed choices about institutions. If this information were combined with other teaching PIs, such as wastage and value-added data, we might hope to see greater public awareness of the differences between teaching quality in institutions of higher education, and, perhaps, some market-led diversion of resources away from prestigious research departments which provide poor quality undergraduate teaching towards those departments, distinguished or not, where teaching is taken more seriously. Although it is usual to think that excellent teaching and high research output go hand in hand, the connection is by no means inevitable, as differences in the relative quality of polytechnic and university teaching in several subject areas suggest (see Ramsden, 1983). A very noticeable finding in the Australian PI study was that numerous departments which had high research reputations were rated poorly by their undergraduate students.

Performance assessment of teaching: some conclusions

Few teachers in higher education will believe that performance indicators and academic staff assessment have been created with their welfare in mind. Attitudes to both are undoubtedly unwelcoming (see Thomas, 1989; Pollitt, 1990). They are seen to be chiefly about accountability to central government, and they serve its interests; they are also about a general shift of academic power to the centre, and so they accommodate the interests of academic executives who see themselves as corporate managers (see Elton, 1988). However, we shall have to live with accountability; I do not think we can long survive if we take the extreme position that *any* formal criteria of performance are such threats to academic freedom that we should have nothing at all to do with them, either for measuring teaching or research. But living with accountability does not mean accepting all its manifestations. Nor does it mean adopting the view that outside pressures are necessary and desirable conditions for improving teaching, as some educators seem to have done.

I have tried to suggest our best strategy for dealing with teaching accountability pressures to our advantage. This is to challenge with great firmness the validity of appraisal (which has, in practice, next to nothing to do with improving instruction), to adopt a wary attitude to attempts to assess the teaching performance of individual academic staff (which in theory are possible but in their implementation mostly invalid, and would probably not improve teaching even if they were more accurate), and to make the best of performance indicators of teaching. These last at least have some potential for helping us to do our jobs better and for helping our clients to receive better consideration. Using student ratings like this also happens to be potentially fairer and less threatening to individual members of staff, particularly junior ones. In the next chapter I suggest some alternatives to appraisal as a means of better academic management.

EVALUATING THE QUALITY OF TEACHING AND COURSES

> Evaluation is often viewed as a test of effectiveness – of materials, teaching methods, or whatnot – but this is the least important aspect of it. The most important is to provide intelligence on how to improve these things.
>
> (Bruner, 1966, p. 165)

It is now appropriate to move our attention to what we might do as teachers in higher education to evaluate the quality of our own work, with the overriding aim of improving the quality of student learning. The fact that a theory 3 way of understanding teaching defines evaluation as being about the process of making teaching better cannot be overemphasised. Evaluation is not at heart about collecting evidence to justify oneself, nor about measuring the relative worth of courses or teachers. It is about coming to understand teaching in order to improve student learning.

From this point of view, then, the comparative and classifying aspects of evaluation represented by the various forms of performance assessment ought to be secondary to its major purpose of helping lecturers to learn how to teach better. The following premises, whose educational basis will be familiar from previous chapters, should apply:

1 Evaluation implies finding out how students and others (including yourself) see your teaching and courses.
2 It requires the collection of evidence from several sources. These sources must always include the students, who are in a unique position to comment on teaching.
3 It involves the *interpretation* of this evidence prior to action being taken. The quality of this interpretive process is critically important to the success of the subsequent measures.
4 Although it is always satisfying to observe positive results, the main focus of evaluation should be on identifying problems rather than proving that something works. It is best seen as a kind of intellectually curious activity, almost a form of research, seeking to disprove hypotheses about the effects of teaching on students' learning and to establish fresh ones.
5 Evaluation is part of our responsibility as teachers towards our students. We should take the major role. We might ask for assistance from external experts, but we should never let ourselves be dominated by them.
6 Evaluation is a continuous and continuing process. It should occur before a course, during it, and after it. Evaluation on the first two occasions is generally more important than on the third. Certainly, evaluation at the end of a course cannot replace evaluation during it.
7 Evaluation is often better if it is a cooperative activity which permits teachers to learn from one another.
8 All evaluation methods, if they are to help teachers to learn, should seek to minimise the threat occasioned by a display of their strengths and weaknesses.
9 The techniques of collecting evidence are less important than the motivation for evaluative activity and one's understanding of these principles.

All these ideas follow naturally from our understanding of effective teaching and assessment. They embody a professional development approach to evaluation in higher education – one which emphasises cooperation, self-monitoring, intrinsic rewards, and egalitarianism. It will be clear that these standards are not easily combined with a process of performance appraisal linked to rewards and punishments.

One way of concluding this chapter would be to examine the various techniques that can be used to apply these ideas. But these techniques have already been described in some detail in a previous book, namely *Improving Teaching and Courses: A Guide to Evaluation* (Ramsden and Dodds, 1989), where I looked at a variety of procedures, ranging from student questionnaires to cooperative peer evaluation of lecturing performance, and from external experts' comments on the curriculum to the analysis of the results of student assessments, that might be used to evaluate the aspects of teaching considered in chapters 8, 9, and 10 of the present volume. As I have been at pains to stress the interpretive understanding of principles as the road to better teaching, and as the techniques are readily available in *Improving Teaching and Courses*, I do not propose to repeat what was said there. Instead, I shall look at how some of the lecturers whose teaching we observed in chapters 8–10 went about applying the ideas.

In chapters 9 and 10 I spoke of effective teaching and assessment as a kind of conversation between lecturers and students. The same reasoning applies to evaluation – although the 'conversation' in this case is widened to include other teachers and reflection on one's own experiences as well as the students, as the examples will show. Another important thing we can learn from these teachers' experiences is that evaluation does not finish when information has been collected. Evaluation is not about handing out questionnaires. The most significant and challenging aspects of evaluation comprise interpretation of results and the action that follows to improve teaching.

Evaluating a materials technology course

We saw in chapters 8–10 how Elaine Atkinson's new materials technology course was based on her evaluation of the previous version. The revised course abandoned the 'information dispensing' view of the subject and sought to introduce methods that would lead students actively to link their knowledge of materials to professional practice. Atkinson described the improvements as 'a continuous process of development' (p. 172). Notice how a good teacher, who cares for students, always conceptualises evaluation as a continuing endeavour, never a one-off activity. We also noted in chapter 10 how Atkinson, like Eizenberg and Dunn, used the results of student assessments as part of the process of evaluation. This enabled her to learn about students' misunderstandings and to structure the course around the problems that students experienced in grasping the key concepts in the subject. Listening to and learning from your students is an essential component of all teaching and of any evaluation.

It is not necessary to use questionnaires to evaluate courses. Other techniques of obtaining student feedback may be as good or better, depending on what you want to find out. During the first year that the revised course ran, Atkinson organised a session based on Graham Gibbs's 'Structured Group Feedback' method (see Gibbs *et al.*, 1988b; also Ramsden and Dodds, 1989, pp. 18-20). She asked each member of the class to write down their answers to each of the following questions:

1 What was the BEST feature of the course for you?
2 What was the WORST feature of the course for you?
3 In what ways do you think the course could be IMPROVED?

She then asked students to discuss their responses in groups of four, and to record the points on which they could reach agreement. The comments were then collated by the teacher in front of the whole class. She asked each group in turn to report a 'best feature' and checked that the rest of the class agreed with it before writing it up on an overhead transparency, and then went on to questions 2 and 3.

After a break, she reported to the class what she intended to do with the information. During the break she compared the comments with her own perceptions of the strengths and weaknesses of the course. This is the most critical part of evaluation – the careful collation and interpretation of the data. Acting on student feedback does not necessarily mean complying with what students say they want. The teacher should remain in control. This does not, however, imply any dismissal of students' comments. It means understanding their meaning in relation to the whole course.

For example, Atkinson was told that students felt insecure at the start of the course; they said they didn't get enough factual material in what they thought was a 'fact-based' subject. The teacher concluded from her own observations of students' work, and her course aims, that students were unclear about what was expected of them and the standard to be reached. She explained her interpretation to the class, and obtained their agreement that it was a reasonable one. She then described what she proposed to do about the problem. This mainly involved providing more individual support at the beginning of the course so that students were helped to become aware of her requirements, and moving one of the assignments to the beginning of the course to provide early feedback on progress.

Evaluating a problem-based engineering course

Like Atkinson's design course, the problem-based engineering course described by Cawley (1989) also illustrates the apparently paradoxical fact that evaluation should often be done *before* a course starts. As we saw in chapter 8, the course was a response to difficulties in student learning (the students focused on theoretical and technical skills separately from their application to real engineering problems; they lacked diagnostic abilities and the capacity to communicate solutions in vibration analysis). The aims and objectives were written with these issues in mind, and the teaching strategies chosen to address them.

Evaluation continued during the new course's implementation, using a variety of methods. These included the probing, by tutors, of students' grasp of the subject of the problem which the group was tackling, in order to determine whether students were using surface approaches in the course; the administration of a comprehensive questionnaire at the end of the first year of the new scheme, using both numerical gradings and open-ended comments; observation by the teachers during the tutorial group sessions of students' level of interest, quality of understanding, and extent of retention of key points; and an analysis of the final marks awarded.

What were the findings and how were they interpreted? The different sources of evidence pointed towards similar conclusions. Students clearly enjoyed the challenge of the course. They felt they were dealing with real problems and that they had been treated in a mature way. Moreover, compared with conventional courses, this one was better in terms of the amount and quality of student learning. The workload of the course was not seen to be greater than that of conventional courses. So far, so good. But evaluation is properly concerned with problems, not plaudits; the focus should primarily be on improvement. It emerged that there was a very small spread of marks in the final grading. Nevertheless, it was clear from tutorial discussions that some students' grasp of the subject was much better than that of others. Some students felt that the group assessments led to certain of their colleagues not pulling their weight. Putting together these different pieces of evidence, the teacher concluded that the assessment should be changed so that students' grasp of the basic principles of the subject was tested. This led to the one-hour 'test of understanding' mentioned in chapter 10 which accounted for 30 per cent of the whole assessment.

When the next cohort of students was asked to comment on this test, very few negative observations were made. They felt that the style of questions used (see chapter 10) was appropriate. The spread of final marks was greater and the test results correlated well with tutors' impressions of students' contributions. However, it was also apparent in this second year of the course that students found it much more time-consuming than a conventional course. Cawley speculates that this occurred because of increased assessment requirements in the other courses that students were taking at the same time. This point illustrates the important fact that no course can be evaluated in isolation from the remainder of a student's programme. Eizenberg (1988) noted, for example, that many of the educational advantages of his anatomy course were diminished by the excessive workloads in other parts of the medical programme (see also chapters 8–10). Cawley points out that .t may be necessary to restructure the whole final year timetable in order to accommodate the problem of an increased assignment workload.

Evaluating a humanities course

The idea that an external team of experts can 'evaluate' a course is completely alien to a theory 3 approach to teaching. However, this does not mean that professional advice and support is unnecessary or unhelpful, particularly if it comes from a source that has been involved in the development of the programme. Lybeck and Yencken's course is an example. Devised in cooperation with members of an educational methods unit, its evaluation was carried out as a cooperative process. A sample of students was interviewed at the beginning and the end of the course in order to gauge their reactions to the group work and assessment procedures, and in order to examine changes in students' conceptions of art history and the Renaissance. The educational methods staff also collected data on attendance and withdrawal. The findings provided a very comprehensive picture of students' approaches and learning outcomes, and were discussed several times with teachers and students. When interpreted in relation to the teachers' own experiences, the staff were able to form a clear picture of the strengths and weaknesses of the course.

The high attendance and low dropout rate; the positive comments of students on their experiences of working cooperatively in the groups, and their own descriptions of developments in their critical thinking and writing skills; the evidence of changes in students' understanding of important concepts; the information derived by the teachers about the quality of students' work from their assessments – these different sources pointed to the fact that the course was achieving many of the goals it set out to achieve. On the other hand, it was clear that some students found the early experiences of the groups unsettling, that the lecture programme (based on visiting lecturers and organised well before the decision to restructure the group work) was not properly related to the seminars, and that some of the essay questions, based on a narrow set of readings, were not in line with the course aims. As a result, the teachers decided to build more direction into the course, to require students to read more widely and imaginatively, to spend more time on developing student confidence and expertise in the groups, and to reorganise the lecture series.

Notice once again in this example how effective evaluation involves collecting and interpreting evidence from a variety of origins (students' comments on their experiences are only one part – though an essential part – of the information needed to evaluate teaching) and how the identification of problems is not ignored despite evidence of the course's success.

CONCLUSION

This chapter has ranged widely over numerous issues of accountability and evaluation of the quality of education. Its most
important conclusion is that the potential of any method of
evaluation or performance assessment to improve the quality of
higher education depends on the professional activity undertaken by lecturers. However elaborate the system of appraisal or
evaluation, its effectiveness stands or falls by the way in which
academic staff interpret it. Educational excellence cannot be
bought by the threats and promises of performance appraisal, but
only by creating the conditions in which teachers can excel.

As students' perceptions of our teaching determine the quality
of their learning, so lecturers' perceptions of evaluation policies
determine the effects of these policies on the quality of their
teaching. Ignoring these educational realities can only result in
pressures for accountability having the opposite effects to their
intentions. Our aim should be the development of a self-critical,
reflective academic community which constantly seeks internal
and external comment on the quality of its teaching, and has the
knowledge base and the sense of inner security to act wisely and
temperately in the light of the judgements it makes of itself.

Chapter 12

What does it take to improve teaching?

If there is no place for pleasure in teaching, surely our learning has failed us altogether.

(Kenneth Eble, 1988)

In the preceding chapters I have maintained that the way to improve teaching is to study our students' experiences of learning. In justifying this approach to improving the quality of higher education, I have been stating explicitly what good teachers know and do naturally. Lecturers who teach well think carefully about their students' understanding of the subject matter and their students' reactions to how it is taught, and they are able to apply this knowledge in the classroom through a variety of different strategies. They are willing to listen to and learn from their students.

In the last chapter of the book, I want to show how the ideas about good teaching that follow from an understanding of our students' learning can be applied to the task of educating ourselves to teach better. If we follow the principles of effective teaching and the developed theory of instruction outlined in chapters 6 and 7, how might we go about improving the quality of teaching? How should we teach lecturers to teach?

THE GOALS OF EDUCATIONAL DEVELOPMENT

The first problem to address is the same one as in all teaching: what do we want the learners to know? In other words, what changes in understanding do we wish to see occurring? Evidently our desire is to change lecturers' understanding and experiences of teaching, away from a theory of teaching as telling or transmitting knowledge, and towards a theory of teaching as intervening to help the students change their understanding. Excellence in teaching demands unremitting attention to how the subject is comprehended by one's students, and the ability to use the results of tests and assignments to change instruction so that it more accurately addresses students' errors and misunderstandings. It means knowing how to devise activities that will increase the probability that students will adopt deep approaches to learning. It means always being on the alert for discrepancies between students' perceptions of our requirements and our own expectations.

We shall want lecturers to enjoy finding out more about the nature of good teaching in their subject area, and to delight in its practice. Needless to say, it will not be enough for them to learn about the theoretical aspects of good teaching and learning: lecturers should be able to apply their knowledge in a range of different contexts, and must recognise and understand the reasons for inconsistencies between the predictions of the theory and what happens in their classes. And, if they are responsible for running a course taught by several teachers, or for running an academic department, we shall expect them to apply analogous principles to their supervision of the academic staff involved; they should manage teachers in a way that is consistent with the principles of effective teaching. Even if they are not so responsible, they should be expected to understand the elements of academic management so that they can encourage informed discussion among their colleagues and productively criticise existing teaching policies. In a democratic organisation, in the words of Pericles, 'although only a few may originate a policy, we are all able to judge it'.

Like conceptual development in students, these processes of changing understanding will be gradual and hesitant. Lecturers will pass through cycles of experiment, error, and progress towards more complete comprehension. As we noted in the cases of several teachers whose experiences were described in chapters 8 to 11, the processes are also continuing ones. No one can ever know enough about how to teach. We shall hope that lecturers come to understand how little they know about teaching, and how their authority rests not on dogmatic assurance, but rather on their knowledge of how little they know.

THE CONTEXT AND PROCESS OF EDUCATIONAL DEVELOPMENT

These goals of development in teaching may be summarised in

terms of a shift from a simple way of understanding teaching to a complex, relativistic, and dynamic one. In the latter, the application of theoretical knowledge is integrated with its practice. This model implies a recognition that learning how to teach is a process that never ends.

These changes emulate those which higher education lecturers, especially those in professional subjects, desire to see in their undergraduate students, and it may be helpful to conceptualise the process of learning how to teach in similar terms. The level of difficulty of this process, for lecturers with an average understanding of teaching, is probably about the same as an undergraduate programme of study. We are not talking about a few survival tips on lecturing and assessment presented in a one-day staff development workshop, useful as these may be for beginners, but about a lengthy and demanding progression towards professional competence.

From our knowledge of the theory of teaching and learning described repeatedly in this book, we are able to see the outlines of how we should proceed to instruct academic staff, at all levels of seniority, so that these goals may be attained. Two related issues must be addressed: the context which will encourage lecturers to use deep approaches to learning about teaching; and the form of intervention that is best suited to encouraging changes in conceptions of teaching. In fact, we can think about ways of undertaking educational development in higher education in terms of different theories of improving teaching.

REWARDS AND PUNISHMENTS: A NAIVE UNDERSTANDING OF IMPROVING TEACHING

It should be apparent from what I said in the last chapter that contemporary policies of appraising academic staff, and linking the quality of a member of staff's teaching to various extrinsic rewards, mostly operate from an unworldly conception of improving teaching – one which is almost diametrically opposed to our practical and theoretical knowledge of how to improve student learning. The idea of incentives and penalties for individual lecturers as a means of making teaching better is deeply embedded in most current thinking, however, and cannot be lightly dismissed. Almost a generation ago the Prices and Incomes Board argued that if the pay and promotion system of university teachers were linked to the effectiveness of teaching, as well as to research, then the quality of teaching would improve. They were far from being the first people to say so. Observations of this kind have been a regularly recurring part of debates about the standard of teaching in higher education, not only in the United Kingdom, but also in North America and Australia. They have become more frequent in the last few years as pressures for accountability and appraisal have increased. The conviction that there is a link between poor teaching and lack of incentive to perform seems to be an area of common ground between staff associations, employers, and educational development lobby organisations.

Sadly, much slack thinking characterises this debate. The argument that there should be tangible rewards for excellence in teaching, such as merit payments, bonuses, prizes, and promotion, is easily mixed up with the very different argument that good teaching in higher education should be recognised and that support for improving teaching ought to be visible. It is sometimes also confused with the idea that there are too many rewards for research and scholarship, and not enough for teaching. It is asserted that the relative priorities of the system are unbalanced, and that lecturers will continue to be bad teachers as long as they get most of their benefits (prestige and promotion) from research, while only lip service continues to be paid to teaching.

But what are the facts about incentives in higher education? The idea that material rewards will in themselves improve teaching does not stand up to much scrutiny. Promotions, salary increases, and prizes for teaching may have some symbolic value, in that they communicate the values of the institution to its staff and to the world at large, but their direct effect on good teaching is negligible (there may however be negative effects: see below). This is undoubtedly an unpalatable truth to some administrators and politicians. The search for higher quality education would be so much simpler if the academic beast responded positively to sticks and carrots.

Studies of academic motivation indicate that most of our desire to do well, as researchers or teachers, comes from within. We must believe in what we are doing if we are to excel at it. Beyond a certain minimum – we nearly all work for a salary as well as for the love of it – extrinsic rewards are relatively unimportant in stimulating academic staff to work harder.

McKeachie (1982) and Miller (1988) found no evidence that merit pay and other awards for teaching effectiveness enhanced quality and productivity in US higher education. Intrinsic interest and a sense of personal control, together with the belief that the organisation cares for a teacher's welfare, a sense of intellectual stimulation, and supports for efforts to improve, are crucial.

Once again an analogy with students and grades is appropriate. An understanding of student learning helps to explain the conditions for excellence in teaching. Academic staff and their students work within a context defined by their perceptions. Most students work for marks and want their assignments to 'count towards the degree' in order to put their best work into them (Elton and Laurillard, 1979); but increasing the emphasis on grades cannot compensate for lack of interest in what is being learned, the opportunity to be self-directed, and the feeling that your teachers care about you. External dissatisfaction (low pay, poor work conditions, doing work that doesn't count) prevents effective learning and teaching; a greater quantity of external satisfaction emphatically does not create them.

While there is no evidence that increasing extrinsic incentives and sanctions makes staff teach better, there is distinct evidence that it may make them teach worse. McKeachie (1982), for example, points out that extrinsic inducements diminish staff motivation in the long run: there are only so many material rewards you can receive. Prizes for teaching are readily interpreted in a cynical light as token and divisive gestures by a fundamentally hostile institutional management. Sanctions, such as extended probation and merit bars, have a more immediate effect: they increase academics' propensity to see teaching as a private activity and they provide disincentives to admitting and sharing problems.

There is nothing particularly surprising about all this: it is quite logical. What *is* surprising is that advocates of prizes and punishments ignore it. As the research into the correlates of surface approaches to learning outlined in chapters 4 and 5 so clearly showed, it is easy to change student learning for the worse by ill-considered amendments to the educational environment. Cynical messages about what will and will not be rewarded in assessments, creating excessive anxiety, and a perceived emphasis on recall of detail and trivial procedures: all these conduce to superficial approaches. Just as an inappropriate context of learning encourages surface approaches to learning, so an inadequate context of teaching will push staff towards superficial strategies focused on minimising penalties and maximising rewards. Neither sticks nor carrots will force students to understand: neither reprimands nor bonuses will force academics to improve their teaching. Unless our aim is to produce the corps of efficient pedants and dullards that Whitehead dreaded, these aspects of academic reality must be embodied in any programme for improving the quality of learning and teaching.

Improvements in the reward system depend not so much on handing out prizes and penalties, but on a change of attitude towards recognition of the professional teacher's role in higher education and an understanding that teaching can be a challenging and satisfying activity. Once we understand that the 'rewards imply greater productivity' equation is part of a naïve conception of improving teaching in higher education, we can begin to appreciate the alternative better. The alternative commits us, like so many of my recommendations about improving student learning, to travelling a harder road. The alternative approach is to create an environment – to construct a context of teaching – in which academic staff can perform to their maximum ability, while at the same time trying to change their understanding of what teaching means. Recognition of good teaching, both at individual and at department level, by various means which I shall describe in a moment, is part of this approach to management and educational development.

LEARNING TO TEACH BETTER: A MORE ADVANCED UNDERSTANDING OF IMPROVING TEACHING

If the implications of our theory of learning and teaching are accepted, changes to the context of teaching in higher education, and interventions designed to encourage teachers to learn, should be carried out in a variety of different ways, and at multiple levels of the higher education system. There can be no single right answer to the problem of improving the quality of teaching. That this perspective is by no means generally accepted is easily shown by reference to many policies of performance appraisal and staff development. The ideology of staff appraisal presents a one-dimensional model of better teaching which focuses narrowly on the quality of individual lecturers' performances and inter-lecturer competition for excellence. Staff development that is focused on training lecturers to use teaching techniques is driven by an equally simplistic theory which says that if we add extra skills to each lecturer's repertoire, then we will get better teachers.

A more practical as well as more intellectually satisfying approach would be to focus on good teaching rather than good teachers. We ought to be able to reach this conclusion from our knowledge of effective learning, even if we do not know about the literature on what makes educational innovations successful. Cooperation between members of staff and peer feedback within a team assists learning and motivation. There are many examples in the literature, in anecdote, and in my personal experience of how course groups, departments, and faculties have worked together as teams to produce better teaching and learning. Changing how we think about teaching is more than changing individual lecturers; although it must imply changes in how they experience teaching. Recall that theories of teaching are 'relational': they describe ways of *experiencing* and conceptualising the activities of instruction, rather than phenomena inside teachers' heads. It is quite meaningful to speak of changes in theories of teaching in the context of a course or department. A problem-based curriculum embodies a different conceptualisation of teaching and learning from a traditional one, for instance. An institutional context which represents in its official pronouncements and reward systems a theory 3 understanding of teaching ('teaching as making learning possible') will tend to shift individual lecturers towards a similar understanding. Educational development therefore involves efforts to change the policies of institutions and departments towards the promotion of good teaching.

It is possible, however, to carry the argument for changing the institutional context and working at the structural level too far. This would also lead us to a too-simple and pessimistic conclusion. While such changes are desirable because they alter the context of teaching – and therefore make it easier to teach well – it is not necessary for every lecturer who is interested in improving on the limitations of conventional small groups and lectures (for example) to wait for an institutional revolution. It is not essential to abandon a traditional curriculum entirely in favour of problem-based learning. Nor is it necessary to wait for more knowledge about teaching and learning to be generated from educational research. It is feasible for individual lecturers and small teams to work within the constraints and yet to have highly positive effects on the quality of learning. Although it may seem at first sight a perplexing observation, our study of the context of learning and teaching demonstrates how much of the process of higher education is the responsibility of individual teachers and students.

We saw some illustrations of this educationally optimistic view in the case studies reported in chapters 8 to 10, as well as in the example of Ms Ramsey's teaching in chapter 6. Peter Cawley's engineering course, for example, was an innovation that was fitted into a conventional programme, and it worked well. Hazel Lybeck and Barbara Yencken's art history course was similarly designed within a department whose teaching was otherwise quite conventional.

Further support for the view that good teaching in adverse settings is achievable can be found in a study of secondary school science teachers by Ken Tobin and Barry Fraser (Tobin and Fraser, 1988). Tobin and Fraser document the existence and effectiveness of 'exemplary teachers' in unfavourable environments – environments constrained much more than is usual in higher education by external examinations. The exemplary teachers used, in the terms of our model of different ways of understanding teaching, a theory 3 approach to their work. They all understood teaching as facilitating student learning, and they all believed that students created their own knowledge as a result of active engagement with the subject matter. These teachers were receptive to ideas for change; they thought and talked about what they did. They acted very much in accordance with the principles of good teaching laid down in chapter 6: although the exact methods they employed varied (some used individual and small group activities more than others, for example), each of these teachers created a setting where students could engage productively with learning tasks. They interacted in a friendly and respectful way with their students, who acknowledged this approach, rarely disrupting their classes. Unlike their less effective counterparts, these exemplary teachers did not focus on transmitting information in order to 'cover' the curriculum in the prescribed time, whether or not learning took place. Instead, they ensured that students understood the content fully by giving them opportunities to comprehend it. They set consistently high expectations for students, and the students responded by doing well.

The critical point is that these successful teachers were subject to the same forces as the less successful:

> These exemplary teachers operated in the same schools as the contrast teachers and their implemented curricula were exposed to the same powerful driving forces as those teachers. For example, the influence of external factors such as tests and examinations were [sic] about the same as those that operated on the classes of the contrast teachers, and factors such as student motivation to learn, student expectations, peer influence, and support of parents were probably similar within a school. Yet these exemplary teachers were able to create a positive learning environment and the comparison teachers generally could not ... they had ... a substantial repertoire of teaching routines available to use with the classes they taught.
>
> (Tobin and Fraser, 1988, pp. 91–2)

Comparable findings were reported by Adrian Leftwich (1987) from his own innovations in undergraduate political science classes. He described amendments which were designed to increase student participation in seminars and to improve the quality of their work; his students responded in a way that we would predict from the understanding of teaching we have been exploring in this book:

> with discipline, responsibility and enthusiasm to challenge, structure and, above all, expectation of high standards and sustained hard work. The experiences confirmed the view that the question of improving or sustaining motivation and interest in learning in higher education is less a matter of overcoming problems to do with alleged deficiencies of students than with the methods we use to engage those interests and to give shape to their expression.
>
> (Leftwich, 1987, p. 322)

Leftwich dismisses the gloomy claims made by some educational reformers that 'real' change in university teaching can only come about through radical structural change. Although he at first received mostly 'amiable indifference' from his departmental colleagues concerning his innovations, there can be no doubt that he was able genuinely to improve the quality of his students' learning.

There is, then, room for manoeuvre in improving teaching and learning. No teacher or educational development adviser may hide behind the belief that real improvement is impossible until drastic change in higher education takes place. Every practising lecturer who is reading this book can start changing his or her teaching tomorrow; and they can expect those changes, if conscientiously performed and compatible with what we know about effective instruction, to have a favourable effect on the quality of their students' learning. Their activity may also influence their colleagues to attempt something different in teaching. As lecturers like Leftwich have reported, relatively modest innovations (especially if they are undertaken within adverse contexts) are often enough to encourage others to try similar ideas. The argument is not that we should discourage either individual initiatives or wholesale changes, but that we should operate at many different levels of the system, remembering always that good educational development should follow the same rules as good teaching. There is no one right teaching method: there is no one correct place to intervene.

How can we encourage more members of staff to improve their teaching, in the way that our case study lecturers and those mentioned in the previous section have done? If appraisal cannot work, what will work? I believe that the answers lie in changes to the management of academic staff as teachers, in a fuller recognition of the practical problems of innovation (including the role of academic development advisers), and in systematic programmes of teacher education which take full account of our knowledge of good teaching.

THE MANAGEMENT OF LECTURERS FOR EXCELLENCE IN TEACHING

The supervision of academic staff for better teaching is a different matter from the management of employees in non-academic organisations. Academic staff are more used to setting their own goals, and to praising and reprimanding themselves, than those in most organisations; in reality, they are rather like the employees in Blanchard and Johnson's *The One Minute Manager* (1983), who have learned to do without managers almost entirely.

To attempt to impose what may be entirely sensible management strategies for less experienced and self-motivated employees on members of staff who have grown out of them is a sure recipe for discontent.

Using academic management strategies that will help teachers teach better implies showing concern for staff *as teachers*; creating a climate of openness, cooperation, and activity rather than one of defensiveness, competition, and passivity; developing an environment in which teachers are likely to learn from one another. Heads of departments ought to become familiar with the extensive literature on this and similar topics, and to build on this knowledge base, recognising always that in higher education most of the motivation to teach well comes from students, colleagues, and within, rather than from external sources. Academic managers, in one phrase, must *learn to manage like a good teacher teaches* (see Eble, 1988, p. 192).

They can learn most, perhaps, about how to run academic departments for the pursuit of high quality learning from the literature on school effectiveness. It is evident that the management style of the head teacher is a vital component of an effective school. Managers of such schools provide an environment in which teachers feel they can teach well because they are aware that tolerance, cooperation, and democratic decision-making are the norm (in this area there are in fact some important parallels with Blanchard and Johnson's ideas). In schools like this, most teachers experiment with new ideas and want to share their experiences with their colleagues. Like Tobin and Fraser's exemplary teachers and our case study lecturers, they think and talk a lot about their teaching and their students' learning. They make mistakes and they are not afraid to make them. They feel they can test out new ideas without fear of their errors being used against them. They are encouraged to show what they have learned from their mistakes. I have found that the same findings apply in the research I have carried out into successful sixth form environments (see Ramsden, 1991a). There is every reason to suppose they apply in higher education as well. There are evident parallels between the effects of independence and freedom in learning on student approaches to studying and the effects of democratic academic management on lecturers' approaches to teaching. Competent academic managers make it possible for their staff to adopt what we might describe, from our earlier discussion of student approaches to learning, as deep approaches to their teaching.

Possibly the most serious unintended consequence of staff appraisal derives from the awesome power it presents to the managers of academic departments to influence the distribution of rewards. That power will tempt many supervisors to manage in exactly those ways which, as we know for certain from the school effectiveness research as well as from the principles of good teaching, will *reduce* the quality of teaching and learning. Better management will require something entirely different: extensive education of supervisors in the characteristics of good teaching, an understanding of how to recognise and reward it productively, and a feel for how to create the trusting environment where teachers believe in what they are doing – so that they find it both challenging and possible to improve their teaching and their students' learning. In particular, managers of departments will need to learn to appreciate that the unsophisticated view of learning and teaching which says that competitiveness is more important for learning than cooperation, and discipline more important than freedom, is an inadequate foundation for improving the quality of teaching. Perhaps all heads of departments should start with A.N. Whitehead's splendid *The Aims of Education and Other Essays*, whose wisdom has been referred to several times in the present volume. There the stories of the essential tension between discipline and freedom in education, and the excitement of imaginative university teaching unfettered by trivial regulation, are wonderfully told.

THE PRACTICAL PROBLEMS OF ENCOURAGING INNOVATION

How can the effort and commitment that teachers put into improving teaching best be recognised? Evidently, departmental and institutional management which is driven by a theory 3 view of instruction will show support for the development of better teaching and learning in several different ways. Perhaps the single most important piece of practical advice they will remember is that improving teaching, like the effective learning of an academic subject, requires much time and effort. Attempts to innovate in teaching when workloads are heavy are likely to result in superficial outcomes.

It is often the case that changes to teaching are implemented without allocating enough time to planning them. But what applies to presenting effective courses for students applies also to effective changes to teaching. It is important to keep the goals of the innovation, which must always be related to changes in the quality of student learning, firmly in mind throughout, and to spend time articulating these goals to everyone involved. Experience shows that if too little time is allocated to making goals clear, the detailed, day-to-day, utilitarian demands of the new assessment or teaching method come to dominate the original intentions of the alterations.

Recognition of efforts to improve teaching must therefore begin by providing academic staff with the time outside their normal teaching and research duties to plan, implement, and discuss the effects of their changes. Time will also be needed to develop new skills, such as those needed to run student-directed groups, to use particular computer software, or to set and mark different types of assessment questions. Time is also required in order to find out about the experiences of people who have made previous attempts to undertake similar changes. Intelligent monitoring of changes is essential if we are to learn from them, as I argued in the last chapter. Proper evaluation demands time to reflect on and talk with colleagues about the innovation, and to plan the improvements that will be made to it next time round.

Staff release schemes, such as those operated in many institutions, are one means of providing teachers with adequate time to pursue improvements in their teaching. The contribution of an educational development adviser or unit can also effectively add to the time available. Such units provide a source of support and practical advice, and a channel for publicising the changes both within the institution and more widely. The recognition of good teaching through resources such as these is an essential means of rewarding excellence.

THE ROLE OF THE ACADEMIC DEVELOPMENT ADVISER

It is less likely that educational development advice will be sought by academic staff, especially those who are anxious about the quality of their teaching, if it derives from a unit which is involved in any way in the performance appraisal of their teaching. Who but a fool would share his or her problems in teaching with colleagues who are involved in gathering information to make judgements about one's professional ability, in matters as important as tenure?

I had always believed this logic to be true, but my belief was originally based chiefly on what many lecturers in my own university, where the unit is not so involved, had said they would do if it were. A few months ago I received a phone call from a lecturer (at another university) who wanted some advice about a change she was thinking of making to the assessment methods of her course. I tried to answer her query as well as I could, and when I suggested that she might go to the educational development unit in her own institution for useful continuing support, she explained that the staff in it were mainly involved in collecting student feedback data which lecturers used when applying for promotion and confirmation of tenure. She and her colleagues would never wish to consult the unit's staff about any problems or weaknesses in their teaching: that was not 'what the educational methods department was about'. A colleague tells a similar story about a lecturer whose teaching had been surreptitiously evaluated by the academic development unit at the request of his head of department. He had subsequently received a formal note from the head requesting a meeting where he would be asked to explain his 'poor student ratings', together with a suggestion that he should seek help from the unit in order to learn some techniques for better teaching! Needless to say, he declined the offer to share his predicament with those who had so brazenly betrayed their professional trust.

The parallels between these approaches to educational development and bad teaching are too obvious to require accentuating. Remember that we are not talking here about a situation analogous to assessing students, where the teacher is inevitably both adviser and judge: the educational developer is not in the same relationship to his or her colleagues in other departments as a lecturer is to students in class, and must recognise this fact by adopting different standards. Experiences of this kind suggest two things: first, that the professional development of personnel in academic methods units is another point of intervention in the system; and that institutions who have arranged for any of the functions of appraisal to be supported by staff in such units should probably think again. In the meantime, many lecturers face a real dilemma in seeking practical advice on better teaching.

TEACHER EDUCATION IN UNIVERSITIES AND POLYTECHNICS

The use of induction or new staff courses in UK and Australian higher education institutions to train novice lecturers is now commonplace. The Warnock Report (1990) recently echoed the recommendations of other reports that introductory courses in teaching methods should be compulsory for all staff, and that induction should continue beyond an initial course.

Plainly, the education of lecturers in methods of teaching should proceed in several ways, as it already does in the best educational development units – through individual, confidential consultations on problems of teaching; by working at department and institution level to ensure that policies for effective evaluation and the recognition of teaching are developed; by helping course teams to plan, teach, and assess the curriculum; through running programmes of workshops and seminars to support course groups and individual lecturers who are engaged in improving their teaching; by offering longer courses in teaching, possibly linked to diploma or master's level qualifications; by encouraging staff to conduct research into teaching and learning their subjects; and so on.

If educational development is about changing lecturers' understanding of teaching, then the methods used to help them to change should reflect the imperatives of a theory 3 approach to instruction. In other words, we ought to teach lecturers in a way compatible with the changes we wish to see them make. The activities used will comprise attempts to integrate professional practice with the process of reflection on that practice, and with the kind of theoretical knowledge reviewed in Part 1 of this book. Skills in the various techniques of teaching will be taught in the context of the understanding that is needed to select a particular technique wisely and to make the skills work. Cooperative activities comparing different teachers' approaches, exercises that highlight inconsistencies in ways of thinking and acting (incongruities between the teacher's goals and what students actually learn in a course, for example), and activities involving monitoring and reporting on the actual application of the ideas in the classroom, will be among the probable methods used. Stimulating interest in the process of improving as a teacher, and encouraging staff to modify their teaching in small, highly practical ways at an early stage in any programme of improvement, will be high priorities.

Instead of describing how each of these interventions might operate from the point of view of what we know about effective teaching in higher education, I want to follow a procedure used earlier and describe a single example of a course for staff, organised by an educational methods unit, which attempts to practise the principles advocated throughout the book. This course might best be described as a continuing professional education course, rather than an induction course – it lasts for one academic year – though many of its ideas are also used in the half-year induction course run within the same unit. It stands in bold contrast to many courses run by other educational methods units, which seem to operate from what I have called a theory 2 approach to teaching. They assume that training in the skills of running groups and giving lectures, and in particular getting teachers and students to *do* things, will in itself lead to higher quality student learning. These courses would seem determined to try and practise the old Chinese proverb: 'I hear, I forget; I see, I remember; I do, I understand.' They would do well to realise that this advice is at best a half-truth, as I have previously argued (see p. 117). In any case, it is now outmoded. A distinguished Hong Kong gynaecologist has recently suggested a better version for his students, which our educational developers might perhaps take to heart: 'I hear, I forget; I see, I remember; *I make a mistake,* I understand.'

I think I have said enough to enable readers who are involved in the professional development of lecturers to apply the principles this course embodies to their own work in the other areas, such as induction courses, mentioned above; the only point to underscore is that the work should always be based on some explicit theoretical understanding of teaching and learning. All too often the work of educational development units, particularly in these days of accountability, is driven more by political expediency and a desire to be seen to be pleasing members of institutional management than by a coherent educational theory. While we all have to work within the limits defined by political demands, I sometimes wish that more of these personnel would be bold enough to put education first.

The course in question lasts for one year, and leads to a certificate of completion which exempts its holders from two units of the Diploma in Education (Tertiary) of the University of

Melbourne.[1] It links the theory of good teaching to its practice in several different ways. The course aims to encourage staff to understand teaching differently: to question their existing teaching methods, to search out reasons for the effects of their teaching on their students' learning, and to apply what they find out in different assessment and instructional methods. Some staff enrol in the programme because they are dissatisfied with their students' performance ('Why don't students understand the things I've told them in lectures?'); some because they feel they are competent teachers, but want reassurance; some because they feel they are not good enough; some because they want to be recognised as expert teachers; and some for a mixture of two or more of these motives.

By continually questioning the validity of teachers' ideas and practices – though in a supportive and helpful way – this course provides a model which the teachers can emulate in their own teaching and especially in their feedback on students' work. Each participant is interviewed individually by the course leader at the beginning of the programme in order to provide her with an understanding of their theory of teaching and their expectations of the course. Early in the course, their teaching is observed: suggestions are made for simple improvements (such as techniques for gaining students' attention in large classes) that will help develop their confidence. The course leader also correlates the information collected during the observation with what each lecturer said during the initial interview. This enables her to confront the teachers with possible discrepancies between their preferred ways of teaching and what they actually do in the classroom, as well as to gain a more complete understanding of their conceptions of teaching which will be drawn upon in subsequent instruction. Moreover, the participants are required to provide feedback on the course leader's own teaching in order to develop their experience of giving as well as receiving constructive criticism of teaching performance.

The first half of the programme includes many of the topics dealt with in this book, such as the effects of assessment on student learning, different teaching strategies, and course development. During the second half of the year, participants teach a course or course component that they have redesigned in the first half. They present their experiences, including a self-evaluation of the course, to the rest of the group on two occasions. They are also involved in leading a seminar for colleagues in their own department. The aim of this seminar is to stimulate discussion of educational issues at departmental level.

The programme is assessed by pass/fail gradings in four ways:

1 A written assignment considering aspects of research into student learning for redesigning a part of the curriculum
2 An outline of the new course or course component, with teaching notes; the course or course component must cover at least six hours of contact time
3 A written evaluation of the course or course component, including an indication of how the teaching might be improved in subsequent years
4 An evaluation of each participant's teaching by the course staff, including observation of class teaching.

A TEACHER'S EXPERIENCE OF EDUCATIONAL DEVELOPMENT

As we approach the end of a book which has stressed so much the student's perspective on learning and teaching, it would seem appropriate to hear from a lecturer who describes (in an evaluation interview) the effects of the one-year course in improving teaching (see pp. 263–4). She speaks of a change in her way of experiencing teaching squarely in accordance with the aims of the course and the theory of instruction on which it is based; and it should be emphasised that observation of her teaching confirmed that she was applying her understanding in practice. Her comments will make my point about the value of applying the principles of good teaching to the education of members of academic staff more forcefully than any further description I could give:

> I think it has changed the way I have thought about teaching a lot. I mentioned to you before that the fundamental realisation for me was that teaching should only be considered in relation to learning. When you are teaching, unless you are constantly monitoring that learning, and trying to address what you understand from that in the practice of your teaching, then it really seems to become some sort of a performance where you really don't care what the critics say or what the critics understand. I realise now that this is the only basis on which you should try to understand the detail of teaching methods and curriculum design.

I learned what it meant to say that you have to start off with what students think and not what you think they think. You have to find out what *they* understand, about their ways of seeing the content. If your teaching is not based on that reality, it can be a long way off the mark. You also have to devise ways of understanding the perceptions that they have of your teaching, and addressing those. Those sorts of things were introduced in the course at the beginning, and I think that that was the most fundamental shake up, if you like.

At first it was uncomfortable to face up to this way of looking at teaching, but we got a lot of support from you to get through it. It took time to learn how to use it and understand it properly. I found the reading that was provided in the early stages extremely useful. It backed up everything that we did. I guess the other thing that was quite clear right from the beginning, which I found extremely useful and have drawn on it a number of times, was just how you ran the class and what you did. Then, when I was trying to think about what I might do in my own class, I would think about how you had run yours. It provided a model which I could work with; it gave me a starting point. Of course my own teaching is different – I've got 60 of them in a different subject – but I could adapt the ideas I'd experienced.

The fact that all the participants came from different subject areas has been of immense use. When you're working in your own area you don't know how other people do things. When you're confronted with the different sorts of problems that they have, you have to think about them from an educational perspective, because you haven't got the usual excuse – that we'll just do it a certain way because we always have in this subject. You also know you have got backup if you run into some disaster or you have got a real problem. We've made contacts which enable us to say, listen, I want to try this – what do you think? We've been able to help each other and learn from each other about teaching.

CONCLUDING SUMMARY

Throughout the previous chapters we have regularly experienced a contrast between two different ways of looking at the subject matter of academic disciplines and at the process of education itself. Roger Säljö described a process of development from purely quantitative views of learning subject matter (adding quanta of facts and procedures to one's store of knowledge) towards a qualitative conception of learning as understanding, relating theory to practice, and abstracting meaning. Similarly, William Perry looked at the process of students' intellectual development, from dualistic to relativistic views of subject matter; while Marton described a distinction between deep-holistic and surface-atomistic approaches and outcomes in studying which can be seen to parallel the contrast between 'imitation' and 'real' subjects drawn so eloquently by Sawyer. In the area of assessing student learning, Biggs's SOLO scheme and the categories derived from analysis of the physics interviews (see pp. 208–10) embody the same theme. The main line of progress is from simple to complex, from black-and-white to shades of grey, from simply accepting what authorities say to questioning and making personal sense, from separate parts to the articulation of parts within a system. In SOLO, for example, relational responses differ from multistructural ones in that they imply a bringing together of isolated parts under an overarching system, while extended abstract responses go even further to question the system itself. And in fact the general trend of the movement in all these examples is away from the search for right and wrong answers towards an understanding and acceptance of the necessary tension of opposites, and a recognition that today's knowledge, however valuable, represents a partial and transitory perspective on reality. It must, like its progenitors, be superseded.

These differences, of course, correspond to lecturers' own descriptions of their aims for student learning, and you will surely see by now what it means to say that good teaching in higher education may be defined by the quality of learning it encourages. The development of good teaching involves an exactly analogous process of change from simple to complex, from absolute to relative, from the unquestioning acceptance of authority to a search for personal meaning, from discrete techniques to the expression of skills within an ordered, yet ultimately provisional system. And – to move to a yet higher level of generality – the education of lecturers so that they can become good teachers implies that those who educate them must comprehend and apply these truths.

In order to improve teaching in higher education, it is

necessary to bear in mind one deceptively simple rule. *Encouraging students to learn and helping lecturers to teach involve identical principles. Therefore, if we understand how to help students, we understand how to improve teaching.* Bad teaching makes the subject matter seem monotonous and difficult, and makes the students frightened and insecure. It leads inexorably to the learning of imitation subjects. As with bad teaching, so with bad evaluation and bad educational development. They neither touch the imagination nor enhance the ability to reason. They sap our energy, they divide us, and they nurture our fear of change. They focus on a procession of signs and meaningless rules rather than on the things those rules and signs are supposed to signify. And not the least of their shortcomings is that they are deadly dull.

If you are able to accept this general line of reasoning, you will find it as depressing as I do to observe in British and Australian higher education the continuing endorsement and use of methods for improving teaching which we know for certain are detrimental to student learning. These include training in techniques of 'getting more information into students' memories' and the absurd stick-and-carrot approach to motivating academic staff represented by performance appraisal and financial rewards for good teachers. Yet their use is understandable in the context of timid or educationally naïve responses to pressures for accountability. It seems that many people, including the makers of high institutional policy as well as some of the educational specialists themselves, have much to learn about the conditions for good teaching and learning. We should be more active in helping them to learn.

The greatest tragedy of the present climate of accountability is not its damaging effect on the profession of higher education teaching, painful though that is. It is rather that these conditions retard the application of our understanding of the educational process to the improvement of learning. This book has shown that we have enough knowledge of the essence and substance of good teaching in higher education to alter the quality of learning out of all recognition. What is needed in the long run is the institutional spirit and the political commitment to apply the principles.

But, as I argued earlier, we do not have to wait for the whole system to change. Despite the rather dismal picture that surrounds us in the higher education of the late twentieth century, there are teachers who are teaching excellently and teachers who are learning to teach excellently. I hope it will be clear from the experiences reported in this book that many of the improvements can begin straight away. There is no need to delay until the millennium of educational development, or to wait for more enlightened approaches to accountability, to use what each of us knows. It is up to us as teachers to take control of improving teaching, especially by listening respectfully to our students about how we can help them to learn. In the process of improvement, I hope we shall realise a conception of teaching and learning as an imaginative, arduous, but *pleasurable* process. There can be no excellent teaching or learning unless teachers and learners delight in what they are doing.

Appendix

Course experience questionnaire

COURSE EXPERIENCE QUESTIONNAIRE

The purpose of this questionnaire is to collect students' opinions of teaching and assessment in particular courses and subjects.

My course is in the Department/School/Faculty of . . . .

My major subject (if applicable)* is in the Department/School of . . . .
*if double major, select one only

Your responses are **strictly confidential** and will not be seen by members of staff. The questionnaire items are based on comments that students have often made about their experiences of tertiary teaching. They have been specially chosen to reflect aspects of teaching and courses that are generally important across a wide range of subjects.

HOW TO ANSWER
Simply circle the number beside each statement that most accurately reflects your view.

1	means that you definitely agree (✓✓)
2	means that you agree, but with reservations (✓)
3	means that you are not sure or that it doesn't apply (?)
4	means that you tend to disagree (✗)
5	means that you definitely disagree (✗✗)

Please answer **all** the questions.

	✓✓	✓	?	x	xx
1. It's always easy here to know the standard of work expected of you	1	2	3	4	5
2. There are few opportunities to choose the particular areas you want to study..	1	2	3	4	5
3. The teaching staff of this course motivate students to do their best work......	1	2	3	4	5
4. The workload is too heavy	1	2	3	4	5
5. Lecturers here frequently give the impression that they haven't anything to learn from students	1	2	3	4	5
6. You usually have a clear idea of where you're going and what's expected of you in this course	1	2	3	4	5
7. Staff here put a lot of time into commenting on students' work	1	2	3	4	5
8. To do well on this course all you really need is a good memory	1	2	3	4	5
9. The course seems to encourage us to develop our own academic interests as far as possible.....................	1	2	3	4	5
10. It seems to me that the syllabus tries to cover too many topics	1	2	3	4	5

	✓✓	✓	?	×	××
11. Students have a great deal of choice over how they are going to learn in this course............	1	2	3	4	5
12. Staff here seem more interested in testing what we have memorised than what we have understood	1	2	3	4	5
13. It's often hard to discover what's expected of you in this course	1	2	3	4	5
14. We are generally given enough time to understand the things we have to learn............	1	2	3	4	5
15. The staff make a real effort to understand difficulties students may be having with their work	1	2	3	4	5
16. Students here are given a lot of choice in the work they have to do............	1	2	3	4	5
17. Teaching staff here normally give helpful feedback on how you are going	1	2	3	4	5
18. Our lecturers are extremely good at explaining things to us............	1	2	3	4	5
19. The aims and objectives of this course are not made very clear	1	2	3	4	5
20. Teaching staff here work hard to make their subjects interesting to students....	1	2	3	4	5
21. Too many staff ask us questions just about facts............	1	2	3	4	5

	√√	√	?	x	xx
	1	2	3	4	5

22. There's a lot of pressure on you as a student here...................... 1 2 3 4 5

23. Feedback on student work is usually provided ONLY in the form of marks and grades.................... 1 2 3 4 5

24. We often discuss with our lecturers or tutors how we are going to learn in this course........... 1 2 3 4 5

25. Staff here show no real interest in what students have to say............... 1 2 3 4 5

26. It would be possible to get through this course just by working hard around exam times........... 1 2 3 4 5

27. This course really tries to get the best out of all its students................... 1 2 3 4 5

28. There's very little choice in this course in the ways you are assessed 1 2 3 4 5

29. The staff here make it clear right from the start what they expect from students 1 2 3 4 5

30. The sheer volume of work to be got through in this course means you can't comprehend it all thoroughly 1 2 3 4 5

THANK YOU FOR YOUR HELP

Notes

CHAPTER 1

[1] The theory underlying this view is that of phenomenography, which in turn derives from phenomenological philosophy. Phenomenography applied to education describes the phenomena of students' experiences of learning and, by extension, their teachers' experiences of teaching. For further details, see Marton (1981), Laurillard (1990), and Ramsden *et al.* (1991).

CHAPTER 10

[1] The project has received financial support from the Australian Research Council (ARC) and The University of Melbourne. The principal investigator for the ARC project was Dr Geofferey Masters. The following have also contributed substantially to the work: John Bowden, Gloria Dall'Alba, Diana Laurillard, Elaine Martin, Ference Marton, Andrew Stephanou, and Eleanor Walsh.

CHAPTER 12

[1] The course is led by Elaine Martin and is for academic staff of the Royal Melbourne Institute of Technology.

References

Andreson L.W., Powell, J.P., and Smith, E.M. (1987) 'Competent teaching and its appraisal', *Assessment and Evaluation in Higher Education* 12: 66–72.

Ashby, E. (1973) 'The structure of higher education: A world view', *Higher Education* 2: 142–51.

Aulich, T. (1990) *Priorities for Reform in Higher Education* (Report by the Senate Standing Committee on Employment, Education and Training), Canberra: Australian Government Publishing Service.

Balla, J.I. (1990a) 'Insights into some aspects of clinical education – I. Clinical practice', *Postgraduate Medical Journal* 66: 212–17.

Balla, J.I. (1990b) 'Insights into some aspects of clinical education – II. A theory for clinical education', *Postgraduate Medical Journal* 66: 297–301.

Balla, J.I., Stephanou, A., and Biggs, J.B.(in preparation) 'Development of a methodology for assessing medical students' ability to integrate theoretical and practical knowledge'.

Balla, J.I., Biggs, J.B., Gibson, M., and Chang, A.M. (1990) 'The application of basic science concepts to clinical problem-solving', *Medical Education* 24: 137–47.

Barnett, S.A., Brown, V.A., and Caton, H. (1983) 'The theory of biology and the education of biologists: A case study', *Studies in Higher Education* 8: 23–32.

Baxandall, M. (1972) *Painting and Experience in Fifteenth Century Italy*, Oxford: OUP.

Beard, R.M. and Hartley, J. (1984) *Teaching and Learning in Higher Education*, London: Harper & Row.

Becker, H.S., Geer, B., and Hughes, E.C. (1968) *Making the Grade: The Academic Side of College Life*, New York: Wiley.

Biggs, J.B. (1987) *Student Approaches to Learning and Studying*, Hawthorn, Victoria: Australian Council for Educational Research.

Biggs, J.B. (1988) 'Approaches to learning and to essay-writing', in R.R. Schmeck (ed.) *Learning Strategies and Learning Styles*, New York: Plenum.

Biggs, J.B. (1989) 'Approaches to the enhancement of tertiary teaching', *Higher Education Research and Development* 8: 7–25.

Biggs, J.B. (1990) 'Teaching: Design for learning', keynote paper,

Annual Conference of the Higher Education Research and Development Society of Australasia, Griffith University, Brisbane, July.

Biggs, J.B. and Collis, K.F. (1982) *Evaluating the Quality of Learning: The SOLO Taxonomy*, New York: Academic Press.

Black, P.J., Bliss, J., Hodgson, B., Ogborn, J., and Unsworth, P.J. (1977) *Small Group Teaching in Undergraduate Science*, London: Heinemann.

Blackburn, R.T. and Pitney, J.A. (1988) *Performance Appraisal for Faculty: Implications for Higher Education*, University of Michigan: National Center for Research to Improve Postsecondary Education and Learning.

Blanchard, K. and Johnson, S. (1983) *The One Minute Manager*, London: Willow Books.

Bligh, D. (ed.) (1982) *Professionalism and Flexibility in Learning* (Leverhulme Series no. 6), Guildford: Society for Research into Higher Education.

Bliss, J. and Ogborn, J. (1977) *Students' Reactions to Undergraduate Science*, London: Heinemann.

Bloom, B.S. (1976) *Human Characteristics and School Learning*, New York: McGraw-Hill.

Bloom, B.S., Engelhart, M.D., Furst, E.J., Hill, W.H., and Krathwohl, D.R. (1956) *Taxonomy of Educational Objectives: Cognitive Domain*, New York: McKay.

Bork, A. (1987) 'Interaction: lessons from computer-based learning', in D. Laurillard (ed.) *Interactive Media: Working Methods and Practical Applications*, Chichester: Ellis Horwood.

Boud, D. (1989) 'The role of self-assessment in student grading', *Assessment and Evaluation in Higher Education* 14: 20–30.

Boud, D., Dunn, J., and Hegarty-Hazel, E. (1986) *Teaching in Laboratories*, Guildford: SRHE & NFER-NELSON.

Bowden, J.A. and Martin, E. (1990) *Report on Validation Study of Course Experience Questionnaire*, Wollongong, NSW: Centre for Technology and Social Change.

Brennan, J. and McGeevor, P. (1988) *Graduates at Work: Degree Courses and the Labour Market*, London: Jessica Kingsley.

Broady, M. (1970) 'The conduct of seminars', *Universities Quarterly*, Summer.

Brown, G. (1978) *Lecturing and Explaining*, London: Methuen.

Brumby, M. (1982) 'Medical students' perception of science', *Research in Science Education* 12: 107–14.

Bruner, J.S. (1966) *Toward a Theory of Instruction*, Cambridge, Mass.: Harvard University Press.

Cave, M., Hanney, S., Kogan, M., and Trevett, G. (1988) *The Use of Performance Indicators in Higher Education*, London: Jessica Kingsley.

Cawley, P. (1989) 'The introduction of a problem-based option into a conventional engineering degree course', *Studies in Higher Education* 14: 83–94.

Centra, J.A. (1980) 'The how and why of evaluating teaching', *Engineering Education* 71: 205–10.

Crooks, T.J. (1988) 'The impact of classroom evaluation practices on students', *Review of Educational Research* 58: 438–81.

Dahlgren, L.O. (1978) 'Qualitative differences in conceptions of basic principles in economics', paper presented at the Fourth International Conference on Higher Education, University of Lancaster, September.

Dahlgren, L.O. (1984) 'Outcomes of learning', in F. Marton *et al.* (eds) *The Experience of Learning*, Edinburgh: Scottish Academic Press.

DES (1987) *Higher Education: Meeting the Challenge*, London: HMSO.

DES (1989) 'In pursuit of quality: an HMI view' in *Quality in Higher Education. A report on the HMI, Invitational Conference*, London: DES.

di Sessa, A. (1982) 'Unlearning Aristotelian physics: A study of knowledge-based learning', *Cognitive Science* 6: 37–75.

Dunkin, M. (1986) 'Research on teaching in higher education', in M.C. Wittrock (ed.) *Handbook of Research on Teaching* (3rd edn), New York: Macmillan.

Eble, K.E. (1988) *The Craft of Teaching* (2nd edn), San Francisco: Jossey-Bass.

Eizenberg, N. (1988) 'Approaches to learning anatomy', in P. Ramsden (ed.) *Improving Learning: New Perspectives*, London: Kogan Page.

Elton, L.R.B. (1982) 'Assessment for learning', in D. Bligh (ed.) *Professionalism and Flexibility in Learning* (Leverhulme Series no. 6), Guildford: Society for Research into Higher Education.

Elton, L.R.B. (1988) 'Accountability in higher education: The danger of unintended consequences', *Higher Education* 17: 377–90.

Elton, L.R.B. and Laurillard, D.M. (1979) 'Trends in research in student learning', *Studies in Higher Education* 4: 87–102.

Engel, C.E. and Clarke, R.M. (1979) 'Medical education with a difference', *Programmed Learning and Educational Technology* 16: 70–87.

Entwistle, N.J. (1984) 'Contrasting perspectives on learning', in F. Marton *et al.* (eds) *The Experience of Learning*, Edinburgh: Scottish Academic Press.

Entwistle, N.J. (1988) 'Motivational factors in students' approaches to learning', in R.R. Schmeck (ed.) *Learning Strategies and Learning Styles*, New York: Plenum.

Entwistle, N.J. (1990) 'How students learn, and why they fail', paper presented at the Conference on Talent and Teaching, Bergen, Norway, May.

Entwistle, N.J. and Marton, F. (1984) 'Changing conceptions of learning and research', in F. Marton *et al.* (eds) *The Experience of Learning*, Edinburgh: Scottish Academic Press.

Entwistle N.J. and Percy, K.A. (1974) 'Critical thinking or conformity? An investigation into the aims and outcomes of higher education', in *Research into Higher Education 1973*, London: SRHE.

Entwistle, N.J. and Ramsden, P. (1983) *Understanding Student Learning*, London: Croom Helm.

Entwistle, N.J. and Tait, H. (1990) 'Approaches to learning, evaluations of teaching, and preferences for contrasting academic environments', *Higher Education* 19: 169–94.

Entwistle, N.J., Hounsell, D.J., Macaulay, C., Situnayake, G., and Tait, H. (1989) *The Performance of Electrical Engineers in Scottish Higher Education*, Report to the Scottish Education Department, Centre for Research on Learning and Instruction, Department of Education, University of Edinburgh.

Eraut, M., Mackenzie, N., and Papps, I. (1975) 'The mythology of educational development: Reflections on a three-year study of economics teaching', *British Journal of Educational Technology* 6: 20–34.

Feldman, K.A. (1976) 'The superior college teacher from the student's view', *Research in Higher Education* 5: 243–88.

Fitch, J.G. (1979) *The Art of Questioning* (9th edn), Syracuse, NY: C.W. Bardeen.

Fransson, A. (1977) 'On qualitative differences in learning. IV – Effects of motivation and test anxiety on process and outcome', *British Journal of Educational Psychology* 47: 244–57.

General Medical Council (1987) *Report of a Working Party of the Education Committee on the Teaching of Behavioural Sciences, Community Medicine and General Practice in Basic Medical Education*, London: General Medical Council.

Gibbs, G. (1982) *Twenty Terrible Reasons for Lecturing*, SCEDSIP Occasional Paper 8.

Gibbs, G. (1990) *Improving Student Learning Project: Briefing Paper for Participants in the Project*, Oxford: The Oxford Centre for Staff Development.

Gibbs, G. and Jenkins, J. (1984) 'Break up your lectures', *Journal of Geography in Higher Education* 8: 27–39.

Gibbs, G., Habeshaw, S., and Habeshaw, T. (1988a) *53 Interesting Ways to Assess Your Students*, Bristol: Technical and Educational Services Ltd.

Gibbs, G., Habeshaw, S., and Habeshaw, T. (1988b) *53 Interesting Ways to Appraise Your Teaching*, Bristol: Technical and Educational Services Ltd.

Gunstone, R.F. and White, R.T. (1981) 'Understanding of gravity', *Science Education* 65: 291–300.

Habeshaw, S., Habeshaw, T., and Gibbs, G. (1984) *53 Interesting Things to do in Your Seminars and Tutorials*, Bristol: Technical and Educational Services Ltd.

Hale, E. (1964) *Report of the Committee on University Teaching Methods*, London: HMSO.

Hart, A. (1987), 'The political economy of interactive video in British higher education', in D. Laurillard (ed.) *Interactive Media: Working Methods and Practical Applications*, Chichester: Ellis Horwood.

Hartnett, A. and Naish, M. (1990) 'The sleep of reason breeds monsters: The birth of a statutory curriculum in England and Wales', *Journal of Curriculum Studies* 22: 1–16.

Heath, R. (1964) *The Reasonable Adventurer*, Pittsburgh: University of Pittsburgh Press.

Heath, T. (1990) 'Education for the professions: Contemplations and reflections', in I. Moses (ed.) *Higher Education in the Late Twentieth Century: Reflections on a Changing System*, University of Queensland: Higher Education Research and Development Society of Australasia.

Hegarty, E.H. (1982) 'The role of laboratory work in science courses: Implications for college and high school levels', in M.B. Rowe (ed.)

Education in the 80s: Science, Washington, D.C.: National Education Association.

Hodgson, V. (1984) 'Learning from lectures', in F. Marton *et al.* (eds) *The Experience of Learning*, Edinburgh: Scottish Academic Press.

Hounsell, D.J. (1984) 'Learning and essay-writing' in F. Marton *et al.* (eds) *The Experience of Learning*, Edinburgh: Scottish Academic Press.

Hounsell, D.J. (1985) 'Learning and essay-writing', *Higher Education Research and Development* 3: 13–31.

Hounsell, D.J. and Ramsden, P. (1978) 'Roads to learning: An empirical study of students' approaches to coursework and assessment', in D. Billing (ed.) *Course Design and Student Learning*, Guildford: SRHE.

Johansson, B., Marton, F. and Svensson, L. (1985) 'An approach to describing learning as change between qualitatively different conceptions', in L.H.T. West and A.L. Pines (eds) *Cognitive Structure and Conceptual Change*, New York: Academic Press.

Johnson, D., Maruyama, G., Johnson, R., Nelson, D., and Skon, L. (1981) 'The effects of cooperative, competitive and individualistic goal structures on achievement: A meta-analysis', *Psychological Bulletin* 89: 47–62.

Knapper, C. (1990) 'Lifelong learning and university teaching', in I. Moses (ed.) *Higher Education in the Late Twentieth Century: Reflections on a Changing System*, University of Queensland: Higher Education Research and Development Society of Australasia.

Knapper, C. and Cropley, C.K. (1985) *Lifelong Learning and Higher Education*, London: Croom Helm.

Kogan, M. (1985) 'The "Expectations of Higher Education" project', in D. Jaques and J.T.T. Richardson (eds) *The Future for Higher Education*, Guildford: SRHE & NFER-NELSON.

Kohl, H. (1976) *On Teaching*, New York: Shocken Books.

Laurillard, D.M. (1984) 'Learning from problem-solving', in F. Marton *et al.* (eds) *The Experience of Learning*, Edinburgh: Scottish Academic Press.

Laurillard, D.M. (1987) 'Pedagogical design for interactive video', in D. Laurillard (ed.) *Interactive Media: Working Methods and Practical Applications*, Chichester: Ellis Horwood.

Laurillard, D.M. (1988) 'Computers and the emancipation of students: Giving control to the learner', in P. Ramsden (ed.) *Improving Learning: New Perspectives*, London: Kogan Page.

Laurillard, D.M. (1990) 'Phenomenographic research and the design of diagnostic strategies for adaptive tutoring systems', The Open University: Centre for Information Technology and Education, Report No. 124.

Leftwich, A. (1987) 'Room for manoeuvre: A report on experiments in alternative teaching and learning methods in politics', *Studies in Higher Education* 12: 311–23.

Linke, R.D. (1991) *Report of the Research Group on Performance Indicators in Higher Education*, Canberra: Australian Government Publishing Service.

Lochhead, J. (1985) 'New horizons in educational development', in E.W.

Gordon (ed.) *Review of Research in Education 12*, Washington, DC: AERA.

Lonsdale, A. (1990) 'Achieving institutional excellence through empowering staff: An approach to performance management in higher education', in I. Moses (ed.) *Higher Education in the Late Twentieth Century: Reflections on a Changing System*, University of Queensland: Higher Education Research and Development Society of Australasia.

McDermott, L.C. (1984) 'Research on conceptual understanding in mechanics', *Physics Today* 37: 24–32.

McKeachie, W.J. (1982) 'The rewards of teaching', in J. Bess (ed.) *New Directions for Teaching and Learning: Motivating Professors to Teach Effectively*, San Francisco: Jossey-Bass.

McKeachie, W.J. (1983) 'The role of faculty evaluation in enhancing college teaching', *National Forum* 63: 37–9.

Marris, D. (1964) *The Experience of Higher Education*, London: Routledge & Kegan Paul.

Marsh, H.W. (1987) 'Students' evaluations of university teaching: Research findings, methodological issues, and directions for future research', *International Journal of Educational Research* 11: 255–378.

Martin, E., Ramsden, P., and Bowden, J.A. (1989) 'Students' experiences in Year 12 and their adaptation to higher education', in H. Edwards and S. Barraclough (eds) *Research and Development in Higher Education 11*, Sydney: Higher Education Research and Development Society of Australasia.

Marton, F. (1981) 'Phenomenography – Describing conceptions of the world around us', *Instructional Science* 10: 177–200.

Marton, F. (1988) 'Describing and improving learning', in R.R. Schmeck (ed.) *Learning Strategies and Learning Styles*, New York: Plenum.

Marton, F. and Ramsden, P. (1988) 'What does it take to improve learning?', in P. Ramsden (ed.) *Improving Learning: New Perspectives*, London: Kogan Page.

Marton, F. and Säljö, R. (1976) 'On qualitative differences in learning. II – Outcome as a function of the learner's conception of the task', *British Journal of Educational Psychology* 46: 115–27.

Marton, F. and Säljö, R. (1984) 'Approaches to learning', in F. Marton *et al.* (eds) *The Experience of Learning*, Edinburgh: Scottish Academic Press.

Marton, F., Hounsell, D.J., and Entwistle, N.J. (eds) (1984) *The Experience of Learning*, Edinburgh: Scottish Academic Press.

Masters, G. N. (1988) 'Partial credit model', in J.P. Keeves (ed.) *Educational Research, Methodology, and Measurement: An International Handbook*, Oxford: Pergamon.

Masters, G. N. (1989) 'Improving the assessment of clinical reasoning', in J. I. Balla, M. Gibson, and A.M. Chang (eds) *Learning in Medical School: A Model for the Clinical Professions*, Hong Kong: Hong Kong University Press.

Mathews, R.L., Brown, P.R., and Jackson, M.A. (1990) *Accounting in Higher Education: Report of the Review of the Accounting Discipline in*

Higher Education, Canberra: Australian Government Publishing Service.

Medawar, P. B. (1977) 'Unnatural science', *New York Review of Books*, 3 February: 13–18. .

Miller, R.I. (1988) 'Merit pay in United States postsecondary institutions', *Higher Education* 17: 219–32.

Muir, R. (1943) *An Autobiography and Some Essays*, London: Lund Humphries.

Newble, D. and Clarke, R.M. (1985) 'The approaches to learning of students in a traditional and in an innovative problem-based medical school', *Medical Education* 20: 267–73.

Nisbet, J. (1986) 'Staff and standards', in G.C. Moodie (ed.) *Standards and Criteria in Higher Education*, Guildford: SRHE & NFER-NELSON.

Novak, J.D. (1981) 'Applying psychology and philosophy of science to biology teaching', *American Biology Teacher* 42: 280–5.

Perry, W. G. (1970) *Forms of Intellectual and Ethical Development in the College Years*, New York: Holt, Rinehart & Winston.

Perry, W. G. (1988) 'Different worlds in the same classroom', in P. Ramsden (ed.) *Improving Learning: New Perspectives*, London: Kogan Page.

Pirsig, R.M. (1974) *Zen and the Art of Motorcycle Maintenance*, London: The Bodley Head.

Pollitt, C. (1987) 'The politics of performance assessment: Lessons for higher education?', *Studies in Higher Education* 12: 87–98.

Pollitt, C. (1990) 'Measuring university performance: Never mind the quality, never mind the width?', *Higher Education Quarterly* 44: 61–81.

Popper, K. (1966) *The Open Society and its Enemies*, (5th revised edn) London: Routledge & Kegan Paul.

Popper, K. (1972) *Objective Knowledge*, Oxford: OUP.

Powell, J.P. (1985) 'The residues of learning: Autobiographical accounts by graduates of the impact of higher education', *Higher Education* 14: 127–47.

Prosser, M. and Millar, R. (1989) 'The "how" and "why" of learning physics', *European Journal of Psychology of Education* 4: 513–28.

Ramsden, P. (1981) 'A study of the relationship between student learning and its academic context', unpublished PhD thesis, University of Lancaster.

Ramsden, P. (1983) 'Institutional variations in British students' approaches to learning and experiences of teaching', *Higher Education* 12: 691–705.

Ramsden, P. (1988a) 'Context and strategy: Situational differences in learning', in R.R. Schmeck (ed.) *Learning Strategies and Learning Styles*, New York: Plenum.

Ramsden, P. (ed.) (1988b) *Improving Learning: New Perspectives*, London: Kogan Page.

Ramsden, P. (1990) *Report to the Higher Education Performance Indicators Project on the Course Experience Questionnaire Trial*, Wollongong, NSW: Centre for Technology and Social Change.

Ramsden, P. (1991a). 'Study processes in grade 12 environments', in B.J.

Fraser and H.J. Walberg (eds), *Educational Environments*, Oxford: Pergamon.

Ramsden, P. (1991b) 'A performance indicator of teaching quality in higher education: The Course Experience Questionnaire', *Studies in Higher Education* 16: 129–50.

Ramsden, P. (in preparation) 'Persistence and change in students' approaches to learning: A longitudinal study of adaptation to higher education'.

Ramsden, P. and Dodds, A. (1989) *Improving Teaching and Courses: A Guide to Evaluation*, Melbourne: Centre for the Study of Higher Education, The University of Melbourne.

Ramsden, P. and Entwistle, N.J. (1981) 'Effects of academic departments on students' approaches to studying', *British Journal of Educational Psychology* 51: 368–83.

Ramsden, P. and Moses, I. (1991) 'Associations between research and teaching among Australian academic staff', unpublished paper based on ARC-funded survey.

Ramsden, P., Beswick, D.G., and Bowden, J.A. (1986) 'Effects of learning skills interventions on first year university students' learning', *Human Learning* 5: 151–64.

Ramsden, P., Masters, G., and Bowden, J.A. (1988) *An Investigation of First Year Assessment*, Report on Research Promotion Grant 1987, University of Melbourne.

Ramsden, P., Marton, F., Bowden, J.A., Dall'Alba, G., Laurillard, D.M., Martin, E., Masters, G.N., Stephanou, A., and Walsh, E. (1989) 'A phenomenographic study of students' conceptions of simple projectile motion', paper presented at the Third European Conference for Research on Learning and Instruction, Universidad Autónoma de Madrid, September.

Ramsden, P., Marton, F., Laurillard, D.M., Martin, E., Masters, G.N., Stephanou, A., and Walsh, E. (1991) 'Phenomenographic research and the measurement of understanding: An investigation of students' conceptions of speed, distance and time', *International Journal of Educational Research* 14.

Roth, K. and Anderson, C.W. (1988) 'Promoting conceptual change learning from science textbooks', in P. Ramsden (ed.) *Improving Learning: New Perspectives*, London: Kogan Page.

Rowntree, D. (1977) *Assessing Students*, London: Harper & Row.

Rowntree, D. (1981) *Developing Courses for Students*, London: McGraw-Hill.

Russell, T. and Johnson, P. (1988) 'Teachers learning from experiences of teaching: Analyses based on metaphor and reflection', paper presented at the Annual Conference of the American Educational Research Association, New Orleans, April.

Säljö, R. (1979) 'Learning in the learner's perspective. I. Some common-sense conceptions', *Reports from the Institute of Education, University of Gothenburg*, 76.

Säljö, R. (1984) 'Learning from reading', in F. Marton *et al.* (eds) *The Experience of Learning*, Edinburgh: Scottish Academic Press.

Saunders, P. (1980) 'The lasting effects of introductory economics courses', *Journal of Economic Education* 12: 1–14.

Sawyer, W.W. (1943) *Mathematician's Delight*, Harmondsworth: Penguin.

Schmeck, R.R. (1983) 'Learning styles of college students', in R. Dillon and R. Schme :k (eds) *Individual Differences in Cognition*, New York: Academic Press.

Schön, D.A. (1983) *The Reflective Practitioner: How Professionals Think in Action*, New York: Basic Books.

Scriven, M. (1987) 'The validity of student ratings', keynote paper, Annual Conference of the Higher Education Research and Development Society of Australasia, Curtin University, Perth, September.

Smith, D.M. (1988) 'On academic performance', *Area* 20: 3–13.

Snyder, B.R. (1971) *The Hidden Curriculum*, New York: Knopf.

Svensson, L. (1977) 'On qualitative differences in learning. III – Study skill and learning', *British Journal of Educational Psychology* 47: 233–43.

Svensson, L. and Högfors, C. (1988) 'Conceptions as the content of teaching: Improving education in mechanics', in P. Ramsden (ed.) *Improving Learning: New Perspectives*, London: Kogan Page.

Tang, K.C.C. (1990) 'Cooperative learning and study approaches', paper presented at the 7th Annual Conference of the Hong Kong Educational Research Association, University of Hong Kong, November.

Thomas, A. (1989) 'Further education staff appraisal: What teachers think', *Assessment and Evaluation in Higher Education* 14: 149–57.

Tobin, K. and Fraser, B.J. (1988) 'Investigations of exemplary practice in high school science and mathematics', *Australian Journal of Education* 32: 75-94.

Van Rossum, E.J. and Schenk, S.M. (1984) 'The relationship between learning conception, study strategy and learning outcome', *British Journal of Educational Psychology* 54: 73–83.

Warnock, M. (1989) *A Common Policy for Education*, Oxford: OUP.

Warnock, M. (1990) *Report of the Committee of Enquiry into Teaching*, London: Polytechnics and Colleges Funding Council.

Watkins, D.A. (1983) 'Depth of processing and the quality of learning outcomes', *Instructional Science* 12: 49–58.

Watkins, D.A. and Hattie, J. (1981) 'The learning processes of Australian university students: Investigations of contextual and personological factors', *British Journal of Educational Psychology* 51: 384–93.

West, L.H.T. (1988) 'Implications of recent research for improving secondary school science learning', in P. Ramsden (ed.) *Improving Learning: New Perspectives*, London: Kogan Page.

West, L.H.T., Fensham, P.J., and Garrard, J.E. (1985) 'Describing the cognitive structures of learners following instruction in chemistry', in L.H.T. West and A. L. Pines (eds) *Cognitive Structure and Conceptual Change*, New York: Free Press.

West, L.H.T., Hore, T., Eaton, E.G., and Kermond, B.M. (1986) *The Impact of Higher Education on Mature Age Students*, Canberra: Commonwealth Tertiary Education Commission.

Whelan, G. (1988) 'Improving medical students' clinical problem-solving', in P. Ramsden (ed.) *Improving Learning: New Perspectives*, London: Kogan Page.

Whitehead, A.N. (1967) *The Aims of Education and Other Essays*, New York: Free Press (first published by Macmillan in 1929).

Williams, B. (1988) *Review of the Discipline of Engineering*, Canberra: Australian Government Publishing Service.

Wright, B.D. (1988) 'Rasch measurement models', in J.P. Keeves (ed.) *Educational Research, Methodology, and Measurement: An International Handbook*, Oxford: Pergamon.

Woodforde, J. (1981) *The Diary of a Country Parson*, Oxford: OUP

Index

academic departments, 4, 7, 11, 78-81, 87, 88, 103-8, 110, 118, 135-6, 147, 148, 151, 157, 167, 202, 221, 222, 229, 236, 237-9, 249, 253, 254-6, 258, 259, 261-2, 265

academic myths, 87-90, 137, 176, 220

accountability, 2, 3, 11, 103, 124, 150, 219, 222, 223-40, 247, 251, 263, 268, 269

accountancy, 32-3, 37, 50, 61, 103, 106

aims and objectives, 9, 21-4, 61, 84, 123-37, 139, 141-9, 150, 167, 168, 170, 171, 172-6, 182, 188, 189, 190, 192, 198, 200, 202-3, 211, 220, 221, 244, 246, 265

aims of education, 17-24, 60-1, 45, 72, 82, 207, 213, 259, 267

appraisal and staff assessment, 1, 2, 3, 124, 218, 219, 222, 223-40, 241, 242, 247, 250, 251, 253, 257, 259, 260, 261, 268

approaches to learning, 38-61, 62-84, 87, 87, 94, 96, 101, 108, 110, 111, 112, 115, 123, 128, 131, 132, 133, 144, 148, 151, 155, 159, 162, 164, 166, 167, 174, 175, 182, 185, 186, 188, 191, 197, 200, 204, 205, 217, 244, 246, 249, 250, 252, 253, 259

approaches to studying, 46-7, 50-3, 56, 58, 61, 103, 118, 258, 267

approaches to teaching, 127, 157, 164, 165, 169, 190, 245, 255, 258-9, 262, 263

architecture, 50, 163

art history, 76, 145-6, 170-2, 189, 201-3, 246, 255

assessment, of academic staff, *see* evaluating teaching and courses; appraisal and staff assessment

assessment, of students, 15, 28, 35, 37, 48, 52, 55, 56, 60, 62, 63, 64, 65, 67-73, 76, 78, 79, 80, 81, 84, 86, 87, 89, 99, 102, 104, 110, 113, 124, 125, 128, 136, 143, 144, 145, 146, 150, 151, 171, 172, 176, 178, 181-213, 218, 210-20, 221, 225, 226, 227, 229, 234, 242, 243, 245, 246, 250, 252, 260, 261, 262, 264, 265, 267; assignments, 46, 48, 63, 66, 71, 76, 101, 118, 136, 155-6, 173, 190, 193, 194, 196-7, 212

essays, 40, 46, 47, 48, 50, 55-6, 61, 66, 70, 77, 110, 125, 184, 186, 192, 194, 203; examinations, 28, 30, 32, 34, 40, 45, 46, 48, 50, 57, 58, 60, 63, 64, 68, 70-1, 72, 73, 113, 118, 124, 126, 136, 148, 184, 186, 188, 189, 190, 192, 193, 194, 198, 199, 202, 203, 212; group assessment, 176, 192, 200-1, 206, 212

multiple choice/objective tests, 60, 124, 125, 160, 183, 184, 192,

194–5, 198, 211; problems, 18,
22, 23, 24, 31, 33, 36, 40, 46–50,
51, 56, 65, 68–9, 77, 149, 175–6,
187, 199, 200–1, 204, 205, 208,
209, 210; reports, 46, 64, 176,
184, 190, 192, 194, 197, 200–1,
203; self-assessment, 192, 193,
197, 211; see also feedback on
progress
'Atkinson, Elaine' (example of
good teaching), 142–4, 172–3,
199–200, 242–4
attitudes to learning and studying,
27, 29, 32–3, 58–9, 68, 69, 73,
80, 96, 98, 145, 163, 164, 171,
186, 196

Balla, J.I., 35, 56, 164, 207–8
Biggs, J.B., 45, 51–3, 55–6, 57, 59,
110, 152, 267
Biology, 34–5, 67, 136
Black, P.J., 162, 168, 169–70
Bruner, J.S., 100, 109, 115, 150,
240

Cawley, P., 148–9, 175–6, 200–1,
202, 244–5, 255
chemistry/biochemistry, 33, 49, 65,
90, 130, 132, 145, 189, 195, 210
competition, 28, 101–2, 183, 185,
192, 212, 222, 223, 224, 227,
234, 254, 258, 259
computer studies, 48
conceptions of learning, 5, 25–7,
30, 31, 33–7, 40, 45, 55, 56, 110,
126, 128, 145, 151, 153–4, 168,
198, 205, 206, 208, 209–10, 267
conceptions of teaching, 4, 16, 17,
88, 110, 114, 129, 130, 148,
153–4, 183–5, 190, 191, 205,
212, 218, 229, 250, 253, 264,
269, see also theories of teaching
context of learning, 6, 45, 47, 50,
57, 62–85, 93, 94, 96, 101, 110,
114, 118, 123, 129, 151, 157,
159, 166, 187, 192, 250, 252–3,
254, 255–9, 262
cooperation in learning and
teaching, 29, 37, 89, 101, 114,

152, 163, 166, 167, 168, 170–2,
173, 175, 178, 192, 196, 200,
203, 205, 227, 241, 242, 246,
254, 258, 259, 262
Course Experience Questionnaire
(CEQ), 103–8, 127, 193, 271–4
critical thinking, 18, 19, 20, 22, 23,
25, 31, 37, 38, 72, 113, 129, 133,
145–6, 171–2, 175, 246

'Dunn, John' (example of good
teaching), 146–8, 176–8, 203–5

Eble, K.E., 6, 98, 158, 167, 248, 258
economics, 22, 36, 40, 72, 73, 76,
79, 130, 131, 141, 162, 210
education (subject), 26, 41, 78,
107
educational development, 7, 10,
22, 61, 75, 109, 110, 113, 119,
124, 150, 155, 172, 224, 233,
242, 243, 246, 248–50, 251, 257,
259–69
effective teaching, principles of, 8,
10, 11, 74, 75, 79, 80, 84,
86–108, 124–6, 135, 139, 140–1,
150, 165–7, 190, 193, 198,
218–19, 221, 239, 241–2, 248,
249, 260
Eizenberg, N., 144–5, 172, 173–4,
197–8, 243, 245
engagement with learning, 39, 42,
46, 51, 67, 69, 73, 74, 81, 82, 86,
93, 100–2, 112, 114, 141, 152,
159, 164, 167, 174, 176, 177,
179, 203, 206, 255, 256
engineering, 13–14, 67, 71, 79, 97,
103, 104, 106, 110, 118, 129,
141, 145, 148–9, 154, 163,
175–6, 193, 200–2, 244–5, 256
English, 21, 49, 78, 79, 90, 130, 145
Entwistle, N.J., 20–1, 29, 31, 50,
51–3, 54, 57, 58, 61, 98, 126,
193
environment, educational or
academic, see context of
learning
environmental planning, 22, 146,
176

essays, *see* assessment of students
evaluating teaching and courses, 1,
    5, 6, 7–11, 52, 80, 85, 88, 90–1,
    96, 99, 102–8, 109, 118, 119,
    124, 127, 136, 150, 172–3, 174,
    176, 178, 179, 181, 185, 191,
    208, 213, 217–47, 260, 261, 262,
    264–5, 268
examinations, *see* assessment of
    students
expectations, of employers, 19,
    28–9
    of lecturers, 19, 20–4, 38–9, 61,
    81, 100, 104, 127, 128–9, 133,
    142, 145–6, 163, 166, 168, 185,
    196–7, 249, 256

factual knowledge, 17, 18, 19, 21,
    23, 25, 26, 30, 37, 39, 40, 42, 45,
    48, 52, 53, 54, 60, 67, 70, 71, 72,
    74, 82, 91–2, 94, 96, 114, 143,
    144, 152, 164, 174, 189, 244
feedback on students' progress,
    76, 81, 89, 90, 95, 99, 104, 107,
    118, 125, 165, 178, 179, 180,
    184–7, 193–7, 199–203, 211,
    234, 244, 264
fine arts, 60, 76, 170
Fraser, B.J., 255–6, 258

geography, 47, 179–80
geology, 71
Gibbs, G., 20, 154–5, 179–80, 192,
    195, 243

history, 6, 21, 24, 37, 38, 46, 49, 53,
    56, 74, 77, 79, 145, 170, 181,
    186
Högfors, C., 129, 139, 196
humanities, 30, 31, 36, 49, 50, 71,
    77, 103, 104, 108, 118, 145–6,
    163, 169, 170–1, 201, 203,
    245–6

independence in learning, 20, 27,
    29, 67, 75, 76, 79, 80, 81, 87, 89,
    90, 99, 100–1, 104, 113, 132,
    146, 148, 149, 152, 158, 163,
    165, 175, 185, 190, 191, 196,

    197, 200, 203, 211, 258, 259
induction courses, for academic
    staff, 97, 262–6
industrial relations, 22, 77
innovation, in teaching, 113, 172,
    176, 179, 192, 235, 254, 255–7,
    259–60
interior design, 142–4, 172–3,
    199–200, 242–4

Jenkins, J., 179–80

key concepts, 21, 39, 82, 84, 89, 91,
    93–4, 100, 114, 131, 133, 143–4,
    165, 173, 174, 188, 198, 207, 243

Laurillard, D.M., 68–9, 159, 161,
    275
law, 22, 24, 50, 135
lectures, *see* teaching methods and
    strategies
Leftwich, A., 256, 257
'Lybeck, Hazel' (example of good
    teaching), 145–6, 170–2, 201–3,
    245–6, 255

management and managers (of
    academic staff and
    departments), 2, 4, 7, 224, 227,
    228, 232, 234, 240, 249, 250–3,
    257–9, 261, 263
Marton, F., 31, 41, 44–6, 50, 53–4,
    58, 63, 66, 68, 80, 116, 151, 210,
    267, 275
Masters, G. N., 23, 205, 207, 275
materials science/technology,
    142–4, 172–3, 199–200, 242–4
mathematics, 22, 30, 31, 36, 38, 48,
    51, 60, 146, 147, 205
measurement and testing, *see*
    assessment of students;
    assessment of teachers
medicine, 20, 21, 22, 31, 35, 36, 50,
    53, 56, 130–1, 141, 144–5, 154,
    163, 164, 173–4, 189, 190,
    197–8, 207–8, 245
memorising, 4, 13, 23, 26, 31, 40,
    41, 42, 45, 48, 50, 51, 52, 55, 68,
    70, 71, 72–3, 86, 91, 94, 96, 104,

123, 144, 153–4, 158, 160, 165, 182, 202, 211
motivation of students, 28, 29, 32, 58, 66, 107, 113, 116, 141, 148, 160, 175, 183, 201, 228, 256 of staff, 7, 222, 225, 227, 228, 241, 251–2, 254, 258, 268

orientations to studying, 50–3, 57, 58, 78–80, 84, 103
outcomes of learning, 16, 17, 24–37, 69, 72, 82–4, 96, 101–2, 110, 118, 119, 125, 133, 137, 148, 154, 183, 186, 187, 191, 200, 201, 205, 208, 228, 237, 246, 259, 267

perceptions of courses and teaching, 16, 62–3, 65–8, 72, 76, 79, 80–4, 100, 101, 103–8, 118–19, 185, 191, 218, 234, 235, 238, 243, 247, 249, 252, 266
performance indicators, 80, 99, 103–8, 185, 191, 222, 236–40
Perry, W. G., 25, 26, 132, 267
pharmacology, 22, 189
physics, 21, 23–4, 31–2, 33–4, 37, 47, 48, 49, 56, 61, 69, 70, 71, 78, 79, 110, 13–16, 162, 169–70, 196, 208–10, 267
physiology, 14–15
Pirsig, R.M., 62, 155–6
political science/politics, 14, 49, 67, 110, 151, 178, 256
Popper, K., 17, 35
Powell, J.P., 27–8, 29
problem-based learning, 81, 141, 148–9, 175–6, 189, 200–2, 244–5, 254, 255
problem-solving, 18, 20–1, 22, 27, 30, 31, 36–7, 40, 46, 47, 48, 50, 51, 56, 65, 67, 68–9, 77, 100, 141, 149, 157, 163, 164, 172, 174, 204, 206, 208–10
professional curriculum, 4, 18, 19, 20, 21, 22, 30, 31, 35, 36, 50, 61, 81, 82, 101, 103, 133, 141, 148, 163, 172, 173, 175, 199, 200, 204, 242–4, 250

professionalism, in teaching, 8, 9, 115, 140, 152, 183, 192, 193, 217, 221, 223, 232, 234, 239, 247, 250, 253, 261, 262–5
psychology, 18, 21, 33, 70, 79, 106

qualitative differences in learning, 4, 7, 17–18, 22, 24, 26, 31, 36, 40, 45, 53–8, 59, 61, 62, 64, 69, 71, 72, 78, 84, 86, 101, 110, 207–10, 267
quality of higher education, 3, 4, 6, 7, 10, 11, 15, 28–9, 30, 33, 39, 45, 51, 53, 59, 61, 73, 78, 79–81, 82, 86, 98, 100, 103–8, 109, 112, 117, 124, 130, 137, 138, 152, 155, 160, 165, 176, 182, 185, 186, 194, 217–47, 248–69

Ramsden, P., 23, 29, 32, 33, 34, 49, 50, 51, 54, 57, 63, 67, 75, 80, 81, 103–4, 106, 116, 151, 206, 210, 230, 238, 239, 242, 243, 258, 275
rewards for teaching, 3, 219, 225–7, 234, 236, 242, 250–4, 259, 260, 268
Roth, K., 91–6, 110
Rowntree, D., 130, 136, 161, 162, 181, 185, 189, 192, 206

Säljö, R., 25, 26–7, 31, 41, 45–6, 50, 54, 63, 66, 68, 80, 154, 267
Sawyer, W.W., 38–9, 59, 86, 97, 267
science, 30, 31, 33, 34–5, 36, 46, 49, 50, 57, 61, 68, 75, 91–6, 97, 102, 103, 104, 108, 110, 255–6
sequence of content, 116, 139–41, 145, 148, 174
social science/sociology, 18, 31, 36, 38, 50, 51, 97, 103, 106, 108, 131, 152, 162, 188, 207
SOLO taxonomy (Biggs), 54–5, 207–8, 267
standards, academic, 3, 6, 11, 13, 37, 101, 106, 112, 127, 133, 144, 153, 185, 187, 211, 219, 221, 225, 232, 243–6, 237, 238, 242, 244, 251, 256

statistics, 146–8, 176–8, 203–5
student choice over methods and
    content, *see* independence in
    learning
student ratings, 75, 91, 98, 101,
    118, 229–33, 235, 238–40, 261
Svensson, L., 43, 51, 57, 58, 129,
    139, 196
staff development, *see* educational
    development

teaching methods and strategies,
    2, 8, 9, 10, 13, 62–3, 75, 78, 81,
    86, 89, 101–2, 113–14, 123–6,
    150–80, 196, 218, 221, 226, 238,
    240, 242–6, 248, 255–7, 260,
    262–5; computer assisted, 112,
    159–61, 165, 178, 195 clinical,
    163–4; laboratory and practical
    classes, 62, 64, 65, 95, 101, 136,
    152, 163–4, 168, 172; large
    classes, 153, 156, 167, 179–80,
    191, 194, 264; lectures, 63, 68,
    71, 73, 74, 76, 77, 88, 101, 111,
    112, 139, 142, 152–6, 157, 158,
    167, 169, 174, 176, 177, 178,
    179, 246, 254, 264; with media,
    159–61; projects, 163, 184;
    seminars, tutorials, and small
    groups, 62, 73, 76, 77, 78, 91,
    95, 101, 118, 145, 157–70, 171,
    175–6, 177, 178, 195, 199, 201,
    246, 254, 255, 256, 262;
    textbooks, 64, 70, 71, 73, 92,
    93–4, 145–6, 161–3, 167, 184
theories of teaching, 4, 8, 16, 87,
    109–19, 123, 124, 127, 131, 137,
    154, 155, 156, 157, 160, 164,
    165, 170, 172, 183, 186, 218,
    221–2, 228, 229, 240, 245,
    248–50, 253–5, 259, 262, 263,
    264, 265, 267; *see also*
    conceptions of teaching
Tobin, K., 255–6, 258

understanding, changes in
    students', 4, 5, 6, 7–9, 10, 16,
    18, 20–4, 26–37, 39–42, 44, 45,
    47, 48, 52, 53–6, 58, 59–61, 74,
82, 84, 87, 93, 103, 110, 111,
    114, 116, 117, 128, 129, 131,
    133, 152, 171–2, 206, 210, 213,
    218, 221, 246, 248, 250, 253,
    254, 265–6

variety in teaching and assessment
    methods, 99, 167, 176–8, 190,
    191–2, 198, 199–201, 211, 221,
    248
veterinary science, 21, 35
Visual Arts, 104

Whitehead, A.N., 1, 19, 23, 25,
    109, 115, 123, 138, 217, 253,
    259
workloads, excessive, 71–3, 75, 79,
    80, 84, 104, 137–8, 151, 162,
    245 259

'Yencken, Barbara' (example of
    good teaching), 145–6, 170–2,
    201–3, 245–6, 255